A+ Preparation Companion
Semester 2

Edited by Bonnie Yarbrough

CISCO SYSTEMS

CISCO PRESS

201 West 103rd Street

Indianapolis, IN 46290 USA

A+ Preparation Companion

Copyright © 2000 Cisco Press

FIRST EDITION

Published by:
Cisco Press
201 West 103rd Street
Indianapolis, IN 46290 USA

Printed in the United States of America 1 2 3 4 5 6 7 8 9 0

Library of Congress Cataloging-in-Publication Number: 00-102054

ISBN: 1-57870-251-8

Publisher	*John Wait*
Executive Editor	*Dave Dusthimer*
Managing Editor	*Patrick Kanouse*
Development Editor	*Kitty Wilson Jarrett*
Senior Editor	*Jennifer Chisholm*
Proofreader	*Erich Richter*
Associate Editor	*Shannon Gross*
Team Coordinator	*Amy Lewis*

TABLE OF CONTENTS

INTRODUCTION

A+ Preparation Companion is a two-volume book designed as text for the A+ classroom and lab experience. This text and the classroom activities help students gain A+ certification and enter the workforce with certified skills. The text is particularly helpful when used in conjunction with the online Aries Certified Computer Technician Curriculum.

This book is designed to further train students and instructors beyond the online training materials. It closely follows a pedagogical style and format that enables students to incorporate prior content knowledge and experience into the present curriculum as they progress through each lesson. In addition, the book provides students the opportunity to reflect on and test their understanding of each lesson's content by completing exercises.

Concepts covered in the two volumes of this book include a brief history of computers, number systems, electricity, power supplies, power events, the workplace and tools, the computer case, the motherboard, the microprocessor, voltage settings, memory, drives, video displays, communication devices, networking architecture and configuration, the Internet, input devices, operating systems, network concepts, operating systems, user profiles and system policy, dial-up networking servers and services, boot files and initialization, problem avoidance, troubleshooting and recovery, and plug-and-play hardware.

The goal of this book

The goal of *A+ Preparation Companion* is to prepare readers to take the A+ and Microsoft Certified Professional exams. It is designed for use independently or in conjunction with the online Aries Certified Computer Technician Curriculum.

This book's audience

A+ Preparation Companion is for anyone who wants to prepare to take the A+ and Microsoft Certified Professional exams. The main target audience for this book is students in high schools, community colleges, and four-year institutions. Specifically, in an educational environment this book could be used both in the classroom as a text book companion and in computer labs as a lab manual companion.

This book is also for corporate training faculty and staff members. In order for corporations and academic institutions to take advantage of the capabilities of computer technologies, a large number of individuals have to be trained in computer basics, operating systems, and the use of networks.

Finally, this book is for general users. This book's user-friendly and nontechnical approach should be appealing to readers who prefer material that's less technical than that in most manuals.

This book's features

Many of this book's features, including the following, help facilitate a full understanding of the requirements necessary to prepare for the A+ and Microsoft Certified Professional exams:

- The format of the material—Content is presented in a series of units, each comprised of five lessons. This format allows students to proceed through the material in a sequential manner and creates a solid foundation of knowledge that leads to a thorough understanding of the content.

- Review exercises—Each lesson contains focus and concept questions, as well as vocabulary exercises, that serve as end-of-lesson assessments and reinforce the concepts introduced in the lesson by helping a student test his or her understanding before moving on to new concepts.

- Glossary—Each semester contains a glossary that provides quick, easy reference. Key terms throughout the lessons are highlighted in bold and are defined in the glossary.

This book's organization

Semester 2 of *A+ Preparation Companion* includes 14 units, each of which contains 5 lessons. Each lesson contains focus, vocabulary, and review exercises.

Unit 1 offers a brief introduction to several operating systems, providing a perspective on the places of DOS and Windows among a variety of operating system alternatives. In addition, this unit discusses preinstalling, installing, and starting MS-DOS; DOS configuration; and basic DOS commands and DOS batch files.

Unit 2 describes how to install Windows 3.1x, the components of the Windows interface, the several core components required for Windows to function, and the program configuration components of Windows.

Unit 3 discusses the basics of the operating system, the role of the user interface, and the organization of the Windows 95/98 desktop. In addition, this unit covers managing the desktop, file system objects, and the GUI of Windows 95.

Unit 4 describes the hardware and software requirements for Windows 95/98, and the different types of installation media, as well as the kind of information that is required during the installation process. In addition, this unit covers some of the common problems that arise during the installation process and how to resolve them, and the differences between uninstalling and deleting Windows 95/98.

Unit 5 presents the Control Panel functions, details about hardware and software configurations, how to use the Control Panel to customize settings, the function and structure of the Registry, and how to reconfigure a computer so that it performs as well.

Unit 6 discusses the Windows 95/98 file system and how it manages information, how to optimize and maintain the performance of a Windows-based computer, and how to troubleshoot Windows 95/98 file system problems.

Unit 7 introduces the roles of threads, processes, and multitasking; how various programs operate in the Windows 95/98 environments; how to modify the Windows environment for different types of applications; and how to troubleshoot and resolve application environment problems.

Unit 8 describes Windows 98, and how to install, configure, and manage a local printer on a Windows 95/98 system. It also covers the print spooler and how to configure the Windows 95 printing system, as well as portable technology in the PC industry.

Unit 9 discusses network support architecture and how to configure network components, configure and manage the file system, how to use printer sharing, and how to use user access utilities in peer-to-peer networks. This unit also covers how to use shared files, printers, and resources, and how to optimize a Windows 95/98 system for a network.

Unit 10 covers Windows NT basic concepts, such as logging in and utilizing domain resources in a Windows NT network, sharing and managing Windows 95 resources in the Windows NT domain, and user profiles, system policies, and common troubleshooting problems.

Unit 11 examines the Novell Network, Novell software, and configuration and login to a Novell Network. It also discusses sharing resources and managing them on the NetWare network, as well as resolving problems.

Unit 12 discusses modems and dial-up networking server services, as well as the Internet.

Unit 13 describes the basics of boot and initialization files in Windows 95, and how to troubleshoot problems with them.

Unit 14 presents procedures for problem avoidance, recovery and resources, plug-and-play hardware, and using the system monitor for troubleshooting remote Windows 95 computers.

The Glossary defines the terms and abbreviations related to networking that are used throughout this book.

SEMESTER 2, UNIT 1

- Lesson 1: An Overview of Computer Operating Systems
- Lesson 2: Preinstalling, Installing, and Starting MS-DOS
- Lesson 3: Configuration and Basic DOS Commands
- Lesson 4: An Overview of MS-DOS/PC-DOS Batch Files
- Lesson 5: Unit 1 Exam

SEMESTER 2, UNIT 1, LESSON 1
An Overview of Computer Operating Systems

This lesson provides a brief introduction to several operating systems. An **operating system (OS)** is the software that controls the allocation and use of the hardware in the computer. The user interface, along with the kernel and the **file management system**, form an operating system. It also provides the operating environment with applications used to access resources on the computer. Operating systems perform the basic tasks of recognizing input from the keyboard or mouse, sending output to the video screen or printer, keeping track of files on the drives, and controlling peripherals such as printers and modems.

User interface functionality

The operating system provides users with an interface so that they can enter commands into the computer. The user sends command requests to the computer directly through the user interface. Applications are layered on top of the user interface. Therefore, users can also send command requests to the computer by means of such applications. The kernel, or OS Executive, interprets these requests and directs the appropriate lower-level operating system processes to carry out the necessary operations.

The user interface and the operating system

Most people have produced or written documents and then printed them. Have you ever wondered what happens when you issue a print command? When you tell an application such as Microsoft Word to print a document, you are manipulating the user interface to obtain a specific result: In this case, you have instructed the computer to print.

The user interface gives your command to the operating system kernel, which then interprets the order to print. Next, the operating system kernel takes the output from the application and hands it off to lower-level processes for execution. Soon, your document is printed. Throughout this chain of events, the underlying processes are invisible. The only step you had to perform was to interact with the user interface. Similarly, when you decide to store a document or file and later want to retrieve it, the file management system or file system of the operating system facilitates this process, requiring minimal intervention on your part.

CP/M

In 1973 Gary Kildall wrote the first PC operating system (using the PL/M program language he invented) called **Control Program for Microcomputer (CP/M)**. Initially it ran on the Intel 8008 chip, and later translated to the 8080 chip. CP/M is similar to DOS.

When IBM entered the PC market in 1981, it initially licensed an operating system instead of developing and supporting one of its own. IBM had gone to Kildall for the CP/M operating system, but when Kildall missed an appointment to discuss IBM's possible use of CP/M, the

IBM executive went on to his next appointment—with a company named Microsoft. Bill Gates seized the opportunity immediately. The rest, as we know, is history.

The history of MS-DOS and PC-DOS

The "Quick and Dirty Operating System" (Q-DOS) was first developed by Tim Patterson of Seattle Computer Products, but was purchased by Microsoft for $100,000. Microsoft then refined it and named it **MS-DOS**, short for Microsoft Disk Operating System.

Because Microsoft licensed IBM to use its operating system rather than buy it outright, Microsoft was able to license MS-DOS to other companies as well. As a result, the two most prevalent disk operating systems are IBM PC-DOS and MS-DOS. PC-DOS is the version installed on IBM computers, and MS-DOS is the version used on most other PCs. MS-DOS and PC-DOS are essentially identical, except that in Version 6 the systems have different add-on utilities.

Other types of DOS

Another type of operating system, DR-DOS, was developed by Digital Research. Novell Corporation bought Digital and changed the operating system's name to Novell DOS. Novell DOS has a feature not found in PC-DOS or MS-DOS called *multitasking*, which enables it to run several programs at once. With this feature, users can easily switch between programs.

Comparisons of DOS versions

DOS has evolved from its original incarnation as a text-based program to one that uses a graphical user interface (GUI). With each new program version, DOS software designers have capitalized on improvements in the power and sophistication of PCs. Table 1-1 summarizes this evolution.

Table 1-1   *The evolution of DOS*

MS-DOS Version	Double-Sided Disk	Print Command	Recover Command	Hierarchic Directories	Label Command	3 1/2-inch Floppy Drives	Menus	Edit Command	Enhanced/ Extended Memory
1.0									
1.1	x								
2.0	x	x	x	x					
3.0	x	x	x	x	x				
3.2	x	x	x	x	x	x			
4.0	x	x	x	x	x	x	x		
5.0	x	x	x	x	x	x	x	x	x
6.0	x	x	x	x	x	x	x	x	x
7.0	x	x	x	x	x	x	x	x	x

Microsoft Windows

As early as 1974, Xerox's Alto workstation—with its GUI, mouse, and computer-to-computer communication—pioneered the friendly systems we take for granted today. By the late 1980s, even as DOS was evolving and improving, its limitations were becoming obvious. Computer-using customers, especially at-home, technically unsophisticated users, wanted machines and software designed and written for nontechnical consumers. MS-DOS did not meet the ease-of-access and ease-of-use needs of the modern—and growing—computer customer base.

Apple and Microsoft caught the gist early, incorporating Alto's user-friendly technology into their own software development, modifying Windows and Macintosh operating system software to accommodate user needs. The result: the now-commonplace friendly GUIs of Macintosh and Windows.

Windows 1.x

Looking more graphical than its DOS underpinnings, Windows 1 still did not feature the icons we have in today's GUIs. Menu systems, tiled windows, mouse access, and multitasking are Windows 1 features still offered in subsequent, even more advanced Windows versions.

Windows 2.x

In the late 1980s Windows 2 brought the familiar access-making icons of today's interfaces. Along with the icons, Windows 2 allowed overlapping, not just tiled, application windows. Windows 2 supported **program information files (PIFs)**, giving users configuring power to run DOS applications more efficiently. An enhanced Windows 2—Windows 386, designed to be compatible with Intel's 386 processor—permitted multiple extended memory DOS sessions.

Windows 3.x

In 1990 Windows 3 included File Manager, Program Manager, and network support in its ever-adapting functions. Windows 3.0's 386 Enhanced mode opened up the hard drive to virtual memory, supplementing the computer's RAM. Better graphical and multimedia capability, improved error-protection, and easier application cooperation with **Object Linking and Embedding (OLE)** accompanied Windows 3.1's 1992 introduction. With Windows 3.11's move to a 32-bit environment—Windows for Workgroups—Windows offered support for both 16-bit and 32-bit applications.

Windows 95

As hardware and software continued to improve, DOS became an unfulfilling underpinning to the Windows GUI. In a move to accommodate ever-expanding modern software and hardware capabilities, Microsoft integrated its friendly Windows shell with its operating system. Now, with Windows 95, the friendly interface was not simply underpinned by the operating system: The friendly interface had *become* the operating system.

Since Windows 95 was released in August 1995, Microsoft has made numerous changes and additions to the operating system. There are four versions of Windows 95—an original version, followed by versions A, B, and C. It's easy to determine your Windows 95 version. Click Start, Settings, Control Panel, and then double-click System. The system dialog box displays your Windows 95 version. The original Windows 95 version, numbered 4.00.950, upgraded Windows 3 versions. The following versions followed:

- Windows 95 A—Windows 95 A (4.00.950a) improved on the previous Windows 95 with a Service Pack 1 update.

- Windows 95 B—The enhanced Windows 95 B, also called OSR2, was released to hardware manufacturers for preinstallation on computers that were subsequently sold to customers. OSR2's most important feature is its **FAT32**, with updated disk utilities.

- Windows 95 C—Windows 95 version C supports the universal serial bus (USB) and Internet Explorer.

Windows 98

A major revision to Windows 95 culminated in Microsoft's introducing Windows 98. Operating intrinsically much like its recent Windows 95 ancestor, Windows 98 offers enhanced and useful features. Better Web/Windows Explorer integration, enhanced support for multimedia and multiple monitors, and a helpful Maintenance Wizard are a few of the features of Windows 98 that distance it from Windows 95.

Windows 98's more recent second edition improves network security features and offers a specification utility for removable disks and other storage hardware. It also provides Internet connection sharing, allowing every networked client computer single-host Internet access.

Windows NT

With its wholly 32-bit code and 4-GB RAM potential, **Windows NT** (New Technology) draws high-power-need users who often run large files and sophisticated programs, and who require more security assurance than mainstream desktop computer users. Windows NT offers two versions: **NT Server**, for network servers, and **NT Workstation**, for workstation or standalone computers.

Windows NT 3.1

Microsoft's initial (1993) new-technology operating system, NT 3.1 resembled regular Windows 3.1 in appearance, but worked quite differently underneath. Without its cousin's DOS genes, NT 3.1 was a dependable operating system, but required more hardware to run effectively. NT 3.1 offered 6,000,000 software code lines, and required Microsoft to issue a repair patch file for the more than 90 bugs from which the operating system suffered.

Windows NT 3.5 and 3.51

Increasing software code lines to about 9,000,000, NT 3.5 (1994) upgraded NT 3.1. In 1995 NT 3.51 enhanced the NT operating system to accommodate many Windows 95 programs. Though functionally improved, NT 3.51's Program Manager interface yet retained the old look and feel of its Window 3.1 relatives.

Windows NT 4.0

Microsoft's 1996 introduction of NT 4.0 brought 16,000,000 code lines into its very friendly traditional Windows 95 interface. Maintaining all its predecessors' NT enhancements, NT 4.0 offers Web server capability and allows across-network application distribution. Unlike its similar-looking Windows 95 counterpart, NT 4.0 does not offer plug-and-play support.

Windows 2000

The new **Windows 2000** offers a mainstream Professional desktop and a Server edition. Windows 2000 maintains NT 4.0 network security standards and adds several wide-ranging enhancing features by way of its Windows 98–appearing interface. A few enhanced features include an automatically personalized Start menu, a Network Connections Wizard facilitating computer-to-computer hookup by way of infrared, serial, or parallel port connections, and easier management for network administrators.

OS/2

IBM's updating of DOS led to the emergence of the **OS/2** operating system line. The first OS/2 accommodated at least 286-processor machines. OS/2 version 2 needed at least a 386 processor and offered 32-bit code. OS/2 version 3, called OS/2 Warp, exhibited 486-preferable processor adaptability, 32-bit code, a graphical interface, and preemptive multitasking. OS/2 paralleled the Windows operating system line evolution, and still holds on to some loyal users.

Mac OS

Apple Computer gave its System 7 operating system a new name in 1997: **Mac OS**. The Apple Computer operating system has held on to a piece of the operating system market despite Microsoft's dominance. Mac OS's easy-to-use interface and standard plug-and-play hardware configuring give it high status in the minds of its dedicated users. An important Mac OS downside is that fewer compatible software applications are available than for PCs.

UNIX

For users whose power needs are huge and complex, the **UNIX** operating system offers major complexity and power. UNIX, for example, forms the operating base for the Internet. Although additional software can make UNIX compatible with Windows and DOS applications, UNIX does not generally rate the user-friendly applause of Windows.

Concept Questions   *Semester 2, Unit 1, Lesson 1*

Demonstrate your knowledge of the concepts in this lesson by answering the following questions in the space provided.

1. Explain what an operating system is, how it works, and what it provides for a computer user.

2. Explain why there are a variety of operating systems, and discuss their advantages and disadvantages.

_____

_____

_____

_____

_____

_____

_____

_____

_____

_____

_____

_____

_____

_____

_____

_____

_____

Vocabulary Exercise

Semester 2, Unit 1, Lesson 1

Name: _____

Date: _____   Class: _____

Define the following terms as completely as you can.

CP/M

_____

_____

DOS

_____

_____

file management system

_____

_____

kernel

_____

_____

Mac OS

_____

_____

operating system

_____

_____

user interface

_____

_____

UNIX

_____

_____

Windows 95

_____

_____

Windows 98

_____

_____

Windows NT

_____

_____

Focus Questions

Semester 2, Unit 1, Lesson 1

Name: _____

Date: _____ *Class:* _____

1. Describe CP/M and its function.

_____

_____

_____

2. Describe how MS-DOS and PC-DOS were named.

_____

_____

_____

3. Describe the features of the various versions of MS-DOS.

_____

_____

_____

4. Describe the features of Windows 1.x, Windows 2.x, and Windows 3.x.

_____

_____

_____

5. Describe the versions of Windows 95.

_____

_____

_____

6. Describe some features of Windows 98.

_____

_____

_____

7. Describe the versions of Windows NT.

_____

_____

_____

_____

8. Describe Windows 2000.

_____

_____

_____

9. Describe OS/2.

_____

_____

_____

10. Describe Mac OS.

_____

_____

_____

11. Describe UNIX.

_____

_____

_____

SEMESTER 2, UNIT 1, LESSON 2
Preinstalling, Installing, and Starting MS-DOS

In this lesson you will learn about hardware and software system requirements, preparing a disk for installation, setting up new installations, upgrading previous installations, startup files, and configuring the **autoexec.bat** and **config.sys** files.

Minimum requirements for DOS

The first step in setting up DOS on a computer is to verify the type of computer you have. DOS will only function on IBM and **IBM-compatible** computers that have a processor compatible with the original Intel 8088 model CPU. DOS cannot be installed on Macintosh computers because Apple has its own operating system that is not compatible with DOS. However, a Macintosh system can use DOS with the addition of a special **expansion card**.

DOS will run on some machines because they are **backward compatible** with the 8088 processor. The 486, Pentium Pro, Pentium, Pentium II, and Pentium III processors fit into this category.

DOS requires 7 MB of disk space. You can check available space by using the **dir** command. If there is a version of DOS already installed and you are upgrading, you can type in the command chkdsk.exe, which also shows the available disk space.

Beginning the installation

After you have determined that there is enough disk space available, you can prepare the disk for installation. The first step is to partition the disk. **Partitioning** is a procedure for creating sections within the hard drive to facilitate file organization.

The next step is to format the disk. **Formatting** is an external DOS command that creates a **File Allocation Table (FAT)**, which allows DOS to find files after they have been saved. To simplify the task, you can use the automatic **dos.setup** program to perform both the partitioning and formatting of the disk in an interactive user-friendly procedure.

Configuring a drive with DOS setup

All operating systems require hard drives to be partitioned and formatted. First, you partition the drive to create usable space; then you need to format it to correlate with the operating system. Operating systems vary in the type of formatting they use. For example, Windows NT can use more than one type of format, unlike DOS, which can only use the FAT file system.

Now you are ready to boot the computer. Before you begin, make sure the computer is functional and that all the peripheral devices are attached. Then follow these steps:

1. Insert into the computer's floppy drive the first DOS install disk, which has **command.com**, **io.sys**, and **msdos.sys** files. The boot disk is configured to boot automatically from this floppy disk.

2. Follow the instructions on your screen to set up MS-DOS.

3. If the computer does not boot from the install floppy disk, check the system BIOS to be sure that floppy drive **a:** is defined properly and that it is enabled for booting.

4. Next, setup asks whether you want Setup to configure the drive space for you. Make sure that the Recommended option is checked. If it is not, use the up or down arrows on your keyboard to select it, and then press Enter.

5. Now you should see a dialog box that asks whether you want to restart the computer. Before pressing Enter, make sure that the first setup disk is still in the computer; then press Enter. When you reboot the computer, it resets and reconfigures the hardware and software.

6. After the computer restarts and DOS setup reappears, the screen should verify that it is formatting your hard drive so it can be used by MS-DOS. If the computer shuts down during this procedure, you need to start at the beginning again.

7. When the formatting is done, the computer reboots again, and Setup reappears.

Now your computer is ready to accept the DOS operating system with the actual installation of MS-DOS.

Configuring a drive with fdisk.exe

fdisk.exe (fixed disk setup program) is a DOS program used to configure unused space on any **fixed drive** and allows you to either partition or repartition a hard disk. To run the **fdisk** utility, type c:\dos\fdisk.exe at the command prompt. The **fdisk** Options screen should appear, with four or five options listed. Before making any changes, check the current configuration by completing the following steps:

1. Boot the computer into DOS.

2. When DOS has loaded, type fdisk.

3. Select the fourth option (Display partition information), and press Enter.

4. Notice that the drive has one partition and has been given the drive letter **c:**.

5. Under Usage, the headings shows the percentage of this drive that is being used. It should say 100%.

6. Press the Esc key to go back to the main **fdisk** menu.

After you view the current configuration, you can decide whether you want to delete the existing partition and reconfigure the drive. The first option allows you to create a DOS partition or logical DOS drive. This option takes an area of free space on your disk and configures that space for use by the system.

Creating a partition

To create a partition, follow these steps:

1. Select Option 1.

2. A second menu appears, with three choices:

   a. Create Primary DOS Partition—Choose this if the disk is new.

   b. Create Extended DOS partition—Choose this if there is already a primary partition.

   c. Create Logical DOS Drive(s) in the Extended DOS Partition—Choose this if there is already an extended partition.

3. After you choose one of these options, **fdisk** asks if you want to use the maximum available size (all the free space on the disk) for this partition. If you choose yes, you get one single partition that equals the size of the entire hard drive. If you choose no, you can type in the number of megabytes you want for that partition, and then press Enter. Then you can go back to the main menu and create an extended DOS partition.

Usually you want to use the default setting, which uses all available drive space, when creating an extended partition. DOS can only recognize two partitions; thus, any space left over would be unusable.

Deleting a partition

When you delete a partition, the deletion is permanent, and any data on the partition is unrecoverable. Therefore, before deleting a partition, you should be extremely careful not to delete any partitions on the system that might contain important data. To delete a partition, follow these steps:

1. Select Option 3.

2. A second menu appears, with four choices:

   a. Delete Primary DOS Partition.

   b. Delete Extended DOS Partition—All extended partitions must be deleted before the primary partition.

   c. Delete Logical DOS Drive(s) in the Extended DOS Partition—All logical drives must be deleted before extended partitions.

   d. Delete Non-DOS Partition.

Making a partition active

The final step to making a hard drive usable by DOS is to set the primary partition as the **active partition** for the system. The active partition must have the necessary system files to boot the computer. Setting the partition to be active does not create these system files; it specifically tells the computer where to look for them.

To select the primary partition as active, follow these steps:

1. Select Option 2 from the fdisk main menu and press Enter.

2. **Type** 1 and press Enter. You will see a confirmation message.

3. Press Esc to return to the fdisk main menu.

4. Exit the fdisk routine.

Formatting a floppy disk for DOS

To format a floppy disk for DOS, follow these steps:

1. Boot to DOS so that you have access to the **format** command.

2. Type format a:.

3. Insert the disk and press Enter.When the disk has completed the formatting process, DOS confirms that the disk is formatted and asks for a volume label to identify the disk.

4. Type a name that has 11 or fewer characters, and press Enter to name the disk. Or you can simply press Enter if you do not want to enter a volume label.

5. If you want to format another disk, press **Y** for yes. If not, press **N** for no.

Installing the non-upgraded version of DOS

Three disks (labeled Disk 1, Disk 2, and Disk 3) are used to install MS-DOS. Disk 1 is the bootable disk, which contains the **command.com**, **io.sys**, and **msdos.sys** files. Follow these steps to install the non-upgraded version of DOS:

1. Insert Disk 1 in drive **a:** and turn on the computer.

2. A screen should appear stating that Setup is determining your system configuration.

3. Press Enter to continue with the installation.

4. A screen appears that shows your system settings. Note that the default for the selection bar is These settings are correct. If the Setup routine has made an error, you can change the settings by using the arrow keys on your keyboard. Highlight what you want to change, and then press Enter. You are then asked to enter a new value. When you are done, press Enter to accept the new value. When you are finished making changes, highlight These settings are correct, and press Enter.

5. The next screen asks you where you want to install the DOS files. The default is c:\dos, which is normally the directory you would choose. Press Enter to accept the default directory. If you want to change the location of the DOS directory, press Backspace to delete the existing location, and enter your own location, and then press Enter.

6. When DOS Setup asks you to insert Disk 2, do so, and then press Enter.

7. When Setup asks you to insert Disk 3, do so, and then press Enter.

8. When prompted, remove all disks, and then press Enter to restart the computer in MS-DOS.

Upgrading DOS

Follow these steps to upgrade DOS:

1. Insert Disk 1 from the DOS upgrade set in drive **a:** and turn the computer on.

2. The next screen welcomes you to Setup and gives you the various options you have in running **Install**. Press Enter to start the upgrade.

3. A screen appears that states that because this is an upgrade, you might have some problems. Installation can make duplicates of your old configuration, including an uninstall, on disks. Press Enter to create the uninstall disks. If your upgrade fails, you can use these disks to boot the computer and restore your old version of DOS.

4. After creating the disks, press Enter to continue when prompted.

5. A screen appears that shows your system settings. Note that the default for the selection bar is These settings are correct. If **Installation** made an error, you can change the settings by using the arrow keys on your keyboard. Highlight what you want to change, and then press Enter. You are then asked to enter a new value. When you are done, press Enter to accept the new value. When you are finished making changes, highlight These settings are correct, and press Enter.

6. If your computer has Windows installed, a screen appears, asking you if you want to install the listed programs; press Enter if you do. To change the list, use the arrow keys to highlight a program, and then press Enter.

7. The next screen is similar to the last one. Select the appropriate option and press Enter.

8. If you are ready to perform the upgrade, press **Y** when prompted. **Install** creates an **old_dos.x** directory and starts the upgrade.

9. The computer asks for specific disks; simply follow the **Install** directions.

10. To complete the upgrade, remove all disks from the floppy drives and press Enter to reboot the computer.

Uninstalling DOS

On rare occasions the DOS upgrade may create problems with your system, so you might need to uninstall the upgrade. During the upgrade process, Setup saves your old DOS information on disks. To uninstall DOS, insert the uninstall disk to boot the computer, and follow the instructions. After the process has been completed, your computer will have been restored to your old version of DOS, and the new version will have been completely removed.

Startup

Starting a computer is known as **booting**, which is short for **bootstrapping**, a term used when technology was in its earlier stages. Bootstrapping refers to the expression "pulling oneself up by the bootstraps," which means to start a project from scratch with little or no help.

The booting of the computer begins with a series of hardware and memory checks called the power-on self-test (POST). The POST makes sure that all hardware parts are functioning. Next, it checks the device drivers and searches for an operating system. Then it checks drives **a:** and **c:** for a system-formatted disk. Finally, it begins loading MS-DOS into memory.

As mentioned previously, three files are necessary for a computer to boot up into DOS:

- **command.com** provides a DOS prompt. **command.com** interacts with the user through the keyboard and the screen, and it accepts and carries out the user's commands.

- **io.sys** is classified as a read-only, hidden system file. **io.sys** is part of the operating system that controls the input/output (I/O) functions of the computer. **io.sys** communicates between the hardware components of the computer, such as the hard disk, floppy drive, and printer.

- **msdos.sys** contains startup configuration information to manage program and file management. It is classified as a read-only, hidden system file.

Concept Questions   *Semester 2, Unit 1, Lesson 2*

Demonstrate your knowledge of the concepts in this lesson by answering the following questions in the space provided.

1. Explain the minimum requirements for setting up DOS on a computer.

2. Explain the booting process of a computer.

_____

_____

_____

_____

_____

_____

_____

_____

_____

_____

_____

_____

_____

_____

_____

_____

_____

_____

_____

Vocabulary Exercise   *Semester 2, Unit 1, Lesson 2*

Name: _____

Date: _____   Class: _____

Define the following terms as completely as you can.

backward compatible

_____

_____

chkdsk.exe

_____

_____

FAT

_____

_____

fdisk.exe

_____

_____

format

_____

_____

partition

_____

_____

Focus Questions

Semester 2, Unit 1, Lesson 2

Name: _____

Date: _____   *Class:* _____

1. On what kinds of computers does DOS function?

_____

_____

_____

2. Describe how a Macintosh can use DOS.

_____

_____

_____

3. Which file system can DOS use?

_____

_____

_____

4. Describe the three files that are located on the first DOS installation disk.

_____

_____

_____

5. Describe what you should do if a computer does not boot with the boot floppy.

_____

_____

_____

6. Describe what happens during setup.

_____

_____

_____

7. Describe how you run **fdisk**.

_____

_____

_____

8. How many partitions can DOS recognize?

_____

_____

_____

9. Describe what an active partition is.

_____

_____

_____

10. Describe what booting is.

_____

_____

_____

11. Describe what files are needed to boot, and what functions those files serve.

_____

_____

_____

_____

SEMESTER 2, UNIT 1, LESSON 3
Configuration and Basic DOS Commands

You have learned about the minimum system requirements for hardware and software, preparing a disk for installation, setting up new installations, and upgrading DOS. In this lesson, you will learn about the primary function of DOS, major DOS elements, and how to configure the **autoexec.bat** and **config.sys** files. You will also learn about essential commands for MS-DOS and PC-DOS.

The primary function of DOS

A computer can perform tasks, such as word processing, database management, spreadsheet calculations, and running games. These functions are performed by programs called **applications**. Applications contain files that can be accessed by DOS, which in turn sends instructions to the processor, where the code is executed. Then, the operating system can send instructions to the printer, monitor, or other devices.

File management is another important task of the operating system. Filenames in DOS are limited by the 8.3 convention, which specifies that all filenames must be 8 or fewer characters, and may contain an extension of up to 3 characters. For example, the filename **config.sys** has 6 characters in its filename and 3 in its extension.

DOS users can assign four file attributes that determine the level of a file's interaction with the system. The **read-only** attribute prevents a file from being modified or deleted. Backup programs use the **archive** attribute to determine when a file needs to be backed up. The **system** attribute tells the operating system that the file should not be deleted because it is essential for the operating system to function. Finally, the **hidden** attribute protects essential files from being deleted or removed by preventing them from being seen in the main directory.

Another primary function of DOS is the management of the hard disk drive and floppy disks. DOS enables the user to create and delete partitions on a hard drive, back up disks, format partitions and floppy drives, and compress files.

DOS can also manage a system. For example, DOS offers the option to adjust the date and time, and has built-in utilities to examine the system's hardware configuration and the amount of memory being used.

The major elements of MS-DOS

DOS contains two essential components:

- The I/O system consists of two hidden files: **io.sys** and **msdos.sys**. These two read-only files are the core of MS-DOS, and they are stored on the root directory of the bootable DOS disk.

- The **command.com** file is the most visible portion of MS-DOS, and allows the user and the computer to communicate.

All three of these files are essential because the computer will not even boot without them.

Customizing the autoexec.bat file

autoexec.bat stands for automatically executed batch program. This startup file automatically runs each time DOS is loaded and tells the computer what commands or programs to execute automatically after bootup.

A common command line on the **autoexec.bat** screen is the **prompt** command. This command tells DOS to display the current drive name and the current directory name as part of the prompt. An example of a prompt command is **prompt $ p $ g**. Table 1-2 shows the symbols used after the $ and the resulting output: As you can see in Table 1-2, the **p** informs DOS to include the current drive and path, and the **g** informs DOS to include the greater-than symbol (>).

Table 1-2   *Symbol output*

Symbol	Output
a	&
b	|
c	(
d	Date
e	Esc key
f	)
g	>
h	Backspace
i	<
j	Designates the current drive
k	Designates the current drive and path
l	=

Symbol	Output
m	Blank space
n	Time
o	DOS version currently in use
p	Move the cursor to the next line

You can also use the **prompt** command to place text onscreen instead of using the symbols. For example, if you type in **prompt hi!**, the screen would display **hi!**.

Another command line is the **path** command:

path c: \ ; c: \ windows; c: \ wp 51; c: \ dbase; c: \ 123

The **path** command specifies which drives and directories MS-DOS searches in order to locate the requested files. In the example above it tells DOS to look into five different directories for program files. When you add software to a computer, it sometimes automatically adds a directory to this path during setup, telling DOS where the new application can be located. If you use more than one drive or directory with the **path** command, you must use a semicolon to separate them. If the **path** command is not configured correctly, you get error messages upon bootup which state that you have a bad command or filename.

smartdrive.exe is a disk-caching program that can improve the performance on a DOS system. **smartdrive.exe**'s purpose is to intercept data that is being read from and written to a hard drive, as well as data that is being read from floppy disks. This data is stored in RAM, in a **cache**. This data can then be retrieved from the cache at a faster speed.

Creating a bootable disk

Before customizing your **autoexec.bat** file, you need to make a bootable disk in case your hard drive fails. To create a bootable disk, use the following steps:

1. At the DOS prompt (**c:\ >**) type **format a: / s**. This command erases any files currently on your **a:** drive and copies the three files that are necessary to boot your computer.

2. Make sure the default drive is **c:**. If it is not, type **c:**.

3. To back up the current copy of **autoexec.bat** to the hard disk, type the following at the DOS prompt: **copy autoexec.bat autoexec.bak**.

4. To back up to drive **a:**, type **copy autoexec.bat a:**.

When you are finished, remove the disk and reboot your computer to execute the new **autoexec.bat** file on your hard drive. Because you have a bootable disk, you can now safely customize your **autoexec.bat** file.

Customizing the config.sys file

The **config.sys** file is a system file that you can alter to meet the needs of your system. This file can be used for tasks such as memory management by arranging the memory addresses used by DOS programs. You can also use **doublespace** in a **config.sys** file, which allows the doubling of disk space created through disk compression. Another option is the **vsafe** command, which enables an automatic virus protection.

Before editing the **config.sys** file, you should make a backup in case you need to restore it to its previous settings. To make a backup, type **copy config.sys config.bak** at the DOS prompt.

To restore previous settings type the following commands:

rename config.sys config.old
rename config.bak config.sys

To edit the **config.sys** file, type **edit config.sys** or **edlin config.sys**.

Main commands of config.sys

The following sections describe the most commonly used commands for **config.sys** and how they are used. The commands must follow certain formats.

The file command

The **file** command designates how many file handles DOS can keep open simultaneously. The maximum number of files is 255. You don't want to set this too high because the memory to the computer system is reduced as this number increases. A normal setting is 30 files. An example of the **file** command is **files=30**.

The buffers command

The **buffers** command determines the number of buffers DOS creates to store data in RAM rather than on disk. A buffer is a temporary memory area where data is kept before being written to a hard drive. By adjusting the number of buffers, you can reduce the number of read and writes on the hard drive and speed up the computer system. When the buffer is set to a higher number, it uses more memory. A hard drive of 120 MB or more would use up to 50 buffers. An example of the **buffers** command is **buffers=50**.

The **device** command

The **device** command loads software drivers that are specific to certain applications. It is executed when DOS is booted. DOS finds the driver and loads it into memory. An example of the **device** command is **device=c:\scangal\scanner.sys**. This command informs DOS to look in the **scangal** directory for the file named **scanner.sys**, to store that data into RAM, and to save it there until there is a request to use the scanner.

himem.sys

himem.sys is also loaded into the system from the **config.sys** file. **himem.sys** is a device driver that provides management of extended memory on 286 or higher computers that contain 1 MB or more of memory. You should use the latest version of **himem.sys** to which you have access. To find the most current version, look in the **\dos** or **\windows** directory and select the latest updated version. An example of a **himem.sys** is **device=c:\windows\himem.sys**.

emm386.exe

emm386.exe is a device driver that provides support for expanded memory and the management of upper memory blocks. It is loaded after **himem.sys** and before other device drivers that attempt to use extended memory. This device driver only runs on 386 or better systems. An example of **emm386.exe** is **DEVICE=C:\DOS\EMM386.EXE 4096 RAM X=D800-DFFF**.

Internal commands for DOS

Internal commands are executed through the **command.com** file.

The **dir** command

dir stands for directory. This command brings up a list that contains file information such as name, time, date, and size, as well as the cluster number of the file's beginning location on the computer system. You can also find out how much space is available on a specified drive with this command. To see a directory, type **dir**. A list of files appears onscreen for that particular command prompt. You can also use **dir** to locate a file. To do this, just type **dir** and then the filename.

The **del** command

del stands for delete, and **del** is an internal DOS command that deletes files. For example, to delete the file **chekhov.ext** on the **a:** drive, you type **del a:\chekhov.ext**. If you want to delete all the files in the **word** directory, type **del c:\windows\word**.

The **md** or **mkdir** command

The **md** or **mkdir** command stands for make directory. You use the **md** command to create a directory on a drive. For example, to create a directory in drive **c:** called **mydoc**, you type **md c:\mydoc**.

The **cd** or **chdir** command

Another internal command is **cd** or **chdir**, which you use to change the current directory. For example, to change from **a:** to **c:**, simply type **cd c**.

The **edit** command

You use the **edit** to modify existing files or to create new text files. When you type the **edit** command, MS-DOS Editor appears onscreen, with pull-down menu options. You can use the menus with a mouse, or with the Alt key and the first letter of the menu name.

The **copy** command

The **copy** command copies a file from one location to another. For example, you use **copy bus.doc a:** to copy the file named **bus.doc** to the disk in drive **a:**. You can use this command to copy one file or multiple files. You can also merge and rename files by using the **copy** command.

The **ren** command

ren stands for rename and is used to change the name of a file. **ren** can only be used to rename the file; it cannot be used to move the file to another directory. For example, to change a Word document file in the **music** directory from **mozart** to **beethoven**, you type **ren c:\word\music\mozart.doc beethoven.doc**.

Wildcard characters

You can use **wildcard characters** such as * and ? in place of letters or words. These characters are used when you want to do a particular operation with several files at once. For example, if you want to locate all the files that have an **.exe** extension, you use a wildcard with the **dir** command: **dir *.exe**.

External commands for DOS

External commands have an **.exe** or **.com** extension and are usually located in the **dos** or **windows** directory. To execute an external command, all you need to do is type the command and then press Enter. Before an external command can execute, the system must find the directory where the command is located. The directory is usually included in the system's **path** statement where the command is located. If not, the command must be executed from within the directory in which it resides.

The *attrib* command

The **attrib** command is an external command that displays or sets file attributes. The four file attributes are

- Hidden—Files with this attribute do not appear in the directory.

- System—Files with this attribute should not be deleted.

- Read-only—Files with this attribute cannot be deleted or erased.

- Archive—When files are modified, MS-DOS sets the archive bit to mark files. This is used to save only the modified files to a backup device.

The *msbackup* command

msbackup lets you make copies of important hard disk files, programs, or data. **msbackup** has a pull-down menu feature, and lets you set up various options to back up files. **msbackup** can back up files to disks or other DOS-compatible devices. To start the backup process, type **msbackup** and press Enter. Follow the directions and choose the type of backup that is applicable to your needs. There are three types of backups you can choose from:

- Incremental backup—Backs up only files changed or newly created since the last full or incremental backup.

- Differential backup—Backs up only files that have changed or been created since the last full backup.

- Full backup—Does a complete backup, whereby all the files on the hard drive are backed up each time the procedure is performed. This is the safest type of backup, but it also takes a lot of time.

The *xcopy* command

A command that is similar to **copy** is **xcopy**. **xcopy** is a faster DOS copy program that can copy subdirectories or even a complete disk. **xcopy** is an external command and differs from **copy**, which is an internal command. For example, **xcopy *.*/a:/s** copies all files from the current directory and subdirectories to drive **a:**.

MS-DOS versus PC-DOS

The differences between MS-DOS and PC-DOS are minimal. MS-DOS stands for Microsoft Disk Operating System. PC-DOS is the IBM-specific brand of DOS that stands for Personal Computer Disk Operating System. Most of the differences between the two DOS systems are in the add-on utilities.

Table 1-3 shows some of the advantages of these two operating systems.

Table 1-3   *MS-DOS and PC-DOS comparison*

Program	MS-DOS	Advantages	PC-DOS	Advantages
Backup	**msbackup**	None	**cpbackup**	Contains a scheduler program that can perform unattended backups at a specified time, and also has user experience levels
Data recovery	Data Recovery	A simplified version of Central Point Undelete	**undelete**	Also uses Central Point Undelete, but more effective in recovering data in deleted directories and files
Text editors	**edit**	Easier to use than **pc-dos e**	**pc-dos e**	Contains more functions than MS-DOS
Disk compression	Doublespace and SuperStor	Has a full-screen user interface	Doublespace and SuperStor	Full-screen user interface must be purchased separately
Antivirus programs	**msav**	A simplified version of **cp antivirus**	**ibmavd**	Has the capability to detect twice the number of viruses as **msav**, and can be scheduled to do this automatically

Concept Questions

Semester 2, Unit 1, Lesson 3

Demonstrate your knowledge of the concepts in this lesson by answering the following questions in the space provided.

1. Explain how DOS is configured and the basic commands it provides.

2. Explain how MS-DOS and PC-DOS compare, and discuss their advantages and disadvantages.

_____

_____

_____

_____

_____

_____

_____

_____

_____

_____

_____

_____

_____

_____

_____

_____

_____

_____

_____

Vocabulary Exercise *Semester 2, Unit 1, Lesson 3*

Name: _____

Date: _____ *Class:* _____

Define the following terms as completely as you can.

application

_____

_____

buffers command

_____

_____

cd or chdir command

_____

_____

copy command

_____

_____

del command

_____

_____

device command

_____

_____

dir command

_____

_____

edit command

_____

_____

emm386.exe

_____

_____

file command

_____

_____

himem.sys command

_____

_____

md or mkdir command

_____

_____

ren command

_____

_____

Focus Questions

Semester 2, Unit 1, Lesson 3

Name: _____

Date: _____   *Class:* _____

1. Describe what the 8.3 convention is.

_____

_____

_____

2. Describe the major elements of MS-DOS.

_____

_____

_____

3. Describe **smartdrive.exe**.

_____

_____

_____

4. Describe what the **config.sys** file is.

_____

_____

_____

5. Describe internal commands.

_____

_____

_____

6. Describe wildcard characters.

_____

_____

_____

7. Describe external commands.

_____

_____

_____

8. Describe **msbackup**.

_____

_____

_____

9. Explain the differences between an incremental backup, a differential backup, and a full backup.

_____

_____

_____

10. What are the four attributes, and when are they used?

_____

_____

_____

SEMESTER 2, UNIT 1, LESSON 4
An Overview of MS-DOS/PC-DOS Batch Files

You have learned how to configure the **autoexec.bat** and **config.sys** files and about the essential commands for MS-DOS and PC-DOS. In this lesson, you will learn what a batch file is, and how to create and implement batch files so they run efficiently.

A **batch file** is an **ASCII** text file that contains a series of DOS instructions to the computer, instructing it to perform specific tasks in an efficient manner. An example of a batch file is the **autoexec.bat** file, which contains a series of startup commands. All batch files have the extension **.bat**.

Batch file commands

When creating a batch file, always use the proper syntax for DOS commands, and enter one command per line. The following are some common commands used in batch files:

- The **rem** command allows you to put remarks into a batch file program.

- **if...then** is used in making decisions. For example, **if** the color is red, **then** go to the next screen.

- The **call** command runs a second batch file from within a batch file.

- The **choice** command stops the batch file and allows the user to make a choice. It is usually used with **if...then** statements.

- The **echo** command displays information on the screen, which is usually the line of text following the **echo** command. You can also use this command to eject a piece of paper from a printer.

- The **pause** command displays a "press any key" message and waits for you to press a key before going on to the next command.

- The **goto** command is useful only inside a batch file because it is a programming command to jump to another location in the file.

Batch file parameters

Parameters are also called **variables**, and are used to change the way batch files are executed. There are two types of batch file parameters: DOS parameters and command-line execution parameters. DOS parameters are placed in the **autoexec.bat** file. They are used to specify environmental variables, so they are sometimes referred to as **environmental variables**. Command-line execution parameters are parameters that are passed to a batch file or to a program from a batch file's command line.

Creating a batch file

Follow these steps to create a batch file:

1. Load the text editor on your computer and select New from the File menu.

2. Start entering DOS commands.

3. When you finish, save the file with the DOS extension **.bat**.

Increasing the efficiency of batch files

After you create your batch files, you might find that they don't work as effectively as you wanted. Here are a few guidelines to make your batch files more efficient:

- You can execute batch files to run automatically at startup, just like the **autoexec.bat** file. To do this you use the **call** command to execute another batch file from within **autoexec.bat**.

- If you want to terminate a batch job, hold down the Ctrl key and press Break. DOS then asks if you want to terminate the batch job. Press Y to terminate, or press N to continue. Another way to terminate a batch job is to press Ctrl + C.

- To make batch files easier to use, make sure you use the batch file extension **.bat**. Note that files named with the extensions **.exe**, **.com**, and **.bat** are files that contain programs. Typing one of these filenames without the extension causes DOS to recognize the file type and execute the program.

- Name batch files according to their function.

- When naming batch files, make sure that you don't assign a name that is the same as an existing DOS command, or DOS will search and execute the first one it finds. DOS searches in this order: **.com**, **.exe**, and then **.bat**.

Concept Questions   *Semester 2, Unit 1, Lesson 4*

Demonstrate your knowledge of the concepts in this lesson by answering the following questions in the space provided.

1. Explain what a batch file is and how it is used.

2. Explain how to increase the efficiency of a batch file.

_____

_____

_____

_____

_____

_____

_____

_____

_____

_____

_____

_____

_____

_____

_____

_____

_____

_____

Vocabulary Exercise   *Semester 2, Unit 1, Lesson 4*

Name: _____

Date: _____   *Class:* _____

Define the following terms as completely as you can.

ASCII

_____

_____

batch file

_____

_____

call command

_____

_____

choice command

_____

_____

command-line execution parameters

_____

_____

DOS parameter

_____

_____

echo command

_____

_____

environmental variable

_____

_____

goto command

_____

_____

if...then

_____

_____

pause command

_____

_____

rem command

_____

_____

Focus Questions

Semester 2, Unit 1, Lesson 4

Name: _____

Date: _____ *Class:* _____

1. How many DOS commands can you use per line?

_____

_____

_____

2. Describe some common batch file commands.

_____

_____

_____

3. Describe what parameters are.

_____

_____

_____

4. Describe DOS parameters.

_____

_____

_____

5. Describe command-line execution parameters.

_____

_____

_____

6. Describe how to execute a batch file from within **autoexec.bat**.

_____

_____

_____

7. Describe how to terminate a batch job.

_____

_____

_____

8. What filename extension is used for batch files?

_____

_____

_____

9. What filename extensions designate files that contain programs?

_____

_____

_____

SEMESTER 2, UNIT 1, LESSON 5
Unit 1 Exam

If you have access to the online Aries A+ curriculum, contact your instructor for the Assessment System URL. If you do not have access to the online curriculum, please continue to Unit 2.

SEMESTER 2, UNIT 2

- Lesson 6: Installing Windows 3.x
- Lesson 7: An Overview of Windows Interface Components
- Lesson 8: Windows 3.x Core Components and Configuration
- Lesson 9: Windows 3.x Configuration Utilities
- Lesson 10: Unit 2 Exam

SEMESTER 2, UNIT 2, LESSON 6
Installing Windows 3.x

In this lesson, you will learn how to install Windows 3.x by using both the express setup and the custom setup. This lesson assumes that you are installing Windows 3.x from 3 1/2-inch disks. Windows has prerequisites, similarly to DOS. The computer system needs to have a 286 or better processor to run Windows in standard mode. To run Windows in 386-enhanced mode, a 386 processor or better is required.

It is recommended that you install Windows over a DOS version of greater than 5.0, but it can be installed on MS-DOS or PC-DOS version 3.1 or better. Keep in mind that these prerequisites are the minimum requirements. You can run Windows with these minimum settings, but it will be very slow. Windows 3.1 should have a 386 processor or better, with 4 MB of RAM and 30 MB of free disk space for best performance. Windows 3.1 requires at least 8 MB available disk space. An upgrade from an earlier version would require 5 MB to 6 MB in addition to what the current Windows is already using.

640 KB of **conventional memory** and 1024 KB (1 MB) of **extended memory** are required for 386-enhanced mode. For standard mode, 640 KB of conventional memory and 256 KB of extended memory are required.

Windows requires a mouse in order to run, because not all Windows programs can use keyboard shortcut command keys. Additionally, you need a video card that has a Windows driver and a monitor that is compatible with that type of video card.

The first part of the installation process involves files from floppy disks being copied to the hard drive and **decompressed**. During the setup process, you are asked to remove and insert disks, according to a specific number. After you insert each disk, click Continue or press Enter to allow the installation to continue. For both express and custom setup, you begin the installation process the same way:

1. Place Disk 1, which contains the file **setup.exe** in the computer.

2. Type **a:\setup** at the **c:** prompt. Setup responds with a message that says it's checking the hardware configuration of your computer, and you get a screen that welcomes you to Setup.

3. To read the help information, press F1; otherwise, press Enter to continue. If you need to exit, you can press F3 anytime during the setup process.

The next screen lets you choose which type of setup you want to use: express or custom. The following sections describe these two processes.

Express setup

Express setup automatically chooses the applications and utilities that will be installed. Express makes the following decisions for you:

- Setup automatically configures the mouse, language, keyboard, and network (if applicable).

- Setup configures the **autoexec.bat** and **config.sys** files.

- Setup suggests that you install Windows to **c:\windows**, and if there is a version of Windows already on your computer, it asks if you want to upgrade.

- Setup searches for available disk space to ensure that there is enough to install Windows 3.1. Setup recommends a partial setup if there is not enough disk space available to install the standard installation.

- Setup adds any currently installed printers from Windows 3.0.

- Setup adds icons for any existing Windows, and some DOS, applications that are on your hard disk.

- After Setup has completed the installation process, it offers some basic instructions on how to use a mouse and explains some basic Windows concepts.

To continue the setup process, follow these steps:

1. Choose Express Setup and press Enter. At this point, Setup is copying files to your hard disk.

2. When Setup asks you to insert Disk 2, do so and press Enter.

3. The next step is to enter the user information. Enter your name and company. If you entered the information correctly, click Continue; if not, click Change, and you can enter the correct information.

4. When the install is finished, Setup starts setting up DOS and Windows applications. When Setup searches for DOS and Windows applications, it creates an icon in the Applications program group. Setup asks where you would like to place the MS-DOS Editor (**edit.com**). Click on MS-DOS Editor, and then click OK so that Setup accepts this as a program and creates an icon for it.

5. Next, Setup asks if you want to view the Windows tutorial. You can click Run to see the tutorial now, or skip it and run it later.

Setup is now finished! You have the choice to restart Windows to begin using it or to return to MS-DOS. It is recommended that you return to MS-DOS, and then reboot the computer. If Setup made any changes to **config.sys** or **autoexec.bat**, then these will be corrected. If you don't return to MS-DOS, Windows might not run properly.

Custom setup

This time we are going to choose **custom setup**, so choose C to perform the custom setup, and then follow these steps:

1. Setup asks you to specify which directory to install Windows in. If the directory it chooses is satisfactory, press Enter, or type in a new path. then press Enter to continue.

2. The next screen that appears is the Windows Settings screen. This screen displays your computer system's software and hardware components, which Windows detected during the initial installation. Check this list carefully for any discrepancies. If you need to change an item, use the arrow keys until the setting you want to change is selected, and then press Enter.

3. This brings up another screen, with a list of choices that you can choose from. Select the correct choice and press Enter. When you are finished making changes, highlight The above list matches my computer and press Enter to begin copying files. Note that setup has detected these settings, and they are usually considered accurate (unless your documentation states otherwise).

4. Setup asks you to type in the drive where Disk 2 is located, to insert Disk 2, and to press Enter to continue copying files. When the DOS portion is completed, Windows is executed for the first time, and it starts the Windows setup program.

5. Next, you need to enter user information. Enter your name and company. If you entered the information correctly, click on Continue; if not, click on Change and enter the correct information.

6. The next screen that appears lets you choose the Windows components. To choose an item, click on the box to mark it. All items in the list are checked by default. If you don't want an item, click on the box to unmark it. When you are finished, click Continue.

7. The next screen lets you choose the Windows applications and utilities for your computer. To install a component, click on the box so that it's marked. To uninstall, make sure the box is not marked. If you want to change a file within a component, make sure the component is checked, and then click Files. This brings up a list of all the files you can add or remove. For example, let's say we want to change the Games component. We want to keep Minesweeper, but would like to delete Solitaire. You would first make sure that Games is checked, and then click on Files. Click on Solitaire, and then click the Remove button. When you are finished, click OK to accept these changes.

8. Setup displays the **virtual memory** setting and gives you the option to select the size and type of your swap file. If you have enough contiguous disk space available, Setup automatically chooses a permanent swap file with the best size possible. If you want to change it, click the Change button, and then select the new type and type in the new size. Click on Change to accept the setting and to continue the installation.

Note: Do not check 32-bit Disk Access unless you are using a Western Digital WD1003 or compatible hard disk, or you have a 32-bit disk access driver for your hard disk. This option enables Windows to write directly to the hard disk, bypassing the BIOS. If there is any sector translation occurring, data is corrupted almost instantly on your hard disk. If you do have a 32-bit–compatible driver and want to speed up Windows, you can check this option.

9. The next step in the process is to install a printer. If you have a printer attached to the computer, you need to install and configure a driver. Using the up or down arrows, scroll through the printers listed, and then click on the name of your printer and click Install.

    If the printer you have is not on the list, choose Install unlisted or updated printer, and click Install. The next screen asks you to insert the disk that came with your printer, and then click OK to install the printer driver. After you have installed the new printer, it will show up in the Installed Printers list.

    The default setting for the printer is LPT1. If you need to change the parallel port, select Connect to choose a different port. Repeat as necessary for other printers you plan to install. When you are finished, click Continue to proceed to setting up your Windows applications.

10. Setup searches your hard disk for applications and then sets them up to run with Windows. To choose both the path and the **c:** (local drive), click the first item, and then hold down the Shift key while clicking the last item. Select both items, then click Search Now to start the search.

11. Setup asks you where you would like to place the MS-DOS Editor (**edit.com**). Click on MS-DOS Editor, and then click OK so that Setup accepts this as a program and creates an icon for it.

12. The final step is to view the Windows tutorial. You can press Run to see the tutorial now, or skip it and run it later.

Setup is now finished! You have the choice to restart Windows to begin using it or to return to MS-DOS. It is recommended that you return to MS-DOS, and then reboot the computer. If Setup made any changes to **config.sys** or **autoexec.bat**, then these will be corrected. If you don't return to MS-DOS, Windows might not run properly.

Concept Questions　　*Semester 2, Unit 2, Lesson 6*

Demonstrate your knowledge of the concepts in this lesson by answering the following questions in the space provided.

1. Explain the minimum requirements necessary to run Windows 3.x.

2. Explain why it is necessary to return to the DOS prompt and reboot your computer after completing Windows Setup.

_____

_____

_____

_____

_____

_____

_____

_____

_____

_____

_____

_____

_____

_____

_____

_____

_____

Vocabulary Exercise   *Semester 2, Unit 2, Lesson 6*

Name: _____

Date: _____   Class: _____

Define the following terms as completely as you can.

conventional memory

_____

_____

custom setup

_____

_____

decompressed

_____

_____

express setup

_____

_____

extended memory

_____

_____

virtual memory

_____

_____

Focus Questions

Semester 2, Unit 2, Lesson 6

Name: _____

Date: _____   *Class:* _____

1. Describe the minimum processor requirement to run Windows 3.x in standard mode.

   _____

   _____

   _____

2. How much disk space is required to install Windows 3.1?

   _____

   _____

   _____

3. Describe the components required to install Windows 3.x.

   _____

   _____

   _____

4. To read the help information, what key do you press?

   _____

   _____

   _____

5. If you need to exit setup, what key do you press?

_____

_____

_____

6. Describe what decisions are made for you if you select express setup.

_____

_____

_____

7. Why is it recommended that you reboot to MS-DOS after the completion of Windows 3.x setup?

_____

_____

_____

8. Describe how you choose the virtual memory setting.

_____

_____

_____

9. Describe how you install a printer.

_____

_____

_____

10. Describe how you set up Windows applications.

_____

_____

_____

SEMESTER 2, UNIT 2, LESSON 7
An Overview of Windows Interface Components

You have learned how to install Windows 3.x using the custom setup and the express setup. In this lesson you will learn about the components of the Windows interface, such as the desktop, Program Manager, File Manager, and Print Manager. You will also learn how to set up applications, as well as how to add and remove components in Windows.

The desktop

The Windows 3.x **desktop** displays icons in the Program Manager, such as Main, Accessories, Startup, Application, and Games. You can move the windows and icons by **clicking and dragging** with a mouse. By **double-clicking** on these icons, you can access these programs. To view the desktop on your Windows system, just turn on the computer and start Windows. The desktop is displayed in the background of your screen.

The Program Manager

The **Program Manager** is located on the desktop. **progman.exe** is the file that runs the program manager. Double-clicking on the Program Manager allows the user access to applications and various utilities needed to customize the Windows system.

The Program Manager uses windows and icons. A window is a rectangular display area that provides space where a program or utility can function. Windows are movable, sizable, stackable, and can be hidden behind other windows. Icons are located in the windows and are used to open applications and utilities.

Window features

The following are some features of **windows**:

- The control box is used to minimize, maximize, and close the application.

- The title bar is located at the top of the screen. It displays the name of an open window.

- The active window is the window that is currently being used.

- The menu bar provides access to a menu that contains a list of commands available in a window.

- The toolbar contains buttons that provide easy access to frequently used commands.

Window states

The following are the window states in Windows:

- A maximized window is one that is enlarged to fill your screen to its maximum potential.

- A restored window can be very small, or it can be as large as a maximized window. The size of the restored window is up to the user.

- A minimized window is reduced to an icon on the desktop in Windows 3.1. In Windows 95 and 98, it is reduced to a button on the Taskbar.

Icons

An **icon** is a picture that represents an object such as a program, file, or command. The label, graphic, program location, and working directory location make up the elements of an icon. The label defines the name of the program, and the graphic represents what the program does. When a user clicks on an icon, that icon becomes active.

A user can view the program location and the working directory by looking at the icon's **properties**. To change the properties, click File on the Program Manager menu, and then go to Properties. In some instances, an icon on a computer could have, for example, a label and a graphic that indicates a word processing program, but when you click on this icon, an accounting program opens. In this case, the user might have changed the properties of that particular icon to keep other users ignorant about their desktop contents.

The File Manager

The **File Manager** allows the user to manage files efficiently. The equivalent DOS commands used in the file manager are **dir, move, copy, xcopy, ren, diskcopy, format, cd, del, deltree, attrib, undelete, backup**, and **md**. The File Manager also contains a search option that allows you to locate a file by typing in the name, phrase, or extension associated with that file.

Wildcards can be used to search for all files that contain certain specifics. For example, if you wanted to find all the files that have the extension **.exe** you would type ***.exe** in the search field. The search engine would then locate all the files with that extension, and list them.

The Print Manager

The **Print Manager** is located in the Main window, and it allows the user to install a printer, connect to a logical port, set up the specific printer parameters, and view what print jobs are lined up in the print queue. The Print Manager is also used to delete, pause, and resume print jobs that are in the queue.

Before you can use the Print Manager, a printer needs to be installed. To install a printer, click on the Options menu and go to Printer Setup. Under the list of printers, find one that is compatible with your printer. You might have to use the book that came with your printer to find a compatible printer if your printer is not listed.

After the printer is installed, click Setup. These options will let you configure the paper size, paper source, graphics resolution, copies, memory, and fonts. Complete the options for your settings, and then click OK.

The Control Panel

The **Control Panel** is located in the Main group of Windows 3.1. Typical options in the Control Panel are color, fonts, keyboard, drivers, sound, date and time, printers, and the desktop. Users can design their desktop colors and choose from a variety of different styles of wallpaper. They can also change the date and time, as well as add fonts and drivers to their computer.

The 386-Enhanced Panel

The 386-Enhanced Panel lets you change the performance of your system, using three options: device contention, scheduling, and virtual memory.

Device contention is used to configure how the system should deal with conflicts over resources. The default setting uses an idle time of 2 seconds.

The scheduling option lets the user determine how much of the system's resources are dedicated to the foreground application, which is on top of all the windows, or in front of all the other applications.

The virtual memory button determines the way the system will use space on the hard drive to supplement the physical RAM. With a setting that is too low, you will reduce the size of the swap file. A **swap file** stores information from a special file on disk; when the information is needed, it is "swapped" back to the main memory. If you set its size too high, it will create problems in searching for information and slow down the system. The recommended default value should be left alone because it is pivotal to the performance of the Windows environment.

Windows Setup

Windows Setup is located in the Main group. Most of the time, users do not need to make changes in this location. For technicians, Windows Setup can serve as a useful area to view the input/output devices installed, to change system settings, to set up applications, and to add and remove Windows components.

To change the system settings, select this option and click OK. You need the Windows Setup disks to install new drivers, or if you are installing new hardware, you need the accompanying disk. When you are finished, you need to restart the machine.

To set up applications, click on the Options menu, and then select Setup Applications. If you select Search for applications and click OK, Windows conducts a search of the machine, looking for new application programs. Windows then creates an icon so the application can be accessed.

Another option in Windows Setup is Add/Remove Windows Components. This allows the user to add or delete different Windows components that are optional to the system. You can add or delete by marking or unmarking the appropriate item. The amount of space each component takes up on the hard drive is listed so you know how much space you can free up by deleting the various components.

Concept Questions   *Semester 2, Unit 2, Lesson 7*

Demonstrate your knowledge of the concepts in this lesson by answering the
following questions in the space provided.

1. Describe the various Windows interface components.

2. Explain why the Windows 3.x Program Manager uses windows and icons, and
describe some of them.

_____

_____

_____

_____

_____

_____

_____

_____

_____

_____

_____

_____

_____

_____

_____

_____

_____

_____

Vocabulary Exercise   *Semester 2, Unit 2, Lesson 7*

Name: _____

Date: _____   Class: _____

Define the following terms as completely as you can.

click and drag

_____

_____

double-click

_____

_____

File Manager

_____

_____

icon

_____

_____

Program Manager

_____

_____

properties

_____

_____

swap file

_____

_____

wildcard

_____

_____

window

_____

_____

Focus Questions   *Semester 2, Unit 2, Lesson 7*

Name: _____

Date: _____   *Class:* _____

1. Describe a window's basic elements.

_____

_____

_____

2. Describe the three different states in which windows can exist.

_____

_____

_____

3. Describe the Print Manager.

_____

_____

_____

4. Describe the Control Panel.

_____

_____

_____

5. Describe the 386-Enhanced Panel.

_____

_____

_____

6. Describe a swap file.

_____

_____

_____

7. Describe how you set up applications.

_____

_____

_____

SEMESTER 2, UNIT 2, LESSON 8
Windows 3.x Core Components and Configuration

You have learned how to install Windows 3.1 by using both express setup and the custom setup. In this lesson, you will learn about the several core components that need to interact to make Windows function. You will also learn how the program configures Windows components.

Windows consists of the following files: core component files, program configuration files, **win.com**, **progman.exe**, DLL files, font files, and configuration utilities. All the core components are covered in this lesson, except the configuration utilities, which are discussed later.

Core component files

The core components consume the most resources and carry out the majority of the Windows functions. Generally, when there is a problem, it's usually because one of the core files doesn't have the required resources.

To check the available resources, select Help from the Program Manager, and then go to About Windows Program Manager. At the bottom of this box is the item System Resources that shows the amount of available resources.

The GDI Manager

gdi.exe is the Graphical Display Interface (GDI) Manager, whose primary function is to draw icons and windows. When something needs to be drawn, Windows first contacts **gdi.exe**. It then contacts the video card through the video driver and informs it how to draw the object.

For each open window, **gdi.exe** requires memory. Therefore, when there are many windows open, a lot of memory is being used. Therefore, it's a good idea to close any windows that you are not using.

To increase the performance of Windows, you can purchase video cards that optimize **gdi.exe** performance. These cards contain processors that draw Windows objects very quickly and efficiently, easing the burden on the rest of the system.

User interaction

The **user.exe** file has one primary function—to interact with the user of the computer. **user.exe** takes the input from the user and sends it to the other components of Windows. Any time you use your mouse or the keyboard, you are interacting with **user.exe**. Problems can occur when there isn't enough system memory or when the hardware is incorrectly configured for input.

Kernel files

You have learned that the kernel is part of the operating system, as well as how the kernel launches applications and allocates system resources. The two main kernel files are **krnl286.exe** and **krnl386.exe**. The file that is used depends on the operating mode in which Windows is currently running. **krnl286.exe** runs in standard mode, and **krnl386.exe** runs in 386-enhanced mode.

win.com

To start Windows a file called **win.com** (sometimes referred to as the "loader") is run. The Windows Setup program builds this file when you install Windows. It contains the following three components:

- **win.cnf**—The configuration file that builds **win.com**. This file has information about the PC's configuration.

- **lgo**—An executable file that has the code that switches the PC from text to graphics mode and displays the Windows logo file.

- **rle** (the run length encoded bitmap file)—RLE refers to the form of compression used when creating the bitmap. This file is correlated with the type of video adapter used.

When **win.com** is executed, the following occurs:

1. **win.cnf** detects the system configuration and contacts the graphics mode file to change the video adapter into a graphics mode.

2. Next, the graphics mode file loads the logo file, and **win.com** displays the Windows logo.

3. The kernel file, along with the rest of Windows, is loaded after the logo is displayed.

To start Windows, type **win** at the DOS prompt. You can also change the way Windows starts up by changing the format of the startup switch. The following are some examples:

- To force Windows to start in the 386-enhanced mode, type **win /3**.

- To bypass the display of the Windows startup logo, type **win**.

- To create a **bootlog.txt** file in the startup directory, type **win /b**.

- To start Windows and automatically start another application according to its filename, type **win** and specify the filename.

- To force Windows to start in the standard mode, type **win /s**.

The Windows Program Manager

progman.exe is the Program Manager, which is one of the most important components of Windows. It contains groups, program icons, and menus that are used to organize, run, and start programs. The user can create an unlimited number of group windows and fill them with icons to launch executable programs.

DLL files

Dynamic link library (DLL) files have a **.dll** extension. Microsoft engineers realized it would not be efficient to write a big file for every Windows program. So instead, they wrote a program core component and several files that were common to many programs. These miniature code files are known as DLL files.

Program configuration files

The program configuration information is stored in three main areas: INI files, the Windows Registry, and group files.

INI (initialization) files are text files that are used to store program settings and are identified by the **.ini** extension. Each time you change the application's settings, these changes are written to the INI file. When you don't want a particular line in an INI file to load, insert a semicolon (;) in front of that entry.

The four main INI files are **win.ini**, **system.ini**, **progman.ini**, and **control.ini**. **win.ini** specifies startup defaults for Windows. It contains settings you make in the Control Panel, such as wallpaper, fonts, language, and sound mapping settings. Table 2-1 lists some common **win.ini** entries.

The **system.ini** file contains Windows configuration settings that control the hardware. Windows reads the settings from the **system.ini** upon startup. This is the most important INI file because it contains much of the Windows configuration and many of the drivers that Windows uses. When a new driver is installed, an entry is made in the **system.ini** file. Table 2-2 lists some common **system.ini** entries.

Table 2-1   *Common **win.ini** entries*

Entry	Function
[windows]	Has an effect on a variety of elements in your Windows environment. An example is the cursor blink rate or the border width of windows.
[desktop]	Contains settings that control the appearance of the desktop.
[extensions]	Contains settings that link groups of documents with an application so that upon opening a document, Windows starts the application.
[intl]	Contains country-specific settings such as default language, type of measuring system, and keyboard layouts.
[fonts]	Lists the font files that are loaded by Windows.
[ports]	Lists all the available output ports, COM ports, and the current port settings.
[TrueType]	Lists TrueType fonts and options that control the display.
[mci extensions]	Matches the media filenames with MCI drivers.
[network]	Stores network settings.
[sounds]	Lists the names of sound files that are initiated by system events.
[PrinterPorts]	Lists inactive and active printers.
[devices]	Lists printers that are active.
[colors]	Lists all the color settings in the Control Panel.
[compatibility]	Contains a list of programs that are compatible with Windows 3.1.

Table 2-2   *Common system.ini entries*

Entry	Function
[boot]	Details the parameters for the system startup, including font files, grabber files, and device drivers.
[boot.description]	Stores the names of the devices that are installed.
[keyboard]	Stores information about the keyboard settings.
[mci]	Lists media control interface drivers.
[NonWindowsApp]	Controls parameters for DOS sessions and lists information used by non-Windows applications.
[386Enh]	Contains information used in 386-enhanced mode.
[standard]	Contains information used in standard mode.

progman.ini controls the configuration of the Program Manager. It contains all the icons for all the programs you need to run. **progman.ini** has two major sections: settings and groups. The detailed overall settings of the Program Manager are contained within the settings. Settings such as a window's position and the driver used for a specific application are found here. The group section identifies the locations and names of the groups. By changing the group section, you can load a different set of group windows.

The **control.ini** file controls the configuration of the Control Panel. It is used to change settings that affect a window's appearance. For example, **control.ini** has different colors and wallpapers that you might use to design the desktop. Whenever any changes are made, **control.ini** is modified as well. Table 2-3 lists some common **control.ini** entries.

Table 2-3   *Common **control.ini** entries*

Entry	Function
[patterns]	Contains the patterns that can be used on the desktop.
3.1=?	If the ? = Yes, then Windows 3.1 is installed.
[MMPCL]	Contains the settings for multimedia devices.
[installed]	Contains the Windows version number and lists installed printer drivers.
[current]	Specifies the color scheme that is currently being used.
[color schemes]	Lists the color schemes that Windows can use.

The **Registry** is a centralized database, used to store information necessary to configure the system. This database has registration information that contains detailed information associating the applications with their file extensions. For example, when you double-click on a file, the associated application opens the file that you double-clicked.

The **Registry Editor** is an application that allows the user to edit the entries in the Registry. The Registry Editor program is called **regedit.exe**, and the icon for this must be created manually; alternatively, you can go to the Program Manager and choose File, choose Run, type **regedit**, and click OK.

Program Manager group files

Program Manager group files are the files located in the **windows** directory that specify information about which application icons are contained in which groups. Group filenames always have the extension **.grp**, and their names are similar to the type of program. For example, the Main group has the filename **main.grp**.

Font files

Font files are stored in **c:\windows\system**. A **font** consists of the characters available in a particular style and weight for a particular design; a **typeface** is the design itself. A font has various ways of presenting a letter. Fonts come in different sizes, and the size is measured in points (a point is 1/72 inch). There are three main font files in Windows: vector fonts, raster fonts and printer fonts.

Vector fonts

A **vector font**, also called a **TrueType font**, is a font that contains characters drawn using mathematical arrangements of line segments. To enlarge the fonts, vectors are increased in magnitude and are moved further apart. TrueType fonts have **.ttf** and **.fot** extensions.

Raster fonts

Raster fonts are also referred to as **bitmap** or **screen fonts**. A font is designed through a collection of small, independently controlled dots (pixels) arranged in columns and rows. Each size is stored as a separate file. For example, a 10-point font would be stored in one file, and a 14-font would be stored in another file. Raster fonts have an **.fon** extension.

Printer fonts

Printer fonts contain instructions for the printer to print them. Device fonts, printable screen fonts, and soft fonts are the three types of printer fonts:

- **Device fonts**, also called hardware fonts, print the fastest. Either hardwired in the printer's control circuitry or added with a removable cartridge, device fonts are stored inside the printer.

- **Printable screen fonts** are printer fonts that translate and download the regular TrueType and bitmap fonts from the computer to the printer. They allow the printer to print whatever is onscreen.

- A **soft font**, also known as a downloadable font, is a disk-stored character set sent through a special utility to the printer's memory or hard disk. These fonts are commonly used with laser printers and other page printers.

Concept Questions   *Semester 2, Unit 2, Lesson 8*

Demonstrate your knowledge of the concepts in this lesson by answering the following questions in the space provided.

1. Explain the function of the core components of Windows 3.x and the benefits they provide users.

2. Explain the function of the Program Manager group files and the benefits they provide users.

_____

_____

_____

_____

_____

_____

_____

_____

_____

_____

_____

_____

_____

_____

_____

_____

_____

Vocabulary Exercise *Semester 2, Unit 2, Lesson 8*

Name: _____

Date: _____ *Class:* _____

Define the following terms as completely as you can.

font

_____

_____

gdi.exe

_____

_____

printer font

_____

_____

raster font

_____

_____

typeface

_____

_____

user.exe

_____

_____

vector font

_____

_____

Focus Questions

Semester 2, Unit 2, Lesson 8

Name: _____

Date: _____ *Class:* _____

1. Describe the two main kernel files.

_____

_____

_____

2. Describe the **win.com** file.

_____

_____

_____

3. To start Windows, what do you type at the DOS prompt?

_____

_____

_____

4. Describe the ways you can change the format in which Windows starts.

_____

_____

_____

5. Describe the **progman.exe** file.

_____

_____

_____

6. Describe DLL files.

_____

_____

_____

7. Where is program configuration information stored?

_____

_____

_____

8. Describe the **win.ini** file.

_____

_____

_____

9. Describe the **system.ini** file.

_____

_____

_____

10. Describe the **program.ini** file.

_____

_____

_____

11. Describe the **control.ini** file.

_____

_____

_____

12. Describe the Registry.

_____

_____

_____

13. Describe the Registry Editor.

_____

_____

_____

14. Where are font files stored?

_____

_____

_____

SEMESTER 2, UNIT 2, LESSON 9
Windows 3.x Configuration Utilities

In this lesson you will learn about Windows configuration utilities. You will also learn how to add new hardware and software to Windows 3.1. These utilities are provided by Microsoft to make managing Windows parameters easier. The PIF Editor and **sysedit.exe** are the two main types of configuration utilities.

The PIF Editor

Program information files (PIFs) tell Windows how to handle DOS applications that are running in a Windows environment. A PIF file has a **.pif** extension. The PIF Editor is used to create and edit these files. When a DOS application does not have an assigned PIF, Windows uses the default PIF setting from the **windows** directory.

The PIF Editor is found in the Main program group. Before you create a PIF file for a DOS application, check the installation directory to see if there is an existing PIF file. Another resource to check for an updated PIF file is the Web site of the company that created the application.

The following is a list of the settings in the PIF editor's main screen:

- Windows Title—Defines the text that appears at the top of the window when running the application in Windows.

- Program Filename—The name and path of the DOS executable. When you double-click an icon, Windows looks for the application specified.

- Start-up Directory—The specified list of files that enable the DOS application to locate the files it needs.

- Optional Parameters—The switches after the DOS application name that cause them to run properly.

- Memory Requirements—Defines how much conventional memory is required for the application.

- Video Memory—Defines the video mode the DOS application uses in Windows.

- EMS Memory—Defines the minimum and maximum amounts of expanded memory the DOS application needs.

- XMS Memory—Defines the extended memory.

- Display Usage—Specifies whether the application runs using the full screen or in a window.

- Execution—Defines the multitasking abilities of Windows. When the Background option is checked, the application runs in the background, even when it's not the primary application. When the Exclusive option is checked, no other application can run in the background.

- Close Window on Exit—Clarifies what happens when you close the DOS application. If this is checked, it closes the window automatically.

- Advanced—Takes you to an advanced options screen, which we will talk about next.

The following is a list of the settings in the PIF editor's advanced options screen:

- Multitasking Options—Controls how the application receives processor time. The range of processor time is from 0 to 10,000, with 10,000 indicating the most processor time.

- Memory Options—Specifies the memory settings to run the application in 386-enhanced mode.

- Display Options—Specifies how an application uses video in Windows in 386-enhanced mode.

sysedit.exe

To run the **sysedit.exe** files, go to the Program Manager and choose File, Run. The files that **sysedit.exe** can edit are **config.sys**, **autoexec.bat**, **system.ini**, and **win.ini**. To edit one of the files, just click on the window of the file you want to edit. When you have finished editing the file, choose File, Save.

Adding new hardware and software

Before you add new hardware and software, you should back up your INI files, GRP files, **autoexec.bat**, and **config.sys** to a floppy disk or to another directory. If you run into problems installing, you still have copies of your original files that you can copy back to their original locations.

When you add new hardware, Windows requires specific drivers so that it can run the new hardware. Usually installing a new piece of hardware requires immediately installing new hardware-compatible software, consisting of both a DOS portion and a Windows portion. The DOS portion contains drivers for **config.sys** or **autoexec.bat**, as well as other DOS utilities. The Windows portion contains applications needed to use the new device.

To add new software, follow these steps:

1. Insert the installation disk into the computer.

2. From the Program Manager, choose File, Run.

3. Type **a:\setup.exe** or **a:\install.exe**—whichever applies to the application.

Concept Questions　　*Semester 2, Unit 2, Lesson 9*

Demonstrate your knowledge of the concepts in this lesson by answering the following questions in the space provided.

1. Describe the settings in the PIF Editor.

2. Explain what you should do before adding new hardware or software.

_____

_____

_____

_____

_____

_____

_____

_____

_____

_____

_____

_____

_____

_____

_____

_____

_____

Vocabulary Exercise   *Semester 2, Unit 2, Lesson 9*

Name: _____

Date: _____   Class: _____

Define the following terms as completely as you can.

EMS Memory

_____

_____

Execution

_____

_____

Memory Option

_____

_____

Memory Requirement

_____

_____

Multitasking Option

_____

_____

Optional Parameter

_____

_____

PIF

_____

_____

Start-up Directory

_____

_____

sysedit.exe

_____

_____

Video Memory

_____

_____

Windows title

_____

_____

XMS Memory

_____

_____

Focus Questions

Semester 2, Unit 2, Lesson 9

Name: _____

Date: _____   *Class:* _____

1. When you add new hardware, what does Windows require?

_____

_____

_____

_____

2. How do you add new software?

_____

_____

_____

_____

3. Describe the two main types of Windows configuration files.

_____

_____

_____

_____

4. Describe the purpose of the PIF Editor.

_____

_____

_____

_____

5. Describe PIFs.

_____

_____

_____

_____

6. Describe the purpose of **sysedit.exe**.

_____

_____

_____

_____

7. Describe why it is a good idea to back up **.ini** and **.grp** files, along with **autoexec.bat** and **config.sys**, before adding new hardware.

_____

_____

_____

_____

SEMESTER 2, UNIT 2, LESSON 10
Unit 2 Exam

If you have access to the online Aries A+ curriculum, contact your instructor for the Assessment System URL. If you do not have access to the online curriculum, please continue to Unit 3.

SEMESTER 2, UNIT 3

- Lesson 11: The Windows 3.x, 95, and 98 Desktop
- Lesson 12: Managing the Windows 95/98 Desktop
- Lesson 13: Windows 95/98 File System Objects
- Lesson 14: Getting Under MS-DOS and the Windows 95 GUI
- Lesson 15: Unit 3 Exam

SEMESTER 2, UNIT 3, LESSON 11
The Windows 3.x, 95, and 98 Desktop

In this lesson you will learn the basics of the operating system, the role of the user interface, and the organization of the Windows 95/98 desktop.

Without an operating system, where could anyone go on a computer? It'd be like getting into your car without your key and trying to hotwire it, only to discover that your car has no water in the radiator, no oil in the engine, and no gas in the tank. As you have learned, an operating system (OS) is the software that controls the allocation and use of computer hardware and is composed of the user interface, the kernel, and the file management system. It provides the operating environment with the applications it needs to access resources: performing the basic tasks of recognizing input from the keyboard and mouse, sending output to the monitor or printer, keeping track of files, and controlling peripherals such as printers and modems.

Unless you're a cyborg, you'll need help to relate directly to the computer's inner workings, and that's where the user interface comes in. **User interface** is a fancy term for familiar computer hardware features such as the monitor, keyboard, mouse, and onscreen software features such as menus, screen design, command language, and online help. The interface allows the user to control computer functions such as running applications, managing files, and printing.

If you're old enough, you might remember the days when engineers and computer programmers used to hustle over to the university lab to punch holes in cards, submit them to the giant computer that filled the whole room, and meticulously examine their resulting printouts. Fortunately, those days are long gone. Today you can tell an application such as Microsoft Word to print a document by manipulating the interface to get the results you want. In other words, the typical user no longer has to understand all the inner workings of the computer to use it effectively.

The user interface communicates your command to the operating system kernel, which interprets the command. Next, the kernel hands off the correct information to lower-level processes for execution, resulting in a printed document. No in-depth analysis of the computer's mind is necessary—all you have to do is interact with the user interface. Likewise, when you store a document and later retrieve it, the file system component of the user interface does the work for you, with minimal intervention on your part.

The Windows 95/98 GUI and desktop

Different operating systems use different user interfaces. Because these interfaces are designed independently by different manufacturers, they are sometimes described as being **proprietary**. The proprietary interface you will be learning about here is that of the Windows 95/98 operating system. To understand the proprietary user interface concept, imagine you are driving a Porsche (Windows 95). On the dashboard, your Porsche has an instrument panel with indicators for speed, fuel level, and temperature. Your friend, on the other hand, drives a Ford Taurus (Windows 3.1). His instrument panel looks very different from yours, yet it provides him with the same information and ability to get around. You have another friend who owns a Ferrari (Windows 98), and another friend who is preparing to get a Lamborghini (a future operating system).

The goal of Windows 95 is to give the user a more **intuitive interface** by moving to a more consistent **object** paradigm. Nearly everything in Windows 95 is represented as an icon or object: files, folders, programs, printers, modems, and processes. Windows 98 refines the appearance of Windows 95 with an updated interface that provides fast and user-friendly Internet access through Windows Explorer.

Windows 3.1 proved to be more user friendly than MS-DOS, but Windows 95/98 addresses three interface areas that seemed to cause the most problems for users:

- Window management

- File management

- Mouse management

The following sections describe these areas.

Window management

Many Windows 3.1 users would open numerous windows and become confused and lose their programs in the process. To address this issue Windows 95/98 has a Taskbar. This Taskbar provides quick access to all active programs by displaying a title button for each open program. This makes it easy to move quickly from one program to another. If a program gets hidden by another window, selecting the program's button on the Taskbar brings it to the front of the desktop. Thus, by using the Taskbar, users are not likely to waste memory by starting the same program more than once.

Users can configure the Taskbar to their preference and can drag the Taskbar to the sides or to the top of the screen. To get to the Taskbar properties, right-click on the open part of the Taskbar, or go through the Start menu to Settings. Taskbar options include the following:

- Always on Top—This leaves the Taskbar always visible.

- Auto Hide—This leaves the screen vacant so you can use the full screen for a program. The Taskbar is hidden, but it reappears when the cursor moves over its location.

- Small Icons—This changes the default icons to smaller versions, which is useful when working with low-resolution screens.

- Show Clock—This allows you to switch between hiding and showing the clock on the Taskbar.

File management

With the maze of subdirectories in Windows 3.1, many users would lose files or get lost trying to find their favorite programs. Addressing this challenge, Windows 95/98 stores information in folders and files with a simpler layout. You'll learn more about this later in the lesson.

Mouse management

Users of older operating systems often took a while to master the concept of double-clicking. Single-clicking didn't always start programs or produce results. Thus, Windows 95/98 allows single-clicking to activate programs. Double-clicking still exists as an option.

The Windows 95/98 mouse, with its expanded features, offers both left and right buttons. This applies to both the Windows 95 2.5 universal serial bus (USB) and the Windows 98–supported USB mouse. The primary mouse button (typically the left button for right-handed users and the right button for left-handed users) is used for all the traditional mouse activities of pointing, selecting, and dragging.

The secondary mouse button performs functions different from those of the primary button. Right-clicking on and icon or object opens a menu of choices, including Open, Cut, Copy, Create Shortcut, Delete, Rename, Properties, and Send to (which allows you to send a copy of the object to floppy drives, mail recipients, or your briefcase).

More mouse "tricks" occur when you drag and drop with the secondary mouse button. Common options include Move Here, Copy Here, Create Shortcut(s) Here, and Cancel. You can also get creative with this function by drawing a box around all the objects you want to drag, copy, delete, and so on, which allows you to manipulate them all at the same time.

The Desktop

The desktop is the first screen you see when you log on to the Windows 95/98 operating system. Although any number of objects can reside on the desktop, Microsoft uses certain elements as standard or **default** features. These default elements allow alternate means of managing the objects and accessing system resources. Following are the default elements:

- My Computer—A container object of other objects stored on the system.

- Network Neighborhood—A container object of networked computers.

- Recycle Bin—A container object showing deleted files and folders. (Note that these can be recovered in the file management system.)

- Taskbar—A bar on the desktop to manage active applications.

- Start menu—A hierarchical menu system on the desktop that provides an alternate access point to the operating system.

The Windows 95/98 graphical user interface (GUI) desktop was designed to be intuitive and allow you to easily use the interface to control the operating system. The GUI desktop is the work area where you manipulate objects represented by icons or use your mouse pointer to choose menu options and arrive at a desired program.

Desktop objects, icons, and menus

An object is a link from the desktop to almost anything in the underlying operating system. Remember that the same basic functions occur here as with MS-DOS, but you're driving the Porsche now, and the engine is hidden under a sharp-looking hood. In general, objects can be opened and have properties. Windows 95/98 considers the following to be objects:

- Files

- Folders

- Programs

- Printers

- Modems

- Processes

Objects on the Windows 95/98 desktop have pictorial representations called *icons*. In other words, a program is represented to the user as a picture or an icon on the desktop. Clicking on the icon opens the program.

Because objects are symbolic links to resources in the operating system, they have certain properties, which are characteristics associated with the object resource. These include location, the actual filename, and the operating parameters. We'll discuss properties further in future lessons.

You also find menus on the desktop. A **menu** is a list of related commands that you use to perform tasks in Windows and Windows applications. Menu commands are organized in logical groups and are located below the title bar of any application that uses them. For example, the Edit menu includes Cut, Copy, and Paste, which are very useful when borrowing images for Web documents.

Concept Questions   *Semester 2, Unit 3, Lesson 11*

Demonstrate your knowledge of the concepts in this lesson by answering the following questions in the space provided.

1. Explain how the operating system's three parts work together to execute the user's commands.

2. Explain the three management problem areas that Windows 95's user-friendly interface addresses.

_____

_____

_____

_____

_____

_____

_____

_____

_____

_____

_____

_____

_____

_____

_____

_____

_____

Vocabulary Exercise   *Semester 2, Unit 3, Lesson 11*

Name: _____

Date: _____   Class: _____

Define the following terms as completely as you can.

default

_____

_____

desktop

_____

_____

drag

_____

_____

file system

_____

_____

intuitive interface

_____

_____

menu

_____

_____

object

_____

_____

proprietary

_____

_____

Taskbar

_____

_____

user interface

_____

_____

Focus Questions

Semester 2, Unit 3, Lesson 11

Name: _____

Date: _____   *Class:* _____

1. Describe how the user interface relates to the operating system.

_____

_____

_____

2. Describe the GUI in Windows 95/98.

_____

_____

_____

3. Describe how you access the Taskbar properties.

_____

_____

_____

4. Describe the Taskbar options.

_____

_____

_____

5. Describe the functions of the secondary mouse button.

_____

_____

_____

6. Describe the options available if you drag and drop with the secondary mouse button.

_____

_____

_____

7. Describe the desktop and how you use it to manipulate the operating system.

_____

_____

_____

8. Describe some of the container objects on the desktop.

_____

_____

_____

SEMESTER 2, UNIT 3, LESSON 12
Managing the Windows 95/98 Desktop

You have learned about the basics of an operating system, its relationship to the user interface, the role of the GUI in Windows 95, and the basic architecture of the Windows 95 desktop. The Windows 98 desktop is very similar to the Windows 95 desktop, but has changed the interface to make it faster and easier for users to access the Internet.

Desktop objects

There are two kinds of objects in the Windows 95 desktop:

- Shortcuts

- Default system icons

These objects are described in detail in the following sections.

The shortcut function

The **shortcut** function allows the user to create a link within Windows 95/98 to a resource in the operating system such as a program, printer, file, or folder. It uses very little disk space and acts as a "dummy" file that can launch the original. Creating shortcuts differs from copying and moving in that the shortcut is only a pointer to the original object. Changes in the program must take place in the original object.

You can distinguish a shortcut icon from a normal icon by its appearance: Look for a curved arrow on top of the shortcut. The properties for a shortcut object indicate its type as Shortcut, and the MS-DOS name has an **.lnk** extension that shows where to find the original icon.

You can create a shortcut file almost anywhere on your system, which frees you from having to navigate to the actual location of the resource. This is different from moving the original object around or from copying the object to another location. In short, shortcuts are powerful tools for convenient access to resources. Three of the main ways to create shortcuts follow:

- Using the File menu:

    1. Click the original file.

    2. Choose Create Shortcut from the File menu.

    3. Drag the shortcut where you want it.

- Using the mouse (variation 1):

  1. Locate the original object.

  2. Hold down the right mouse key.

  3. Drag the object onto the desktop.

  4. Release the mouse button.

  5. Select the menu option Create Shortcut Here.

- Using the mouse (variation 2):

  1. Locate the original object.

  2. Hold down the right mouse key.

  3. Release the mouse button.

  4. Select the Create Shortcut menu option.

  5. Drag the shortcut where you want it.

You can also create a shortcut from by selecting File, New, Shortcut to start the Create Shortcut Wizard.

As you can see, Windows 95/98 has made shortcuts very user friendly. A shortcut icon has an arrow across it to indicate that it is a link rather than the original resource. Double-clicking with the primary mouse button or single-clicking with the secondary mouse button and selecting the Open menu option accomplishes different actions depending on the object:

- Programs or applications are automatically launched.

- For files, the associated application is launched, and the file is loaded into it.

- Folders are opened as desktop windows, with the files displayed as objects.

- Printers are opened as job queues showing print jobs.

Default system icons

The **default system icons** include the My Computer, Network Neighborhood, and Recycle Bin icons. They contain classes of common-purpose objects that are grouped for the user's convenience.

My Computer is a container object that holds all the resources available on the local computer, including the following:

- Icons that represent the local drives on your system—hard drives, floppy drives, and CD-ROM drives

- A **Control Panel** folder that contains the utilities you need to customize the computer's configuration

- A Printers folder that contains the printers that are set up to run through the operating system

- A **Dial-Up Networking** folder that contains the modem dialup links to external Internet hosts

Network Neighborhood is another container object that holds all the network devices accessible by the system, including the following:

- Other systems in your immediate workgroup

- An Entire Network folder showing all the other workgroups, servers, and shared resources available on these systems

The **Recycle Bin** is a container object that contains files deleted from the local system hard disk drive. You can recover them if you want, or expunge them from the system permanently. This helps protect you against accidental deletions.

Opening these containers via a double-click of the mouse or via the Open menu makes these resources immediately available. The functions of these system objects are explored in subsequent lessons.

The Taskbar

The Windows 95/98 multitasking operating system allows you to have several tasks or applications running on your desktop at the same time, resulting in several overlapping windows. Thus, the user needs a tool to sort these applications and to be able to switch back and forth between them: the **Taskbar**. The Taskbar exists by default at the bottom of the desktop screen and works as a program shell that contains an open program title box for each program running on the desktop. Clicking on a tile box or right-clicking and selecting an action from the menu allows you to control the program on the desktop. When you have many programs open on the desktop, simply click on the appropriate title box in the Taskbar to bring that program to the screen.

Another nifty method of switching from application to application on the desktop is to press the Alt and Tab keys simultaneously. This function has been improved from Windows 3.1 so that it displays icons representing all the applications currently running, much like the Taskbar.

On the Taskbar you can find a small notification area just to the left of the system clock. Small icons load at startup or when programs are launched to provide real-time displays about the state of the program running in the operating system. Again, you are just a double-click away from controlling the resources these icons point to.

The Start menu

The Start menu provides a menu-driven alternative to the icon-based desktop for initiating activities on the system. This menu offers a convenient entry point for the entire computer system. Simply click the Start Menu button at the far left of the Taskbar and scroll with the mouse to select the desired program.

The Start menu's default features are as follows:

- Shut Down—Presents a choice of shutting down, rebooting, or logging out of the system.

- Run—Presents an alternative to the DOS command line for running programs. It also contains a cache of commands that have been carried out in the past.

- Help—Launches the help facility.

- Find—Launches the find utility.

- Settings—Presents choices of submenus in the Control Panel, Printers folder, and Taskbar to allow you to change the various settings and configurations.

- Documents—Presents a list of the most recently used documents created on the computer.

- Programs—Presents a comprehensive container object with many program folders or shortcuts. In short, all programs and applications installed on the computer can be accessed through this menu.

Customizing the Taskbar and Start menu

You can easily customize the Taskbar. You can change its position on the desktop, and you can change various properties of the Taskbar. To change its position, drag it with the mouse to the desired edge of the screen. You can also customize the width of the Taskbar by positioning the mouse pointer on the edge of the Taskbar until the pointer changes to a double-arrow. Then click the mouse and drag the bar to the desired width.

A large Taskbar tends to get in the way, so you might want to hide it or to change various other preferences. To do so, do one of the following:

- Go to the Start Menu, select the Settings feature, and select the Taskbar & Start Menu icon.

- Go to a blank area of the actual Taskbar, right-click, and select Properties from the menu.

The resulting dialog box, Taskbar Properties, provides options to suit your preferences, including the following:

- Always on top—Causes the Taskbar to always be visible on the desktop.

- Auto hide—Causes the Taskbar to disappear when not used, until the mouse cursor is moved over the typical location. (This can be extremely useful for small monitors.)

- Show Small Icons in Start Menu—Causes the embedded icons in the Start menu to shrink to a smaller size. (This is very helpful on lower-resolution screens where larger icons cause the menu to extend beyond the desktop size.)

- Show clock—Allows the clock to show or be hidden in the Taskbar notification area.

You can also easily customize the Start menu. You can add a shortcut to the top segment of the Start menu, above the Programs icon, by locating and dragging the shortcut icon from its current location. You can add, remove, or modify Start menu utilities and programs by selecting the Settings feature and choosing the Taskbar and Start Menu option.

Windows 98 browsing tools

Windows 98 has added a feature to make it easier to browse the computer system and the Internet more efficiently by using browsing tools. Simply add the Explorer bar to any window or toolbar, and Windows 98 automatically detects information that is present in the window.

Concept Questions   *Semester 2, Unit 3, Lesson 12*

Demonstrate your knowledge of the concepts in this lesson by answering the following questions in the space provided.

1. Explain the benefits of using Windows 95 desktop objects and how they function.

2. Explain how the Windows 95 Taskbar facilitates multitasking.

_____

_____

_____

_____

_____

_____

_____

_____

_____

_____

_____

_____

_____

_____

_____

_____

_____

_____

Vocabulary Exercise   *Semester 2, Unit 3, Lesson 12*

Name: _____

Date: _____   *Class:* _____

Define the following terms as completely as you can.

default system icon

_____

_____

Dial-Up Networking

_____

_____

Printers

_____

_____

Recycle Bin

_____

_____

shortcut

_____

_____

Focus Questions

Semester 2, Unit 3, Lesson 12

Name: _____

Date: _____   *Class:* _____

1. Describe how shortcuts function.

_____

_____

_____

2. Describe how you distinguish a shortcut icon from a normal icon.

_____

_____

_____

3. Describe how you create and use shortcuts.

_____

_____

_____

4. Describe the My Computer container object.

_____

_____

_____

5. Describe the Taskbar and its function.

_____

_____

_____

6. Describe the notification area and its function.

_____

_____

_____

7. Describe the Start Menu and what it does.

_____

_____

_____

8. Describe how you can customize the Taskbar.

_____

_____

_____

9. Describe how you can customize the Start menu.

_____

_____

_____

10. Describe the Windows 98 browsing tools.

_____

_____

_____

SEMESTER 2, UNIT 3, LESSON 13
Windows 95/98 File System Objects

You have learned to organize your desktop, Start menu, and Taskbar settings, and how to create shortcuts. You will now learn the basics of file system object navigation and manipulation.

Most people are very familiar with clicking, double-clicking, and dragging the mouse to navigate. By clicking on your right mouse button on a desktop object's icon, you arrive at an Object menu, which provides a number of choices: Open, Cut, Copy, Create Shortcut, Delete, Rename, Properties, and possibly Send To. These are pretty self-explanatory, but one interesting thing occurs when you decide to modify an object. Examining and/or modifying objects in Windows 95 requires neither rocket science technology nor tremendous artistic creativity. You merely need to get to the properties sheet of the embedded object. Besides right-clicking the object and choosing Object Properties on the menu, you can also get there the following ways:

- Select the object and pressing Alt + Enter.

- Select the object and choosing Object Properties from the Edit menu (if there is one on this object).

You can change the object's icon, the icon's caption, and the icon's display size. Even if you're happy with the default icon, you might want to replace the default caption with something more descriptive. Of course, more commonly you are going to use the objects to navigate around the computer system.

Object navigation and manipulation with Windows Explorer

Windows 95 allows a variety of simple ways to navigate through the user interface. You can use the mouse or the find feature, which allows you find files and computers locally and on the network, which was traditionally done by using the filename. Windows 95 has expanded the Find feature to allow you to also find files by using the following:

- **Folders**, which contain files and other folders and are very similar to DOS directories.

- **Dialog boxes**, which allow easier access to files.

- **Windows Explorer**, which displays the files and directories of the system and can tunnel through directories into files. This replaces the File Manager from previous systems.

Whereas the Start menu allows you to access commonly used programs and utilities, Windows Explorer displays a structured map of the entire system. Windows Explorer functions just like the trees you experienced with the MS-DOS system, but the tree is now replaced with a series of graphical representations of folders and files.

You can access Windows Explorer two ways:

- Through the **Start menu**

- By right-clicking a desktop object (but note that right-clicking a shortcut doesn't get you to Explorer)

Navigating the file system through Explorer is pretty simple. After selecting Windows Explorer, you see all the files and directories in relation to the whole computer system. You see a double-pane window. The left side presents files and folders, in the hierarchy of the entire system. The right side presents an object as if it were opened. Thus, you can find any file, folder, or object that exists on your computer through Windows Explorer.

If you like one-stop shopping, you'll enjoy using Windows Explorer to manipulate the file system. All the folders and files are there, so it's just a matter of learning a few tricks, and you'll have things organized the way you want them. Windows Explorer has a very useful help section that will probably answer most of your questions.

Following are some of the common functions you can do from the Explorer. Note that in performing any of the actions described, you can select more than one file or folder by holding down the Ctrl key and clicking the items you want to move. To select all the items in a folder, select one item with the mouse and then press Ctrl + A.

Creating a folder

To create a folder, follow these steps:

1. Open the folder in which you want to create a new folder.

2. On the File menu, point to New, and then click Folder.

3. Type a name for the new folder, and press Enter.

Moving a folder or file

To move a folder or file, follow these steps:

1. Click on the file or folder you want to move.

2. From the Edit menu, click Cut.

3. Open the folder where you want to put the file or folder.

4. From the Edit menu, click Paste.

Copying a folder or file

To copy a folder or file, follow these steps:

1. Click on the file or folder you want to copy.

2. From the Edit menu, click Copy.

3. Open the folder where you want to put the file or folder.

4. From the Edit menu, click Paste.

Deleting a folder or file

To delete a folder or file, follow these steps:

1. Click on the folder or file you want to delete.

2. On the File menu (or after right-clicking), click Delete.

You can also drag the file or folder icon to the Recycle Bin. And you can delete the item without having it stored in the Recycle Bin by pressing Shift while dragging.

Finding objects in the file system

Traditional find utilities have allowed only name searches. The find utility has been upgraded in Windows 95/98 to allow searching by the following:

- Time parameters (including modification dates)

- Text contents

- Type of object

- Size

So you can find an item even if you're not sure about its exact location or name. Find can also locate specific computers on the network or other specific objects in the Microsoft Network. One challenge many users face is simply finding the find utility. Here are two ways to get there:

- From the Start Menu click Find, and then Files or Folders.

- Right-click an object, and then click Find.

Between the find utility and Windows Explorer, you should find it easy to navigate around the system and manipulate the objects to suit your needs.

Concept Questions   *Semester 2, Unit 3, Lesson 13*

Demonstrate your knowledge of the concepts in this lesson by answering the following questions in the space provided.

1. In what ways has navigation been improved in Windows 95/98?

2. For what can you search by using the Windows 95/98 find feature?

_____

_____

_____

_____

_____

_____

_____

_____

_____

_____

_____

_____

_____

_____

_____

_____

Vocabulary Exercise   *Semester 2, Unit 3, Lesson 13*

Name: _____

Date: _____   *Class:* _____

Define the following terms as completely as you can.

dialog box

_____

_____

folder

_____

_____

Start menu

_____

_____

Windows Explorer

_____

_____

Focus Questions   *Semester 2, Unit 3, Lesson 13*

Name: _____

Date: _____   *Class:* _____

1. How do you access an object menu?

_____
_____
_____

2. What kinds of actions are performed on objects?

_____
_____
_____

3. How do you navigate to find objects?

_____
_____
_____

4. How can you access the Windows Explorer?

_____
_____
_____

5. How do you create a folder?

_____
_____
_____

6. How do you move a folder or file?

_____

_____

_____

7. How do you select more than one file or folder at a time?

_____

_____

_____

8. How do you copy a folder or file?

_____

_____

_____

9. How do you delete a folder or file?

_____

_____

_____

10. How do you delete a folder or file without having it stored in the Recycle Bin?

_____

_____

_____

11. How do you locate objects in the file system?

_____

_____

_____

SEMESTER 2, UNIT 3, LESSON 14
Getting Under MS-DOS and the Windows 95 GUI

You have learned how to navigate through the user interface and make modifications. Now you will look under the GUI of Windows 95 and discover how it compares with the MS-DOS **command.com** file.

The GUI versus the command line

Although Microsoft emphasizes its GUI, it really runs as a DOS 7 system. In fact, you can easily separate DOS 7 out, and run Windows 95 or Windows 3.11 under it. It's a good thing for a computer technician to know, and knowing the DOS commands has some useful applications.

Some older computer gurus became a little bit distressed when GUIs came out and made it easy for regular people to relate to computers. The gurus' exclusive realm could now be invaded by novices. No longer could new users be intimidated with threats of binary code in Pascal or FORTRAN lingo.

Although the MS-DOS **command.com** appears technical to some users, it is simply the visible portion of MS-DOS. It shows the accessible files of the system and provides a pathway to them. Likewise, Windows 95 shows its accessible files and provides a pathway through them via its GUI. It does have a larger number of ways to access files: through the Start menu, Taskbar, shortcuts, Windows Explorer, and various dialog boxes.

Another way to look at the difference between the two software products is to imagine your Porsche with only the frame, the engine, the electrical system, and other components needed to drive the car (MS-DOS). Contrast that vision with your loaded Porsche—its sleek body, comfortable seats, snazzy dashboard, stereo system, and radar detector (Windows 95). A mechanic or technician might prefer MS-DOS for certain functions, because of the system and program access it provides, but a casual user will find it much more comfortable to cruise along in Windows 95.

Even though Windows may appear more attractive than MS-DOS, there are some advantages to running Windows program under DOS. Some users are more comfortable with DOS and prefer it, and certain programs (often games) require it. So, it's essential to know how to use both systems well and be able to switch between them.

Using the DOS command line

The simplest way to get to the MS-DOS **command line** is by selecting Start, Programs, MS-DOS Prompt. Then you can use MS-DOS commands from a DOS window. When you want to return to Windows 95, just enter the command **exit** or press Alt + Tab to close the window and return to the GUI.

Suppose you want to work in DOS instead of working from Windows 95. There are a two ways to do so:

- From Windows, choose Shut Down from the Start Menu. You will be offered several options. Choose Restart the computer in MS-DOS mode.

- You can boot up in DOS:

  1. If you have dual-boot enabled, press F8 when you see the message Starting Windows 95 and highlight Previous version of MS_DOS, or simply press the F4 key.

  2. If you have dual-boot enabled, press F8 when you see the message Command prompt only.

  Using both of these methods, you will have the Windows version of the **config.sys** and **autoexec.bat** DOS commands, but not the GUI DOS command. To enable this, you must load **mscdex.exe** and your mouse driver by hand.

Reconfiguring to run off MS-DOS 6.2x

To reconfigure to run off MS-DOS 6.2x, follow these steps:

1. Find the text file called **msdos.sys** in your root directory.

2. Get rid of the Hidden, System, and Read-Only file attributes.

3. Bring up an editor on this file and make two changes: Change the line **BootGUI=1** to **BootGUI=0**, and add the line **LOGO=0**.

Your **msdos.sys** file now looks like this:

[Paths]
WinDir=C:\WINDOWS

WinBootDir=C:\WINDOWS
HostWinBootDrv=C

[Options]
BootMulti=1
BootGUI=0
Network=1
Logo=0
LoadTop=0

Using the GUI alternative to the command line

Now that you know how to convert your Windows–configured machine to MS-DOS, you need to remember how to go back to the Windows GUI. As mentioned previously, you can simply type the command **exit** at the MS-DOS prompt, or press Alt + Tab. Another method is to use the command **win** to reload the GUI.

MS-DOS systems utilize the **open** command to open existing files, and Windows 95 utilizes a similar device from its Start Menu: **Run**. You can use the Run command to launch any program, open any document, and open any folder. It is especially useful when you want to rerun or reopen a recently used program or document or the program needs a command-line parameter. The Run command is very user friendly. If you don't know the name of the program or document you want, click on Browse, and you can access all the programs and files on the computer.

Concept Questions   *Semester 2, Unit 3, Lesson 14*

Demonstrate your knowledge of the concepts in this lesson by answering the following questions in the space provided.

1. Explain how you access the MS-DOS prompt while running Windows 95 and return to the Windows environment from MS-DOS.

2. Explain the common purpose of the GUI and the command line.

_____

_____

_____

_____

_____

_____

_____

_____

_____

_____

_____

_____

_____

_____

_____

_____

_____

_____

Vocabulary Exercise   *Semester 2, Unit 3, Lesson 14*

Name: _____

Date: _____   *Class:* _____

Define the following terms as completely as you can.

command line

_____

_____

command.com

_____

_____

Run

_____

_____

Focus Questions   *Semester 2, Unit 3, Lesson 14*

Name: _____

Date: _____   *Class:* _____

1. Describe the reasons you might run MS-DOS.

_____

_____

_____

2. Describe how you return to Windows 95 from the MS-DOS prompt. Describe how you access DOS instead of working from Windows 95.

_____

_____

_____

3. Describe how you reconfigure to run off MS-DOS 6.2x.

_____

_____

_____

4. When in MS-DOS, how do you go back to the Windows GUI?

_____

_____

_____

5. Describe the Run command in Windows 95.

_____

_____

_____

SEMESTER 2, UNIT 3, LESSON 15
Unit 3 Exam

If you have access to the online Aries A+ curriculum, contact your instructor for the Assessment System URL. If you do not have access to the online curriculum, please continue to Unit 4.

SEMESTER 2, UNIT 4

- Lesson 16: Preinstallation Decision Making for Windows 95/98
- Lesson 17: The Windows 95/98 Installation Process
- Lesson 18: Troubleshooting a Windows 95/98 Installation
- Lesson 19: Removing Windows 95/98
- Lesson 20: Unit 4 Exam

SEMESTER 2, UNIT 4, LESSON 16
Preinstallation Decision Making for Windows 95/98

You have learned how to manage the Windows desktop as well as how to manipulate file system objects. You have also learned about the difference between the GUI and the DOS command line. In this lesson you will learn about the hardware and software requirements for Windows 95/98. You will also learn the appropriate file system for the installation, as well as the appropriate situations for dual-boot installations.

Hardware requirements for Windows 95/98

Table 4-1 shows the hardware requirements for Windows 95/98.

Table 4-1   *Hardware requirements for Windows 95/98*

Component	Windows 95 Requirements	Windows 98 Requirements	Comments
CPU	386DX or higher CPU	486DX 66-MHz or higher CPU	Windows 95 and Windows 98 both run 32-bit code
Memory	4 MB **RAM**	16 MB RAM	8 MB RAM is recommended for Windows 95, and 32 MB of RAM is recommended for Windows 98
Video card	Video display unit requiring a **video graphics adapter (VGA)**	**Super VGA (SVGA)** or better monitor with graphics card	SVGA recommended for Windows 95
Disk drive	50 MB–55 MB disk space	140 MB–255 MB disk space	Hard drive and either high-density floppy drive or CD-ROM drive required on Windows 95
Mouse/ pointing device	Recommended	Required	A mouse makes it easier to navigate the system
CD-ROM or DVD	Recommended	Required	For multimedia presentations and for easier installation

The Windows 95 file system

The **File Allocation Table (FAT)** is an area on a disk in which information about file location is stored. This is how the operating system keeps track of the files on the hard drive. FAT is the 16-bit file system that is used by MS-DOS. Windows 95 comes with a newer type of FAT, called **FAT32**. Windows 95 installs over existing MS-DOS FAT partitions as long as you have enough space in the partition for Windows 95.

There are some benefits to FAT32. It uses 4 KB of space, versus the 16 KB required by FAT16. FAT32 also makes it possible to have large hard drives that do not have to be divided into partitions. Additionally, FAT32 is compatible with programs designed to run on earlier versions of MS-DOS and Windows. However, many disk utilities that perform low-level maintenance tasks require updating.

On the other hand, FAT32 cannot see drives with other types of formatting, so all your hard drive space must be formatted with FAT32. If you are on a network, all drives that are shared must be either FAT32 or FAT16, not a combination of the two.

The type of FAT

To find out how the hard drive is formatted, follow these steps:

1. Double-click the My Computer icon.

2. Right-click the drive you want to check, and select Properties.

3. Beside the label Type, you see information about how the disk is formatted.

Dual booting

The **dual boot** feature allows Windows 3.x to remain intact in your system so you can run it as needed. This may come in handy when you have an application that doesn't run in Windows 95, or if you have problems installing Windows 95 properly. When Windows 95 does not work, you can boot into Windows 3.x and correct the problem, or remove Windows 95 and reinstall.

Software requirements for Windows 95 upgrading and dual booting

To install a Windows 95 upgrade or dual boot, you need the Windows 95 upgrade disk or CD-ROM, and one of the following:

* MS-DOS or PC-DOS 3.2 or higher

* Windows 3.x

* Windows NT 4.0 with Dual-boot (Windows 95 does not support NTFS Disk Partition)

For a new installation of Windows 95, you need the following:

- Windows 95 boot disk and CD-ROM, or disk set Version A, B, or C

- Necessary patch files from the Microsoft Web site

Installing Windows 95 to dual boot with MS-DOS

The following are some specific requirements before initiating dual booting:

- You must have MS-DOS version 5.0 or 6.0, prior to installing Windows 95.

- You must install Windows 95 into its own directory, which cannot contain any version of Windows 3.x.

- Application programs might need to be reinstalled to work with Windows 95.

To initiate the MS-DOS/Windows 95 dual boot, press the F4 key during the Windows 95 boot sequence. When you press F4, it bypasses the Windows 95 bootup and boots into the old version of DOS. From DOS, you can start Windows 3.x. This will only work if the MS-DOS is version 5.0 or later and the **msdos.sys** file in the root directory contains the line **bootmulti=1**. By default, this line will not be present in the original version of Windows 95 if you upgrade an existing Windows 3.x; however, this line is present in OSR2.

Managing swap space

With Windows 95/98 you no longer need a permanent swap file because the operating system dynamically sizes the swap file space. If you have both Windows 95/98 and Windows 3.x on your computer, you might get error messages that your swap file has been corrupted whenever you start Windows 3.x. To avoid this, you can remove the permanent Windows 3.x swap file with the following procedure:

1. Start Windows 3.x.

2. Double-click the Control Panel in the Program Manager.

3. Double-click the Enhanced icon in the Control Panel.

4. Click Virtual Memory and choose Change.

5. From the drop-down menu select Temporary, click OK, and exit the Control Panel.

6. Close the Windows 3.x to get to the DOS prompt.

7. Type **cd** and press Enter.

8. Type **attrib 386spart.par** and press Enter

9. If step 8 results in a listing of this file, type **del 386spart.par** and press Enter.

Windows 95 setup commands

You can run Windows 95 Setup from your previous DOS version or from Windows 3.1x (but not from Windows 3.0). Table 4-2 lists some common DOS commands.

Table 4-2   *Common DOS commands*

Command	Resulting Action
setup/?	Lists the setup command lines.
setup/d	Does not use existing version of Windows to run Windows 95.
setup/id	Does not check for minimum hard disk space requirement.
setup/is	Runs Setup without first running ScanDisk in case you don't have enough conventional memory.
setup/iq	Runs Setup without first running ScanDisk. (It is recommended to run Setup from DOS.)
setup/im	Skips the available memory check
setup/in	Runs Setup without setting up network components.
setup/ip	Skips the check for any plug-and-play devices.
setup/it	Skips the check of **terminate-and-stay-resident (TSR)** programs that are known to cause problems with Windows 95 Setup.
setup/l	Enables a Logitech mouse during Setup.
setup/n	Causes Setup to run without a mouse.
setup/ndstart	Copies from the Windows 95 source file the minimum Windows 3.x DLLs required to run Windows 95 Setup and then exits to DOS.
setup/t:c:\tmp	Specifies which directory (**c:\tmp**, in this case) Setup copies its temporary files to. If this directory doesn't exit, Setup creates it.

Software requirements for Windows 98 installation

To upgrade to Windows 98, you need to clean up your hard drive and the Recycle Bin, and close the antivirus program. The Windows 98 upgrade software package contains a CD-ROM disk, a bootup disk, and a certificate of authentication. You need to have one of the following software programs on your machine to be able to use the upgrade:

- MS-DOS/PC-DOS with Windows 3.x

- Windows 95

- Windows NT 4.x (FAT partition table only)

Installing Windows 95/98 to dual boot with Windows NT

Before installing Windows 95/98 to dual boot with Windows NT, make sure that the entry **bootmulti=1** is in the **msdos.sys** file in the root directory of your startup drive. Also make sure that the computer is configured to dual boot between Windows NT and MS-DOS. Check your Windows NT documentation for details. Then follow these steps:

1. Start the computer in MS-DOS mode.

2. Run Windows 95 Setup.

To run MS-DOS after Windows 95/98 has been installed, select the MS-DOS option from the Windows NT multiboot menu. Next, go to the Startup menu in Windows 95/98 and select the option Previous version of MS-DOS.

Concept Questions   *Semester 2, Unit 4, Lesson 16*

Demonstrate your knowledge of the concepts in this lesson by answering the following questions in the space provided.

1. Explain FAT32's relationship to Windows 95.

2. Explain what a dual boot is and why you would want to dual boot.

_____

_____

_____

_____

_____

_____

_____

_____

_____

_____

_____

_____

_____

_____

_____

_____

_____

_____

_____

_____

Vocabulary Exercise   *Semester 2, Unit 4, Lesson 16*

Name: _____

Date: _____   *Class:* _____

Define the following terms as completely as you can.

dual boot

_____

_____

FAT

_____

_____

FAT32

_____

_____

SVGA

_____

_____

TSR

_____

_____

VGA

_____

_____

Focus Questions

Semester 2, Unit 4, Lesson 16

Name: _____

Date: _____ *Class:* _____

1. What are the hardware requirements for Windows 95/98?

_____

_____

_____

2. What file system is appropriate for Windows 95?

_____

_____

_____

3. Describe the advantages and disadvantages of FAT32.

_____

_____

_____

4. Describe how you know what file system you have on your computer.

_____

_____

_____

5. Describe the software requirements for Windows 95 upgrading and dual booting.

_____

_____

_____

6. Describe how to install Windows 95 to dual boot with MS-DOS.

_____

_____

_____

7. Describe what happens when you press the F4 key during the Windows 95 boot sequence.

_____

_____

_____

8. What are some common Windows 95 setup commands?

_____

_____

_____

9. Describe the software requirements for Windows 98 installation.

_____

_____

_____

10. Describe how to install Windows 95/98 to dual boot with Windows NT.

_____

_____

_____

SEMESTER 2, UNIT 4, LESSON 17
The Windows 95/98 Installation Process

In this lesson, you'll learn about the different types of installation **media**, as well as the kind of information that is required during the installation process. You will also learn the steps that are necessary to install Windows 95/98, along with how to upgrade to Windows 95/98.

Using a floppy disk or a CD-ROM

Windows 95/98 is available on floppy disks or **CD-ROM** as an upgrade to a previous existing Windows installation. If you have a CD-ROM drive in your computer, the best choice is a CD-ROM because you won't have to swap disks. Additionally, the CD-ROM is faster, it includes administration components, and CD-ROMs are less likely than disks to have faults or produce errors.

Before beginning the installation

Before installing Windows 95/98, you should do the following:

- Read the installation instructions carefully.

- Locate the serial number of the software. You will need this during the installation process. You should also record it in a place where you can find it later if needed.

- Read the software license agreement.

- Close all open programs or windows on your computer.

- Read the Windows 95/98 **readme** and **setup.txt** files on the installation disks for any notes relating to hardware. If any of your hardware is not supported, Windows 95 will choose a generic driver or use the existing one installed on your computer.

- Verify that your computer's hardware and software components meet Windows 95's minimum requirements. If you have access to the Internet, you can view the hardware compatibility and latest release at **www.microsoft.com/hwtest**.

Configuring the floppy disk drive

If you are installing a new floppy disk drive before installing Windows 95/98, you will first need to configure the floppy disk drive. The configuration is stored in the Setup or **complementary metal oxide semiconductor (CMOS)** section of the computer. To configure the floppy disk drive, do the following:

1. When your computer is booting, you see a message that tells you to start the CMOS setup program. Follow the instructions to run the Setup program.

2. Read the Setup program's instructions carefully. Then go to the basic section where the floppy drive is located.

3. After you select the correct drive, save the settings and exit by pressing the Esc or F10 key, as applicable.

4. You get a list of drives and information regarding the date, time, and other devices. Move to the correct section, usually floppy A or B, and then use the arrow keys to move around and use the page up and page down keys to change the settings.

Configuring the CD-ROM drive

When you install Windows 95/98, it automatically detects and installs all the hardware that is currently on your computer. If you are adding new hardware to your computer after installing Windows 95, you can use Add New Hardware to add a new device to your computer system, such as a new disk drive, tape drive, modem, or sound card.

To add a device drive after installing Windows 95, do the following:

1. Choose Start, Settings, Control Panel, Add New Hardware.

2. Click the Next button.

3. Choose Yes to have Windows search and detect your hardware.

4. Click the Next button to proceed to the hardware detection page. The automatic hardware detection looks for your modem.

5. Choose Details to see a list of detected hardware, or you choose Finish to complete the installation.

6. Restart your system so that Windows will support your new hardware.

Options in the installation process

The following are the options in the installation process:

- Typical—This is the default option recommended for most users. This option performs most of the installation steps automatically. The user needs to confirm the directory where Windows 95 will be installed, provide user information, and choose whether to create a startup disk.

- Portable—This is the recommended option for users with portable computers. This option installs the components Briefcase, Dial-up Networking, Direct Cable Connection, and Disk Compression Tools. These optional components provide file synchronization and the software for cable connections for exchanging files.

- Compact—This option is for users who have limited disk space on the computer. This option installs the minimum files required to run Windows 95.

- Custom—This option is recommended for experienced users who want to select the various elements of Windows 95. The users can select application and network components to be installed, and verify the configuration settings for devices.

Backing up system files

Before installing Windows 95, you should back up the following files:

- All **.ini** files in the **windows** directory

- All **.dat** files in the **windows** directory

- All **.pwl** files in the **windows** directory

- All **.grp** files in the **windows** directory

- The **config.sys** file

- The **autoexec.bat** file

- Proprietary network configuration files and login scripts

Installing Windows 95 from MS-DOS

Follow these steps to install Windows 95 from MS-DOS:

1. Windows 95 comes with a bootable DOS disk that allows you to partition your hard disk, format the partitions for DOS, and install the necessary files to boot the computer. Place this disk in your computer and turn it on. The DOS prompt (**c: \>**) should appear on the screen.

2. Insert Setup Disk 1 in the floppy disk drive, or place the Windows CD-ROM in the CD-ROM drive.

3. At the prompt, type the drive letter, followed by a colon (**:**), a backslash (****), and the word **setup**. For example, if you are setting up from a floppy disk, type **a:\setup**, and if you are setting up from a CD-ROM drive, type **d:\win95\setup**.

4. Click OK, then Continue, and Windows performs a routine check of the system and lets you know if you have enough memory available. If Windows reports that you lack conventional memory, click Exit. Refer to the manual that tells how to edit your **autoexec.bat** and **config.sys** files, make the needed adjustments, and restart the computer.

5. Click Continue, and Windows 95 starts the installation process. If you are installing Windows 95 from floppy disks, the system lets you know when to insert a new disk.

6. Click Yes for the software agreement. If you click No, the installation process ends.

7. Make sure that all programs are closed, and click on OK when you are done.

8. Press Enter, or click the Next button to continue.

9. Windows chooses a directory in which to install the program. Click the Next button to choose the **c:\windows** directory.

10. Click the Next button to choose the typical setup.

11. Complete the user information section, and then press Next to continue the installation process.

12. Setup analyzes your computer. If you have any of the devices shown on the screen, click the checkbox and press Next.

13. Windows installs the recommended components.

14. It's a good idea to create a startup disk because it comes in handy when you need to boot your computer when Windows 95 is not running properly. Click on the Next button, and Windows creates a startup disk.

15. Click Next to continue, or click Back to review the Windows 95 settings.

16. Label the disk Windows 95 Startup Disk, and then put it in the **a:** drive and click OK. When the startup disk is completed, remove the disk and click OK.

17. Click the Finish button. When you click the Finish button, Windows 95 restarts your computer and loads Windows 95.

Upgrading to Windows 95

Follow these steps to upgrade to Windows 95:

1. Insert Setup Disk 1 in the floppy disk drive, or place the Windows CD-ROM in the CD-ROM drive.

2. Go to your File Manager or your Program Manager and select File, Run.

3. Type the drive letter, followed by a colon (:), a backslash (\), and the word **setup**. If you are setting up from a floppy disk, type **a:\setup**. If you are setting up from a CD-ROM drive, type **d:\setup**.

4. Click OK, and then click Continue, and Windows performs a routine check of the system to determine whether you have enough memory available. If Windows reports that you lack sufficient conventional memory, click Exit, and then edit your **autoexec.bat** and **config.sys** files and restart the computer.

5. Click Continue to start the Windows 95 installation process. If you are installing Windows 95 from floppy disks, the system lets you know when to insert a disk.

6. Click Yes to agree to the terms of the software agreement. If you click No, the installation process ends.

7. Make sure that all programs are closed, and then click OK when you are done.

8. Click the Next button to continue.

9. Windows now identifies **c:\windows** as the destination for the program. Unless you have a particular reason for installing to a different drive, go with the program recommendations.

10. Click the Next button to choose the typical setup. Again, unless you have a particular reason for doing a custom setup, go with program recommendations.

11. Complete the user information, and then press Next to continue the installation process.

12. Setup analyzes the computer. If you have any of the devices shown onscreen, click on the checkbox and click Next.

13. Click Next, and Windows installs the recommended components.

14. It is recommended that you create a startup disk because this disk comes in handy when you need to reboot the computer when Windows 95 is not running properly. When you click the Next button, Windows initiates the process of creating a startup disk.

15. Click Next to continue, or click Back to review the Windows 95 settings.

16. Label a blank disk Windows 95 Startup Disk, insert it in your **a:** drive, and click OK. When the startup disk is completed, eject it from the drive and click OK.

17. Click the Finish button. Windows 95 restarts the computer, and installation is complete.

Concept Questions   *Semester 2, Unit 4, Lesson 17*

Demonstrate your knowledge of the concepts in this lesson by answering the following questions in the space provided.

1. Explain the Windows 95 installation process and the information that is required before installing Windows 95.

2. Explain how to back up system files.

_____

_____

_____

_____

_____

_____

_____

_____

_____

_____

_____

_____

_____

_____

_____

_____

_____

_____

Vocabulary Exercise   *Semester 2, Unit 4, Lesson 17*

Name: _____

Date: _____   *Class:* _____

Define the following terms as completely as you can.

CD-ROM

_____

_____

CMOS

_____

_____

media

_____

_____

Focus Questions   *Semester 2, Unit 4, Lesson 17*

Name: _____

Date: _____   *Class:* _____

1. Should you use floppy disks or a CD-ROM to install Windows?

_____

_____

_____

2. Describe what kind of information is required during the installation process.

_____

_____

_____

3. How do you configure a floppy disk drive?

_____

_____

_____

4. How do you configure the CD-ROM drive?

_____

_____

_____

5. What is the typical option available during the installation process?

_____

_____

_____

6. What is the portable option available during the installation process?

_____

_____

_____

7. What is the compact option available during the installation process?

_____

_____

_____

8. What is the custom option available during the installation process?

_____

_____

_____

9. Describe the files should you back up before installing Windows 95.

_____

_____

_____

10. Describe how you install Windows 95 from MS-DOS.

_____

_____

_____

11. Describe how you upgrade to Windows 95.

_____

_____

_____

SEMESTER 2, UNIT 4, LESSON 18
Troubleshooting a Windows 95/98 Installation

You have learned about different kinds of software installation media. You have also learned the steps necessary to install Windows 95/98 and how to upgrade to Windows 95/98 from a previous version. In this lesson you will learn about some of the common problems that arise during the installation process and how to resolve them.

When installing Windows 95, there are three points at which the computer can stop or stall: before, during, or after hardware detection. Stopping or stalling is recorded in the **log files** as specified in the Table 4-3.

Table 4-3   *Recording stopping or stalling errors in log files*

Filename	What Occurs	Purpose	File Location
setuplog.txt	This file is created when Setup fails before hardware detection.	Windows 95 recovers by reading this file. This file can also be used for troubleshooting errors that occur during installation.	This file is located in the root directory. It determines where the system stalled, what to redo, and what to skip.
detlog.txt	This is a text file created every time the detection process runs.	This file contains a record of a specific hardware device that was detected and identifies the parameters for the detected device.	This file is located in the root directory when Windows 95 is installed. This file indicates the start of a detection test and if it was completed.
detcrash.log	This is a binary file that is created when Setup fails during hardware detection.	This file records information about the detection module that was running and the memory resources or I/O port it was accessing when it failed.	This file can be read only by Setup. If the detection process completed successfully, this file is deleted.

To avoid **crashing** twice, Windows 95/98 uses log file information and the **detcrash.log** file. You should not delete any of these files when troubleshooting. For example, if **detcrash.log** were deleted, Setup would not be able to recognize a failure and move beyond that point. Log files are useful when you are troubleshooting because you can get information from **setuplog.txt** and **detlog.txt** to check for any devices that might have created the problems.

The Windows 95 startup disk

The startup disk is a bootable floppy disk with a collection of Windows system files and utilities that can be used for troubleshooting. When the hard disk does not boot, the startup disk can be used to boot the computer.

When you installed Windows 95, you should have made a startup disk. This disk can be a lifesaver if you encounter serious problems with Windows 95 after it's installed. If you need to use this disk, insert it into the floppy drive and reboot the computer. A screen with the MS-DOS command line appears, to help you recover the installation.

If you didn't make a startup disk when you installed Windows 95, you can still make one by following these steps:

1. Select Start, Settings, Control Panel, and double-click the Add/Remove Programs icon.

2. Click the Startup Disk tab.

3. Insert a floppy disk and click the Create Disk button.

Troubleshooting specific problems

Table 4-4 lists some specific problems you might encounter and procedures that might help fix them.

Table 4-4   *Troubleshooting problems*

Problem	Procedure
The computer won't boot into Windows.	Reboot the computer and press F8 to start the Startup menu in MS-DOS. Start Windows in safe mode; this boots into Windows, where you can diagnose the problem.
Windows 95 won't start and you want to remove it from the computer.	Boot the computer from the startup disk into MS-DOS and enter **uninstall** at the **a:** prompt.
The setup halts during hardware detection.	Turn off the power to the computer, wait 10 seconds, and then turn the power back on. (Do not press Ctrl + Alt + Del.) When it restarts, use Safe Recovery to restart Windows. This skips the portion of detection that caused the problem.

Problem	Procedure
On the first restart after setup, the computer locks.	If you think it's a hardware compatibility problem, boot into Safe Mode, which loads Windows 95 with a minimal set of drivers.
Setup fails to start.	1. Check the computer for viruses. 2. At the command prompt, type **mem/c/p** to check for sufficient conventional memory and XMS memory. Windows 95 requires 420 KB for conventional memory and 3 MB of XMS. If you need more memory, you can remove unnecessary drivers or TSRs. 3. Check the RAM configuration in **config.sys**. • MS-DOS 4.x or earlier should contain the following setting: **device=himem.sys**. • MS-DOS 5 or later should contain the following command lines: **device=himem.sys** **device=emm386.exe.noems** **dos=high.umb**
A problem occurs during the file-copying phase of Setup.	Exit Setup, restart the computer, and rerun Setup. Then select the Safe Recovery option and click Continue. This should successfully complete the installation process.
Setup fails with error B1.	This message indicates that Setup has detected an older processor and instructs you to upgrade your processor.
Setup starts, but there is an error during the installation process.	1. Restart Windows 95 by using Safe Recovery. 2. Check the **detlog.txt** or the **setuplog.txt** file. 3. Run a virus-detection program and the ScanDisk utility to check for viruses and to verify that all system components are functioning normally. 4. Check the system hardware to see if it's compatible. 5. Check for a damaged or missing files. If it's referenced in an error message, check to see if the file exists and check the file location, size, date, and version.

Concept Questions   *Semester 2, Unit 4, Lesson 18*

Demonstrate your knowledge of the concepts in this lesson by answering the following questions in the space provided.

1. What are the three points during installation where the computer can stop or stall?

2. What are some problems you might encounter in installing Windows 95/98, and what are the corresponding troubleshooting procedures?

_____

_____

_____

_____

_____

_____

_____

_____

_____

_____

_____

_____

_____

_____

_____

_____

_____

_____

Vocabulary Exercise   *Semester 2, Unit 4, Lesson 18*

Name: _____

Date: _____   *Class:* _____

Define the following terms as completely as you can.

binary file

_____

_____

crash

_____

_____

log file

_____

_____

text file

_____

_____

uninstall

_____

_____

Focus Questions   *Semester 2, Unit 4, Lesson 18*

Name: _____

Date: _____   *Class:* _____

1. At what points during the Windows 95 install might the computer stall?

_____

_____

_____

2. Describe how Windows 95/98 avoids crashing twice.

_____

_____

_____

3. Describe how you make a startup disk.

_____

_____

_____

4. Describe what you do if the computer will not boot into Windows.

_____

_____

_____

5. Describe what you do if Setup halts during hardware detection.

_____

_____

_____

6. Describe what you do if after the first restart after setup, the computer locks.

_____

_____

_____

7. Describe what you do if setup fails to start.

_____

_____

_____

8. Describe what you do if a problem occurs during the file-copying phase of Setup.

_____

_____

_____

9. Describe what you do if Setup fails with error B1.

_____

_____

_____

10. Describe what you do if Setup starts, but there is an error during the installation process.

_____

_____

_____

SEMESTER 2, UNIT 4, LESSON 19
Removing Windows 95/98

In this lesson, you will learn about the differences between uninstalling and deleting Windows 95/98, as well as the proper methods of deleting and uninstalling Windows 95/98.

Deleting versus uninstalling Windows 95

There are two ways to remove Windows 95—uninstalling and deleting. The preferred method is **uninstalling** because it restores the computer to its original state. For example, when you uninstall Windows 95 on a dual boot, the machine returns to its previous versions of MS-DOS or Windows 3.x. On the other hand, when you uninstall Windows 95 on a computer that was upgraded from Windows 3.x, you need to reinstall Windows 3.x.

Uninstalling Windows 95 is done in two steps. First, the existing system and configuration files are backed up, and then the uninstalling process begins. If you have installed programs after you installed Windows 95, and then you uninstall Windows 95, you will have to reinstall the other programs. Additionally, some Windows 95 applications might not run under Windows 3.x.

The following are some conditions that must be met before you try to uninstall Windows 95:

- The system files created during setup must be saved, and **w95undo.dat** and **w95undo.ini** should still exist.

- After installing Windows 95, your system and/or boot partition must not be compressed.

To remove Windows 95, you can choose one of the following ways:

- Use the Add/Remove Programs icon in the Control Panel, and choose the Install/Uninstall tab.

- Delete Windows with command-line startup. This procedure is described in the following section.

Deleting Windows 95 with command-line startup

Follow these steps to delete Windows 95 with command-line startup:

1. Turn the computer on and press F8 when the Starting Windows message appears.

2. Select Command Prompt Only.

3. To delete files and directories, copy the Windows 95 version of **deltree.exe** to the boot drive. At the command prompt, type **copy\windows\command\deltree.exe c:**.

4. To use ScanDisk, copy the ScanDisk files from the Windows **command** directory to the root directory. At the command prompt, type **copy\windows\command\scandisk.* c:\.**

5. Use the Notepad to edit **scandisk.ini** in the Windows directory. Change the entries to the following:

labelcheck=on
spacecheck=on

6. To remove all entries in earlier version of MS-DOS, type **scandisk c:.**

7. To delete the Windows 95 directory, type **deltree windows.**

8. To delete the Windows **config.sys** and **autoexec.bat** type

deltree config.sys
deltree autoexec.bat

9. To delete the **winboot.ini** file and **winboot** directory, type **deltree winboot.*.**

10. To delete setup, boot, and detection log files, type the following:

deltree setuplog.*
deltree bootlog.*
deltree detlog.*

11. To delete **io.sys** and **msdos.sys**, type the following:

deltree io.sys
deltree msdos.sys

12. To delete the compression drivers, type **del dblspace.bin.**

13. To delete the command processor, type **deltree command.com.**

14. Place a bootable floppy disk with a suitable version of MS-DOS into drive **a:** and restart the computer.

15. After the booting is done, type **sys c.** If you used compression, copy **dblspace.bin** from the DOS directory to the root directory in version 6.0. If you have a **shell=statement** referencing **command.com** from another directory, you need to copy **command.com** to the root directory. Then remove the disk and restart the computer.

Attempting to delete Windows 95 from the directory may not work because the boot process will locate the Windows 95 boot files, and they in turn will look for the system files. Therefore, the original operating system may have to be reinstalled.

Deleting versus uninstalling Windows 98

When you upgrade the operating system to Windows 98 from an earlier version—Windows 3.x or Windows 95—you have the option to save all your old system files. That means that you can uninstall Windows 98 to restore your earlier version. To do so, follow these steps:

1. Click Start, Settings, Control Panel, Add/Remove Programs. Under the Install/Uninstall tab, click Uninstall Windows 98.

2. Click Yes.

If you want to delete the Windows 98 upgraded version and reinstall a brand new copy of Windows 98 follow these steps:

1. Back up your data with Microsoft Backup, Zip, or Tape.

2. Boot up the computer with the Windows 98 boot disk or CD-ROM.

3. Start and run **fdisk**, and then press Delete, and you see the extended and primary partition table.

4. Restart the system with the Windows 98 boot disk or CD-ROM to install Windows 98.

Concept Questions   *Semester 2, Unit 4, Lesson 19*

Demonstrate your knowledge of the concepts in this lesson by answering the following questions in the space provided.

1. What is the difference between uninstalling and deleting Windows 95?

2. What is the preferred method for removing Windows 95, and why?

_____

_____

_____

_____

_____

_____

_____

_____

_____

_____

_____

_____

_____

_____

_____

_____

_____

_____

_____

Vocabulary Exercise   *Semester 2, Unit 4, Lesson 19*

Name: _____

Date: _____   Class: _____

Define the following terms as completely as you can.

ScanDisk

_____

_____

uninstall

_____

_____

Focus Questions   *Semester 2, Unit 4, Lesson 19*

Name: _____

Date: _____   *Class:* _____

1. Describe the advantage of uninstalling over deleting Windows 95.

_____

_____

_____

_____

2. Describe the steps to uninstall Windows 95.

_____

_____

_____

_____

3. Describe what you should do before uninstalling Windows 95.

_____

_____

_____

_____

4. Describe the ways you can remove Windows 95.

_____

_____

_____

_____

5. Describe how you delete Windows 95 with command-line startup.

_____

_____

_____

_____

6. Describe how you delete and uninstall Windows 98.

_____

_____

_____

_____

SEMESTER 2, UNIT 4, LESSON 20
Unit 4 Exam

If you have access to the online Aries A+ curriculum, contact your instructor for the Assessment System URL. If you do not have access to the online curriculum, please continue to Unit 5.

SEMESTER 2, UNIT 5

- Lesson 21: The Windows 95/98 Control Panel
- Lesson 22: System Hardware and Software Configuration for Windows 95/98
- Lesson 23: The Windows 95/98 Registry and Installation Files
- Lesson 34: Optimizing the Windows 95/98 System
- Lesson 25: Unit 5 Exam

SEMESTER 2, UNIT 5, LESSON 21
The Windows 95/98 Control Panel

In this lesson you will learn about how the Control Panel functions. The **Control Panel** operates as the user's gateway into GUI and system functions. The Control Panel contains icons to access key system objects, to enable you to customize their functions. These customization settings, or **configurations**, are stored in an internal database called the **Registry**. Windows 95/98 allows easy access to the Control Panel from the Start menu.

Going back to our Porsche analogy, suppose you have just purchased a standard European factory model that has some features you'd like to change: a clock set for Greenwich standard time, the steering wheel on the right, and a top speedometer reading of 200 kph. You tell the dealer that you want the following modifications performed by his mechanics (the Control Panel): the clock set for U.S. Central Standard Time, the steering wheel on the left, and a top speedometer reading of 180 mph.

Utilities in the Control Panel

Windows 95/98 has made the Control Panel function easily accessible from a variety of locations:

- The Start menu

- The My Computer object

- Windows Explorer

- A shortcut Control Panel icon on the desktop

Control Panel functions help you configure your machine to suit your needs, and amaze your non–computer-savvy friends with all the cool tricks you can do. The Windows 95/98 Control Panel icons are described in Table 5-1.

Table 5-1   *Windows 95/98 Control Panel icons*

Feature	Windows 95	Windows 98	Details
Accessibility Options	x	x	Alter the workstation for people with hearing, vision, and movement impairments. This includes altering the video display and keyboard functions.
Add New Hardware	x	x	Install new hardware devices or reconfigure hardware settings.
Add/Remove Programs	x	x	Manage Windows 95 programs—create a startup disk, and add and remove programs and components.
Date/Time	x	x	Change the system date, time, and time zone.
Display	x	x	Specify the background, screen saver, and visual appearance of the programs.
Fonts	x	x	View existing fonts and install new ones.
Internet	x	x	Configure settings for Internet Explorer.
Keyboards	x	x	Specify speed, pointer keys, language, and keyboard type.
Mail and Fax	x	x	Specify settings for mail, fax, and other messaging services.
Microsoft Mail Postoffice	x	x	Administer a Microsoft Workgroup Postoffice.
Modems	x	x	Install a new modem or configure existing ones.
Mouse	x	x	Customize buttons, pointer, animation, and the type of device.
Multimedia	x	x	Specify multimedia settings.

Feature	Windows 95	Windows 98	Details
Network	x	x	Install or customize network settings, adapters, services, and protocols.
Passwords	x	x	Change passwords, enable remote administration, or determine user profile usage.
PC Card	x	x	Configure and stop PC Card devices.
Printers	x	x	Install, view, and manage printers.
Regional Settings	x	x	Specify international settings.
Sounds	x	x	Change system and program sounds assigned to events.
System	x	x	Specify memory parameters. Examine and configure system hardware.
Desktop Themes		x	Administer the desktop.
Find Fast		x	Get Microsoft system information.
Games Controllers		x	Use to configure and test game controller.
Infrared		x	Use the infrared monitor for portables.
Power Management		x	Use power management for portables.
Telephony		x	Set dialin properties.
User		x	Add user account and PIN.
32 Bit ODBC		x	Administer ODBC data services.

Concept Questions   *Semester 2, Unit 5, Lesson 21*

Demonstrate your knowledge of the concepts in this lesson by answering the following questions in the space provided.

1. Explain the function of the Control Panel and why it is an important utility.

2. Explain how you access the Control Panel in Windows 95/98.

_____

_____

_____

_____

_____

_____

_____

_____

_____

_____

_____

_____

_____

_____

_____

_____

_____

_____

Vocabulary Exercise   *Semester 2, Unit 5, Lesson 21*

Name: _____

Date: _____   *Class:* _____

Define the following terms as completely as you can.

configuration

_____

_____

Control Panel

_____

_____

Registry

_____

_____

Focus Questions   *Semester 2, Unit 5, Lesson 21*

Name: _____

Date: _____   *Class:* _____

1. Describe the Accessibility Options feature.

_____

_____

_____

2. Describe the Add New Hardware feature.

_____

_____

_____

3. Describe the Add/Remove Programs feature.

_____

_____

_____

4. Describe the Date/Time feature.

_____

_____

_____

5. Describe the Display feature.

_____

_____

_____

6. Describe the Fonts feature.

_____

_____

_____

7. Describe the Internet feature.

_____

_____

_____

8. Describe the Keyboard feature.

_____

_____

_____

9. Describe the Mail and Fax feature.

_____

_____

_____

10. Describe the Microsoft Mail Postoffice feature.

_____

_____

_____

11. Describe the Modems feature.

_____

_____

_____

12. Describe the Mouse feature.

_____

_____

_____

13. Describe the Multimedia feature.

_____

_____

_____

14. Describe the Network feature.

_____

_____

_____

15. Describe the Passwords feature.

_____

_____

_____

16. Describe the PC Card feature.

_____

_____

_____

17. Describe the Printers feature.

_____

_____

_____

18. Describe the Regional Settings feature.

_____

_____

_____

19. Describe the Sounds feature.

_____

_____

_____

20. Describe the System feature.

_____

_____

_____

21. Describe the Desktop Themes feature.

_____

_____

_____

22. Describe the Find Fast feature.

_____

_____

_____

23. Describe the Games Controllers feature.

_____

_____

_____

24. Describe the Infrared feature.

_____

_____

_____

25. Describe the Power Management feature.

_____

_____

_____

26. Describe the Telephony feature.

_____

_____

_____

27. Describe the User feature.

_____

_____

_____

28. Describe the 32 Bit ODBC feature.

_____

_____

_____

SEMESTER 2, UNIT 5, LESSON 22

System Hardware and Software Configuration for Windows 95/98

You have learned that the Windows 95/98 Control Panel is the utility that helps you configure and reconfigure hardware and software settings to suit your needs. So the Control Panel is the place to go for computer customization. In this lesson you will learn some details about hardware and software configurations, using the Control Panel to customize the settings.

Installing and configuring a new device

If you've just installed a new hardware device, you can immediately go to the Control Panel and click on the Add New Hardware icon. This starts the Add New Hardware Wizard. (If you make a mistake, are unprepared to configure the hardware, or get scared, you can always cancel or go back.) To proceed, click Next, and you arrive at the first working screen.

Ideally, Windows automatically detects any new devices you have plugged in, so the Yes button is selected by **default**. Simply click Next and let the computer take over. This part of the process may take several minutes, and occasionally might even lock up your computer. Don't panic. No harm will be done. Simply press the **restart** button to regain control.

If you know exactly what hardware you want to add, you can save some time by clicking No before clicking Next, and then proceed with the directions.

For each device that is detected or specified, you choose a **driver**. On the left pane of the window, drivers are organized by manufacturer or developer, and on the right by the specific model or version.

If you have a hardware device that is not installed properly, the **interrupt request (IRQ)** begins to wave its flag for attention. It literally interrupts the computer from whatever it is doing and demands that the problem be attended to.

If the device is **plug-and-play** compatible, Windows does all the work for you; however, if it is not plug-and-play compatible, you might be required to physically manipulate a card, move jumpers, or flip switches to choose IRQ and I/O addresses.

Managing hardware profiles

Conflicts or problems with hardware devices can affect a system's performance adversely, sometimes without you knowing about it. To check out your system's Hardware profile, click on the System icon in the Control Panel. After the general panel of system properties, you can click the **Device Manager** to find information on all your system's hardware, listed by categories.

Whenever the hardware changes on a plug-and-play computer, Windows 95 creates a new hardware profile upon **system** restart. It detects the hardware profile and loads the appropriate drivers. Conversely, on computers that do not support plug-and-play, you must create hardware profiles by hand. Upon startup you are prompted to select a hardware profile, and then Windows takes over and loads the drivers for the devices. Occasionally you might need to change a device's configuration. If this is the case, using the Device Manager can help you avoid the errors that can occur if you attempt to edit Registry entries directly.

Controlling display properties

To change the monitor's settings and appearance, click the Display icon in the Control Panel. From here you can change the type of display driver being used, as well as the driver settings, which include the following:

- Background settings, including patterns and wallpaper

- Screen saver settings, including password protection and energy-saving monitor features

- Appearance settings, including font sizes and color schemes

The display options are very user friendly, and you can use them to change the video card driver, the appearance of the desktop, the video resolution, and other visual display items.

Installing and controlling modems

When you first install Windows 95 or if you buy a new modem (or switch to a new serial port), you need to go to the Modems option in the Control Panel. You can take advantage of the Standard Modem Devices option and let Windows take care of the details. Afterward you can change any details to suit your needs. Table 5-2 lists options you can configure from the General tab.

Table 5-2   *Configurable modem options*

Use This Option	To Configure This
Port	The COM or LPT port to which the external modem is attached, or a COM port name assigned to an internal modem
Speaker Volume	The volume for the telephone speaker
Maximum Speed	The speed at which Windows 95 communicates with the modem, which is limited by the CPU speed of the computer and the speeds supported by the modem and the COM port

Configuring multimedia devices

The Control Panel's Multimedia Device option enables you to control the following:

- Audio—Configure installed sound cards for playback and recording, and set the volume, the recording qualify, and the preferred device for operation.

- Video—Change the default display for video to full or windowed screen.

- MIDI (Musical Instrument Digital Interface)—A standard for digital synthesizer communications. The MIDI tab has two main functions: Allowing configuration of MIDI output settings and providing access to the Add New Instrument Wizard.

- CD Music—Select the CD-ROM drive and set the volume for the drive's headphone port.

Adding and removing operating system components

Windows 95 includes optional components as well as essential ones. These optional components include screen savers, wallpaper images, accessory programs, and the **Microsoft Network (MSN)**. To make adjustments, start by double-clicking the Add/Remove Programs icon in the Control Panel. Windows lists the optional components in the dialog box, along with a categorical listing of disk space that is currently being used. To add or remove a component, select a category and then click the Details button. Installed items are flagged with checkmarks. Uncheck a box to remove an item, and check a box to install it.

Desktop themes

Desktop themes allow you to change the system desktop, screen saver, pointing devices, and sound effects in the desktop. You can also change the font, color, and wallpaper. To reconfigure your desktop, double-click the Desktop Themes icon.

The Find Fast feature

Find Fast allows you to find information about the system. It has technical support for specific words and phrases in the help topic. To use Find Fast, double-click the Find Fast icon.

Configuring a Windows 95/98 network

Follow these steps to configure a Windows 95/98 network:

1. Add a network card and double-click the Network icon.

2. Click Add, Adapter, Have Disk.

3. Insert the drivers disk into drive **a:**, or the drivers CD into the CD-ROM drive.

4. Click Browse and select the network drive.

5. Click OK to load the network drive.

Concept Questions   *Semester 2, Unit 5, Lesson 22*

Demonstrate your knowledge of the concepts in this lesson by answering the following questions in the space provided.

1. Explain the procedure you follow to install and configure a new device using the Control Panel.

2. Explain how the Device Manager can help improve a system's performance.

_____

_____

_____

_____

_____

_____

_____

_____

_____

_____

_____

_____

_____

_____

_____

_____

_____

_____

_____

Vocabulary Exercise   *Semester 2, Unit 5, Lesson 22*

Name: _____

Date: _____   Class: _____

Define the following terms as completely as you can.

driver

_____

_____

IRQ

_____

_____

plug-and-play

_____

_____

Focus Questions

Semester 2, Unit 5, Lesson 22

Name: _____

Date: _____   *Class:* _____

1. Describe what happens if there is an IRQ problem.

_____

_____

_____

2. Describe how you use the Control Panel to manage hardware profiles.

_____

_____

_____

3. Describe how you use the Control Panel to control display properties.

_____

_____

_____

4. Describe how you use the Control Panel to install and control modem devices.

_____

_____

_____

5. Describe how you use the Control Panel to configure multimedia devices.

_____

_____

_____

6. Describe how you use the Control Panel to add and remove operating system components.

_____

_____

_____

7. Describe how you use the Control Panel to manage applications.

_____

_____

_____

8. Describe how you use the Control Panel to remove applications.

_____

_____

_____

SEMESTER 2, UNIT 5, LESSON 23
The Windows 95/98 Registry and Installation Files

You learned how to use the Control Panel to install and configure components and applications in the computer system. After you make these types of changes, the various parameters are stored in the **Registry**. In this lesson you will learn about the functions and structures of the Registry and how to use it. The Registry stores software and hardware configuration settings in a single database. This central repository is built during initial setup and is updated whenever additions, removals, or configuration changes are made to devices or software.

Registry files

Although the Registry is one database, it consists of two different **Registry files** to allow more network configuration flexibility:

- **user.dat**—Contains user-specific information

- **system.dat**—Contains hardware-specific and computer-specific settings

By default these two files are stored in the Windows system subdirectory, but they could be located in different physical locations, depending on how the machine is set up.

The Registry's structure

The Registry is organized into a tree-like structure just like folders and files in a well-organized filing cabinet. It appears very similar to the Windows Explorer directory. The Registry contains six subtrees:

- **HKEY_LOCAL_MACHINE**—Computer-specific information about the type of hardware installed, software settings, and other information.

- **HKEY_CURRENT_CONFIG**—Same information as **HKEY_LOCAL_MACHINE**, with display and printer information

- **HKEY_DYN_DATA**—Status information for various devices as part of the plug-and-play information. It points to the **HKEY_LOCAL_MACHINE**.

- **HKEY_CLASSES_ROOT**—Essential information about OLE, shortcuts, and GUI aspects. It points to a branch of **HKEY_LOCAL_MACHINE**.

- **HKEY_USERS**—Generic and specific information about all the users who log on to the computer, with default settings for applications, desktop configurations, and so on.

- **HKEY_CURRENT_USER**—Points to a branch of **HKEY_USERS** for user currently logged on.

Each subtree contains subkeys—**config**, **enum**, **hardware**, **network**, **security**, **software**, and **system**—which give more specific information about the computer.

The Registry Editor

Although you should use an icon such as Add New Hardware from the Control Panel to make system modifications, you can use the Registry Editor (**regedit.exe**), located in the *win_root* folder, to view and modify Registry settings. You should do this only when absolutely necessary. Any changes made directly to the Registry are immediate and irrevocable, so be sure to back up your current Registry before making changes! As you have likely discovered already, backing up any system or file is a wise precaution.

Viewing the Registry Editor should be relatively safe. Beside each key is a + that you can click to reveal additional subkeys. To view the values for a key, click the key itself. You can add keys and change values by following directions and clicking on the various data values.

Following are commands to work with the Registry Editor:

- Find—A search function that you use by typing the string you want to locate.

- Import/Export—Allows saving in a text file and restoring it on the same or a different computer.

- Connect Network Registry—Allows editing the Registry of a remote computer, as long as you have a Remote Registry service and user-level security.

Concept Questions   *Semester 2, Unit 5, Lesson 23*

Demonstrate your knowledge of the concepts in this lesson by answering the following questions in the space provided.

1. Explain why you should or should not routinely make changes to Registry configurations.

2. What kind of information is stored in the Registry?

_____

_____

_____

_____

_____

_____

_____

_____

_____

_____

_____

_____

_____

_____

_____

_____

_____

_____

Vocabulary Exercise   *Semester 2, Unit 5, Lesson 23*

Name: _____

Date: _____   *Class:* _____

Define the following terms as completely as you can.

Registry

_____

_____

Registry Editor

_____

_____

Registry file

_____

_____

Focus Questions

Semester 2, Unit 5, Lesson 23

Name: _____

Date: _____   *Class:* _____

1. Describe **HKEY_CURRENT_CONFIG**.

_____

_____

_____

2. Describe **HKEY_DYN_DATA**.

_____

_____

_____

3. Describe **HKEY_CLASSES_ROOT**.

_____

_____

_____

4. Describe **HKEY_USERS**.

_____

_____

_____

5. Describe **HKEY_CURRENT_USER**.

_____

_____

_____

6. Describe how often Registry information is updated.

_____

_____

_____

7. Describe how the Registry is structured.

_____

_____

_____

8. Describe the purpose of the Registry.

_____

_____

_____

9. Describe the two files that form the Registry.

_____

_____

_____

10. Describe the six main Registry branches.

_____

_____

_____

_____

_____

_____

SEMESTER 2, UNIT 5, LESSON 24
Optimizing the Windows 95/98 System

You have learned about using the Control Panel and the Registry to change computer configurations. Now it's time to find out why configuring is important. You will learn how to reconfigure your computer so that it performs as well as possible.

Performance factors

We all know what it's like to go to school or to work with a headache, a fever, or allergies. Sometimes you've gone without enough sleep or without eating properly. When these things occur, you have probably been less alert and productive than normal. If you had a complete medical checkup that day, a doctor could probably diagnose some problem areas and offer remedies. The same is true of your computer. If you expect maximum performance, you need to pay close attention to the some performance factors, such as the following:

- Memory—This is the most important performance factor. Check the memory first when performance begins to fail.

- Processor speed—Faster CPUs should mean faster performance, but it depends on available RAM and other factors.

- Hard disk speed—This is important to consider, but not as important as RAM and processor speed.

- Display adapter speed—High-speed display adapters reduce the amount of time spent drawing graphics.

- Network adapter speed—Faster network cards transfer data faster.

- **Protected-mode drivers** versus **real-mode drivers**—Protected-mode drivers give the best performance.

Virtual memory

Virtual reality is a computer-based reality that doesn't really exist in the physical realm. Similarly, **virtual memory** doesn't exist in the real RAM realm. Because current applications often require more RAM than computers possess, Windows 95/98 coordinates both RAM and hard disk space to provide temporary (virtual) memory. This allows for the maximum amount of memory your system allows.

To accomplish this task, Windows 95/98 uses a **swap file** (or **paging file**). Using virtual memory, some of the program code is stored in RAM while other information is temporarily swapped to the swap file. The swap file is dynamic—it swaps information back and forth from RAM and gets larger or smaller, depending on system memory requirements and available disk space. It can also occupy fragmented regions of the hard disk without impairing the computer's performance. In fact, a benefit of this invisible activity is that you can run more programs simultaneously than the computer's RAM allows.

You can use the Control Panel's System option to change virtual memory settings. Although the system defaults usually provide the best performance, you can adjust the swap file settings to optimize performance. On machines with multiple hard disk drives, you might want to put the swap file on the drive with the fastest performance or on one that is not very busy. To adjust the virtual memory swap file, follow these steps:

1. Double-click System in the Control Panel.

2. Click the Performance tab.

3. Click Virtual Memory.

4. To specify a different hard disk, click the option Let me specify my own virtual memory settings.

5. Specify the new disk in the Hard Disk box or type new values in the Minimum or Maximum boxes.

6. Click OK.

Optimizing file system performance

Whereas file system drivers were supported by MS-DOS in Windows 3.1, file system drivers are Ring 0 components in the Windows 95/98 operating system. Windows 95/98 supports the following:

- 32-bit FAT (VFAT) driver

- 32-bit CD-ROM file system (CDFS) driver

- 32-bit network redirector for connectivity to Microsoft network servers

- Other drivers added by other vendors

The **Virtual File Allocation Table (VFAT)** driver acts as the primary file system and cannot be disabled. Although hard drive speeds have increased quite a bit over the years, you still might want to speed one up, and there are a few ways to speed them up, primarily through the system **cache**, which stores the most frequently accessed data.

Think of the cache as your kitchen, where you store your favorite foods and snacks. Rather than run to the store every time you want to break out the popcorn and soda, you can simply head to the kitchen cache. The computer operates the same way, storing your favorite locations on the hard disk swap file.

Because Windows 95/98 has a dynamic disk cache, you do not need to configure its size. As shown in Table 5-3, some settings used for Windows 3.x are no longer required and should be removed from the Windows 95/98 configuration files to prevent potential problems because they only waste memory space and actually interfere with Windows 95/98 automatic disk caching.

Table 5-3 *Removing configuration settings to optimize file system performance*

Configuration File	Configuration Setting to Remove
autoexec.bat	SHARE SMARTDRV settings Any entries for other disk cache software
config.sys	SMARTDRV settings (double-buffer driver) Any entries for other disk cache software

Concept Questions   *Semester 2, Unit 5, Lesson 24*

Demonstrate your knowledge of the concepts in this lesson by answering the following questions in the space provided.

1. Explain the factors that affect system performance.

2. Explain which older settings should be removed from Windows 95/98 configuration files and why.

_____

_____

_____

_____

_____

_____

_____

_____

_____

_____

_____

_____

_____

_____

_____

_____

_____

_____

Vocabulary Exercise   *Semester 2, Unit 5, Lesson 24*

Name: _____

Date: _____   *Class:* _____

Define the following terms as completely as you can.

cache

_____

_____

swap file

_____

_____

VFAT

_____

_____

virtual memory

_____

_____

Focus Questions

Semester 2, Unit 5, Lesson 24

Name: _____

Date: _____ *Class:* _____

1. Describe how to adjust the virtual memory.

_____

_____

_____

2. Describe how to optimize file system performance.

_____

_____

_____

3. Describe VFAT and how it functions.

_____

_____

_____

4. Describe how Windows 95/98 allocates memory by using a swap file.

_____

_____

_____

SEMESTER 2, UNIT 5, LESSON 25
Unit 5 Exam

If you have access to the online Aries A+ curriculum, contact your instructor for the Assessment System URL. If you do not have access to the online curriculum, please continue to Unit 6.

SEMESTER 2, UNIT 6

- Lesson 26: The Windows 95/98 File System
- Lesson 27: Managing the Computer's File System
- Lesson 28: Preventive Maintenance for Windows 95/98
- Lesson 29: Troubleshooting the Windows 95/98 File System
- Lesson 30: Unit 6 Exam

SEMESTER 2, UNIT 6, LESSON 26
The Windows 95/98 File System

In this lesson you will learn about the Windows 95/98 file system, file types, how to manage files, and how to browse the system's directory.

The Windows 95/98 file system stores individual files in directories that appear on the screen as folder icons. Folders within folders are called *subdirectories*, or *subfolders*. Files that contain operating instructions for the computer are called *program files*. Files can also contain text documents that you can read. Files, folders, and subfolders can be physically stored on magnetic disks, optical discs, or any data storage medium.

Think of a folder as a container, like a drawer, where files are stored. Folders are used to organize data into categories, the same way that folders in a file cabinet are used to store information.

The Windows 95/98 file system has three main components:

- Drives (hard disk, floppy disk, and CD-ROM), which contain and organize files within directories.

- Folders, which contain files and other folders.

- Files, which hold information such as programs, text, graphics, and numeric data.

File types in Windows 95/98

Files are typically categorized according to the type of information they hold. In Windows a file's type is signified by its **extension**, which is an abbreviation, preceded by a period, that appears at the end of a filename (for example, **.exe**, **.sys**). Files are usually identified as one of the following types:

- Data files—Contain numbers, names, addresses, and other information created in a database or spreadsheet program.

- Font files—Contain a selection of fonts, which you can see by opening the My Computer window.

- Program files—Contain computer-readable code. To start a program file, double-click on the program icon.

- Support files—Contain information that is stored by programs. These files can't be executed or started by double-clicking.

- Text files—Contain alphanumeric characters that follow the American Standard Code for Information Interchange (ASCII). Text files are accessible by a wide range of programs.

- Graphics files—Contain visuals or graphical information, created in programs such as Paint.

Table 6-1 lists commonly used filename extensions and the types of files they're used for.

Table 6-1   *Commonly used filename extensions*

Extension	Description
.qic	Microsoft Backup file
.bas, .frm	Microsoft Visual Basic files
.bmp	Bitmap graphics image
.cda	Audio CD file
.ini	Program settings
.cch, .cdr, .shw	CorelDraw! files
.set	Microsoft Backup file sets
.fon	Font definition
.hlp	Online help file
.ht	HyperTerminal file
.msg	Mail message file
.mmm	Media clip, such as sound and video clips
.mda	Microsoft Access file
.xlc, .xlm, .xls, .xlt, .xlw	Microsoft Excel files
.mpp, .mpv	Microsoft Project files
.doc, .dot, .rtf	Microsoft Word files
.mid, .rmi	MIDI files
.ppt	Microsoft PowerPoint file
.reg	Registration database file

Extension	Description
.txt	Text file
.ttf	TrueType Font file
.avi	Video file
.wav	Windows sound file
.wri	Write document

File management in Windows 95/98

In Windows 95/98, you decide where to create folders and where to place files. With My Computer, you can create folders and subfolders. The following sections describe some of the file management techniques available in Windows 95/98.

Creating folders

To create a new folder directly on the desktop, follow these steps:

1. Double-click the My Computer icon.

2. Double-click the Drive **c:** icon to open its window.

3. Choose File, New, Folder.

4. A new folder should appear on the desktop. Name the new folder by entering its name in the caption box, and then press Enter.

Selecting files

You can select a file by clicking on it. To select files that are adjacent to one another, click on the first file, and then hold down the Shift key and click on the next file. To select two or more files that are not adjacent, click on files one at a time while holding down the Control key. To deselect a file, simply click on it again.

Moving and copying files and folders

In Windows 95/98, it's a simple process to copy or move information. Files are moved or copied from a *source* to a *destination*: The source is the file to be copied and the destination is the file's new location.

Before moving files or folders, be sure both the source and its destination are visible onscreen. To move a file or folder, select it, hold down the Shift key, and drag the file or folder to the destination window. After you release the file or folder, a dialog box will let you know that the command is being executed. If you try to move a file and copy over an existing document, another dialog box will appear, asking for confirmation to replace the existing file.

To copy a file or folder to a different drive, select it, drag it to its destination, and release it. When you are copying a document to a closed folder, drag the item to be copied over the folder's icon until the icon appears highlighted. When you drop it, it is copied into the highlighted folder. A dialog box appears to verify that the file is being copied. Note that you can do a similar procedure by right-clicking the mouse and following the directions on the menu.

To copy an object within the same drive, hold down the Ctrl key as you drag the object; otherwise, you will move it instead of creating a copy.

If you right-click a folder or file and drag it to its destination, when you release it, a menu appears that offers the choice to either copy or move the file. Click on your choice, and the command is executed.

Deleting folders

You can delete a folder in two ways:

- Click the folder to select it, and then press the Delete key.

- Click the folder to select it, and then select File, Delete.

When you delete a folder, you are also deleting all the files that are contained within that folder, so use caution when you delete. Windows 95 displays a message box to confirm any deletions you make, and you have the option to recover deleted folders from the Recycle Bin. However, when a file or folder is deleted from a floppy disk, it is gone forever.

Undeleting files and folders

Folders and files that have been deleted by default go to the Recycle Bin. If you need to restore a folder, double-click the Recycle Bin icon. Choose the files you want to restore, and then select File, Restore. As mentioned previously, this does not apply to files and folders deleted from floppy disks because deleted floppy files are not sent to the Recycle Bin.

If you want to delete a file or folder and get rid of it permanently—without sending it to the Recycle Bin, where it could be reclaimed at a later time—you can bypass the Recycle Bin entirely by holding down the Shift key when you press the Delete key. Just keep in mind that if you do this, the file is gone forever.

Renaming folders

To rename a folder, follow these steps:

1. Click on the folder to select it.

2. Click File, Rename.

3. A caption box appears. Type the new name in it and press Enter.

Another way to rename a folder is as follows:

1. Click on the folder to select it.

2. Click on the name of the folder. A caption box appears around the existing name, and the arrow changes to a cursor.

3. Type the new name and press Enter.

Finding files and folders

To locate a file or folder, follow these steps:

1. Choose Find from the File menu.

2. From the cascading menu that appears, select the Files or Folders option.

3. A dialog box appears that asks you the name of the file you want to locate. Type the name, choose the location, and click Find Now.

File size

File size is measured in small chunks called **bytes**, each about the size of one character. A thousand bytes is called a **kilobyte (KB)**, and a million a **megabyte (MB)**, and a billion a **gigabyte (GB)**. Computer-savvy types frequently toss around terms like *meg* for megabyte, and *gig* for gigabyte.

If you want to see how large a file is, you can check in the My Computer window or Windows Explorer, using the Details view. If you plan to back up a file on a floppy disk later, you can check to make sure it will fit, taking into account the other files that may be occupying space on that disk.

File properties

Windows 95/98 allows you to view the properties of any file by right-clicking the file's icon and selecting Properties from the pop-up menu that appears. The Properties dialog box reveals a great deal of information about the file. Some of this information can be changed by the user, and some is there for reference. A glance at the General tab of the Properties box tells you the name of the file, the type of file it is, where it is located, and its size. You can also see its MS-DOS name and various time-sensitive information, such as when the folder was created, when it was last modified, and when it was last read or accessed.

At the bottom of the Properties dialog box is a list of attributes, each of which can be enabled by checking the box next to it:

- **Read-only**—Read-only means just that: You can open it, read it, and even print it, but you can't make any changes to the file, or even get rid of it. Why would you want this option? We've all had the experience of throwing something out by accident. The read-only attribute protects you from accidentally deleting something important. You can uncheck the read-only box anytime if you want to make changes, and then later you can re-enable it.

- **Hidden**—Hidden means the file is hidden from view in file listings. For those who are secretive, perhaps burning the midnight oil working on those top-secret files meant for your eyes only, this option was made for you. Also, if you work on a computer that is used by a number of different people, you can keep sensitive files out of general view if you tag them as hidden.

- **Archive**—Archive automatically affects any file you change. The file is marked with a flag in the form of the letter *A,* which, when you look at its listing, lets you know that it has been altered and needs to be backed up.

- **System**—System identifies crucial system files. Notice that this option is unavailable (gray). System attributes are assigned by the computer's operating system, and are protected from tampering. System files are hidden in DOS file listings, unless Show All Files has been enabled in the Options dialog box.

You can choose one or more attributes for a file.

File creation date and time

Windows keeps track of when files are created and modified. The exact moment when you save a file for the first time is considered its creation date and time. Subsequent saves are recorded as modification dates. To see a file's creation date, and when it was last modified, go to the General tab in the Properties dialog box. You can find modification dates in My Computer or Explorer, in the Details view.

Keep in mind that in order for file creation and modification times to be correct, the system clock must register the correct time and day.

Browsing system drives and directories

It's important to know how to navigate, or browse, the computer, so you can find things easily. Windows 95/98 makes it very simple to locate a particular folder or file. The Windows 98 operating system has added browsing tools to explore many Windows files and the Network Neighborhood.

Start by double clicking on the My Computer icon on the desktop. With the window open, you can see icons for all the drives on the system, and folders relating to other system functions. First, look at the **c:** drive by double-clicking its icon. Now you can see all the folders residing on that drive. To see what's inside a given folder, follow the same pattern: double-click an icon to open the folder. (Remember that you can check out the properties of a file by right-clicking once on the file's icon.)

You've probably noticed that Windows 95 opens a new window on the desktop every time you double-click an icon. If you are working your way through a series of folders to get to a particular file, you can quickly clutter up the screen with a pile of open windows. This ties up system memory you could be using for other things. If you don't need to look at more than one window at a time, you can tell Windows to reconfigure the desktop so that only one window is open at any given time, and the contents of that window simply change as you continue to open folders or files. In many situations, this can be a more efficient way to browse. To do this, select the View menu in the My Computer window and select Options. A dialog box appears. The Folders tab is the one you want; it offers two browsing options:

- Browse folders by using a separate window for each folder.

- Browse folders by using a single window that changes as you open each folder.

The first option is the default in Windows 95, meaning that the computer is preset to use this option until you tell it otherwise. The second option uses less memory, but allows you to have only one window at a time open on the desktop. Choose the option that best suits your purposes. After you have chosen an option, click OK to make it happen.

Using the toolbar in a folder window

Let's assume that you have efficiently configured the desktop to open only one window at a time. You have browsed from folders to subfolders, and reached the file you were looking for. At this point you are far from the My Computer window, the parent folder you opened when you started. Suddenly you realize that you have to go back, because you need to look at something located there. What you need to do is access the toolbar in the folder window. From the View choose Toolbar. The toolbar, containing a pull-down list and a series of icons, appears across the top of the window. Use the Up One Level button to retrace your steps. You can also browse the pull-down list and locate your destination.

Concept Questions   *Semester 2, Unit 6, Lesson 26*

Demonstrate your knowledge of the concepts in this lesson by answering the following questions in the space provided.

1. Explain the form and purpose of file extensions.

2. Explain how the three main components of the Windows 95/98 file system allow you to work with icons to represent files and directories.

_____

_____

_____

_____

_____

_____

_____

_____

_____

_____

_____

_____

_____

_____

_____

_____

_____

_____

Vocabulary Exercise   *Semester 2, Unit 6, Lesson 26*

Name: _____

Date: _____   *Class:* _____

Define the following terms as completely as you can.

archive attribute

_____

_____

byte

_____

_____

extension

_____

_____

GB

_____

_____

hidden attribute

_____

_____

KB

_____

_____

MB

_____

_____

read-only attribute

_____

_____

system attribute

_____

_____

Focus Questions   *Semester 2, Unit 6, Lesson 26*

Name: _____

Date: _____   *Class:* _____

1. Describe the Windows 95/98 file system.

_____

_____

_____

2. Describe the main components of the Windows 95/98 file system.

_____

_____

_____

3. Describe the file types in Windows 95/98.

_____

_____

_____

4. What are some examples of common file extensions?

_____

_____

_____

5. Describe how files are managed in Windows 95/98.

_____

_____

_____

6. Describe how you create a folder.

_____

_____

_____

7. Describe how you select a file.

_____

_____

_____

8. Describe how you move and copy files or folders.

_____

_____

_____

9. Describe how you delete a folder.

_____

_____

_____

10. Describe how you undelete a folder.

_____

_____

_____

11. Describe how you rename a folder.

_____

_____

_____

12. Describe how you find a file.

_____

_____

_____

13. Describe how you check a file's size.

_____

_____

_____

14. Describe how you view a file's properties.

_____

_____

_____

15. Describe what you see in the file Properties dialog box.

_____

_____

_____

16. Describe how you access a file's creation or modification date.

_____

_____

_____

17. Describe how you browse system drives and directories.

_____

_____

_____

18. Describe how you configure Windows to open only one window at a time.

_____

_____

_____

19. If you have told Windows to open only one window at a time, how do you move
up a level in the folder hierarchy?

_____

_____

_____

20. Describe the Windows toolbar options.

_____

_____

_____

SEMESTER 2, UNIT 6, LESSON 27
Managing the Computer's File System

You have learned about the Windows 95/98 file system and its key components. You have learned about files and folders—how to create them, identify them, protect them from human error—and also how to browse the hard drive to find files and folders when you need them. In this lesson, you'll find out still more about how the Windows 95/98 file system manages information.

Disk partitions

A computer permanently stores data on its hard drive. The read/write heads inside the hard drive allow random access to information stored on the drive's magnetic platters. This enables you to retrieve a tremendous quantity of data far more rapidly than was possible with earlier linear media, such as magnetic tape, which could utilize only a relatively small amount of data in a sequential manner.

To make the best use of all this space, computer disks are divided into sections, called **partitions.** Having multiple partitions on the hard drive allows you to

- Quickly retrieve information

- Use multiple operating systems on the same computer

- Physically separate information for organizational and security reasons

You can have up to four separate partitions on any one hard disk. It's also important to know that there are two different kinds of partitions:

- **Primary partitions**—The active primary partition is the one the computer references when it boots up the operating system. If you want to be able to store and use more than one operating system on the hard drive, you must place each one in a different primary partition. Only one primary can be designated as active at any given time. Primary partitions cannot be subdivided into smaller partitions.

- **Extended partitions**—The extended partition uses free hard disk space, and is usually assigned all the available space outside the primary partition(s). The data stored in the extended partition is used by the operating system. There can be only one extended partition per disk, but unlike the primary, it can be subdivided into multiple partitions, called **logical drives.** Each one of these subdivisions can be treated as a separate drive. This allows you to assign them additional drive letter designations.

Partitioning a hard disk

To reconfigure the hard disk into partitions, follow these steps:

1. Use Add/Remove Programs (in the Control Panel) to create a startup disk.

2. Create a backup of all files on the hard disk.

3. Use **fdisk** to repartition the hard drive (you'll learn the details of this step later in the lesson).

4. Format the hard disk (you'll learn the details of this step later in the lesson).

5. Reload the backup files.

Creating partitions

The **fdisk** utility (located in the *win_root* folder) allows you to create partitions. With **fdisk**, you can enable **FAT32** support, create and delete primary and extended partitions, create logical drives within an extended partition, and assign an active partition.

The manufacturer of the computer may have already created partitions for you. If you decide to change them, you can use **fdisk**, but be sure to create a backup of your existing files first, because the originals will be lost when you create new partitions. Keep in mind that actions you perform with **fdisk** are not reversible, so be cautious!

Follow these steps to use **fdisk**:

1. Boot from a Windows 95/98 startup disk or click on the command prompt.

2. Type **fdisk**.

3. The **fdisk** Options screen appears, offering a series of options:

- Create a DOS partition or logical DOS drive.

- Set the active partition.

- Delete a DOS partition or logical DOS drive.

- Display partition information.

Note that if you have more than one hard disk, **fdisk** displays another option, Change current fixed disk drive, which gives you the option to switch to another hard disk.

fdisk also reminds you which hard disk drive you are working on by displaying a current fixed disk drive number on each screen. If you have only one drive, the number is always 1.

Formatting partitions

You've used **fdisk** to create a partition. Now what do you do? The partition must be formatted before it will be ready to accept and store data. To format the partition where Windows 95/98 resides, use the process outlined in the Windows 95/98 startup disk.

Follow these steps to format a partition for a secondary drive:

1. Restart the computer.

2. Open the My Computer window.

3. Right-click the icon of the drive you want to format, and then click Format. The Format dialog box appears.

4. Choose Full as the Format type.

5. Enter **drive** plus the letter of the drive you have chosen for the label (for example, **drive d**).

6. Click Start. The Format dialog box appears, asking you to confirm the formatting action.

7. Click OK. A progress bar appears, and when formatting is complete, a dialog box appears. Click Close.

8. The Format dialog box appears, telling you to run ScanDisk. Click OK.

9. When ScanDisk's Help dialog box appears, click Close.

Deleting partitions

Partitions must be deleted in a certain order. Non-DOS partitions must be deleted first, followed by any logical drives in the extended partition. After that, extended partitions can be deleted, and finally, primary partitions. Again, remember that **fdisk** permanently destroys any files in deleted partitions, so be sure to back up existing files.

To delete a partition, follow these steps:

1. Go to the **fdisk** Options screen as you did earlier in the lesson.

2. Press 3, and then press Enter.

3. When the Delete DOS Partition or Logical DOS Drive screen appears, press the number for the kind of partition you want to delete, and press Enter.

4. Follow the onscreen directions.

5. Repeat these steps to delete additional partitions or drives.

Naming Windows 95/98 files

Those familiar with Windows 3.1 remember the 8.3 filename rule, which limited filenames to eight characters plus a three-character extension that identified the file's type, with no spaces between characters (for example, **articles.doc**). This was fine as long as your ideal filename contained eight or fewer characters, but in many cases it led to squashed, cryptic versions of what the user would have called the file if the naming convention had been more flexible.

Windows 95/98, on the other hand, allows you to use filenames and directory names as long as 255 characters! It wouldn't be terribly practical for you to actually use this many characters, but just being able to enter a filename and use complete words with spaces between them is a thrill for Windows 3.1 veterans.

In Windows 3.1, filenames were limited by MS-DOS and the File Allocation Table (FAT) file system, which could not support anything longer than the 8.3 convention. Even though Windows 95/98 makes long filenames possible, if you are running a 16-bit program on the upgraded system, filenames will be abbreviated by that older program to conform to the 8.3 convention. So, in essence, a Windows 95/98 file actually has two names: its long filename, and an MS-DOS– and Windows 3.1-compatible name that fits the 8.3 rule. This allows older programs to read Windows 95/98 files.

Here's what happens when the abbreviation occurs: The system removes spaces from the Windows 95/98 filename and keeps the first six letters (called the **basis name**), abbreviates the rest by replacing it with ~1 (called the **numeric tail**), and changes all the letters to uppercase. So, a file created in Windows 95/98 named **Term Paper** would show up in Windows 3.1 as **TERMPA~1.DOC** (the identifying **.doc** at the end, remember, is called an extension, which tells you in this case that it's a Microsoft Word document).

How FAT, FAT32, and VFAT affect filenames

A trio of terms circulating around the filename issue might need some clarification at this point: FAT, FAT32, and **Virtual File Allocation Table (VFAT)**. What do they mean, and how do they affect your ability to name files?

FAT is a system that organizes the information stored on disk partitions. Data is separated into clusters that contain sectors. Early FAT systems supported 8- and 16-bit clusters, which restricted filenames to the 8.3 rule.

Later on, FAT32 was created, a 32-bit system that allows partitions larger than 2 GB and that made long filenames possible. However, there are some challenges with FAT32, including the following:

- Windows NT 4.0+ cannot access FAT32 volumes.

- Previous operating systems such as MS-DOS, Windows 3.x, and Windows 95 OSR1 cannot access FAT32.

- It is incompatible with DriveSpace3. (However, you can use a primary partition with FAT32 and put FAT16 on the other, using DriveSpace3 on the 16-bit volume.)

- You cannot run the **checkdsk** command to fix errors on FAT32. (However, you can use ScanDisk to fix errors.)

- There is limited support on the file control block.

- It is inoperable on Interlink.

Whereas FAT32 brought progress by allowing long filenames, VFAT made a great leap in user convenience by operating in protected mode. VFAT is a virtualized 32-bit FAT and allows the FAT to reserve an area of its directory for long filenames. To create long filenames, Windows 95 **concatenates,** or strings together, a series of MS-DOS–compatible directory entries into one filename entry.

Troubleshooting long filename problems

Here are some suggestions for handling difficulties with long filenames:

- Use the MS-DOS prompt in Windows 95 instead of MS-DOS mode.

- Use a Windows 95 disk utility rather than an MS-DOS utility.

- When copying files between directories, use long filenames.

- Perform file management on long filenames only.

- Don't use long filenames in root folders.

Table 6-2 lists some actual problems you might encounter, as well as possible causes and remedies.

Table 6-2 *Common problems with long filenames*

Problem	Possible Cause and Remedy
When I boot to an MS-DOS command prompt, none of my long filenames are available.	Long filenames are unavailable because protected-mode file system drivers support them. Because these drivers are not loaded when the command prompt is booted, long filenames are rendered unavailable. If you instead used an MS-DOS prompt from within Windows 95/98, the long filenames would become visible.
The MS-DOS names for my long filenames have been changed.	When you copy, edit, back up, and restore files, this can change a file's MS-DOS alias.
The MS-DOS names for my long filenames have been deleted.	MS-DOS aliases contain additional information regarding file creation times, dates, and access, which make them different from pre-Windows 95/98 files. Some MS-DOS utilities, when encountering this additional information, think the files need to be repaired and destroy them by mistake. Use a Windows 95/98 disk utility instead of its MS-DOS counterpart.
Some of my long filenames have been destroyed.	If you copy, edit, back up, and restore files using the MS-DOS alias, it destroys the long filename in the process. Manage these functions using long filenames in Windows 95/98.
I can't create additional files or folders in a partition's root folder, even though I know there is plenty of space.	Long filenames take up directory space faster than 8.3 names, so be conservative in your choice of filenames for files that will be stored in the root folder.

Disk compression

Picture yourself out in the woods, enjoying a relaxing weekend camping trip. You've set up the tent and are starting to unpack your gear. Somewhere in your assortment of stuff is a small bag, about the size of a loaf of bread, which holds your rolled-up sleeping bag. You open the drawstring, shake the bag out, and unroll it. When you lay it out on the tent floor, you notice that it's longer than you are tall. At the end of the trip, you roll it up and stuff it back into its small bag. It hardly takes up any space at all in the car. At home, you'll toss it back in the closet, and there it'll stay until you need to use it again. Similarly to the way you can compress your sleeping bag into a very small space, Windows 95/98 provides DriveSpace and DriveSpace3, which compress files so that they take up less space.

DriveSpace

Follow these steps to use the DriveSpace utility:

1. Click on the Start button, click Run, and type **drvspace**.

2. In DriveSpace, click the drive you want to compress.

3. Select the Drive menu, and click Compress.

4. The Compress a Drive Dialog box appears, showing the drive that will be compressed. If you would like to define the space that should be left available for the host drive, and specify whether it will be hidden, click on the Options box, and make modifications as needed. Click OK when you're through. Note that DriveSpace automatically hides the host drive if the amount of free space is less than 2 MB.

5. Click Start to continue.

6. DriveSpace prompts you to back up your files. You can do this by clicking the Back up Files button.

7. Start compression by clicking the Compress Now button.

At the beginning of the compression cycle, DriveSpace checks for disk errors. The process of compression can take up to several hours, depending on how much data is to be compressed and the speed of the hard disk and processor. DriveSpace keeps checking the data as it goes through the compression process.

DriveSpace3

DriveSpace3 is an upgraded version of DriveSpace that comes with Microsoft Plus and Windows 95 OSR2. Keep in mind that OSR2.x, Windows 98, DriveSpace3, and FAT32 are incompatible. Even though DriveSpace3 has been modified to work with FAT32, it cannot itself be compressed.

DriveSpace3 creates compressed files that can hold more data than the original DriveSpace utility, uses Pentium-optimized code, enables higher compression density, and allows the user to adjust the performance/compression ratio.

Concept Questions   *Semester 2, Unit 6, Lesson 27*

Demonstrate your knowledge of the concepts in this lesson by answering the following questions in the space provided.

1. Explain where the computer stores data.

2. Explain the differences between FAT, FAT32, and VFAT.

_____

_____

_____

_____

_____

_____

_____

_____

_____

_____

_____

_____

_____

_____

_____

_____

_____

_____

Vocabulary Exercise   *Semester 2, Unit 6, Lesson 27*

Name: _____

Date: _____   *Class:* _____

Define the following terms as completely as you can.

basis name

_____

_____

concatenate

_____

_____

disk compression

_____

_____

DriveSpace

_____

_____

extended partition

_____

_____

fdisk

_____

_____

logical drive

_____

_____

numeric tail

_____

_____

partition

_____

_____

primary partition

_____

_____

Focus Questions   *Semester 2, Unit 6, Lesson 27*

Name: _____

Date: _____   *Class:* _____

1. Describe how you partition a hard disk.

_____

_____

_____

2. Describe how you use **fdisk**.

_____

_____

_____

3. Describe the hard disk limitation for the primary partition with Windows 95/98.

_____

_____

_____

4. Describe the next step after you create a partition with **fdisk**.

_____

_____

_____

5. Describe how you delete a partition.

_____

_____

_____

6. Describe some rules for naming files.

_____

_____

_____

7. Describe some suggestions when working with long filenames.

_____

_____

_____

_____

_____

_____

8. Describe some common problems and possible solutions for problems with long filenames.

_____

_____

_____

_____

_____

_____

SEMESTER 2, UNIT 6, LESSON 28
Preventive Maintenance for Windows 95/98

You have learned about partitions and how to manage them, how to manage long filenames in Windows 95/98, and about the importance of file compression and how to use the DriveSpace utility to compress files. In this lesson, you'll learn about optimizing and maintaining the performance of a Windows-based computer.

Optimizing file system performance

To make the most of the system's potential, it is essential to get it running as swiftly and efficiently as you can. There are a number of ways you can **optimize** a hard disk and help a system do its best:

- Allow Windows to manage **virtual memory**, and leave enough space on the drive to accommodate it. Windows is designed to efficiently gauge the need for virtual memory.

- Run ScanDisk and Disk Defragmenter regularly, and empty the Recycle Bin frequently so it doesn't use up valuable disk space storing things you no longer need.

- Eliminate real-mode drivers, if possible. Real-mode drivers are older, 16-bit drivers designed for use with MS-DOS and earlier Windows versions. The newer, 32-bit drivers that come with Windows 95/98 are faster and more secure, but if the older ones are still on the system (for example, because you upgraded to Windows 95 from an earlier version), the computer might use them anyway, and this could compromise the system's performance. Eliminating them will ensure that the system is using the newer drivers. Note that Windows 95/98 should automatically unload any real-mode drivers for which it has protected-mode drivers.

- Eliminate device conflicts.

- Refrain from requesting background processing for MS-DOS–based applications unless you need it.

- Be wary of MS-DOS applications that use up available extended memory.

Fixing disk errors

In Windows 95/98 you can use the **ScanDisk** program to repair certain kinds of disk errors. You can use it on hard or floppy disks, including ones that have been compressed using DriveSpace. ScanDisk can help unravel the following dilemmas:

- FAT problems

- Long filename problems

- Lost partition data clusters

- Cross-linked files, which contain clusters that have been mistakenly linked to more than one file (the affected files intersect one another, which can cause problems when you're trying to read them)

- Directory structure problems

- **Bad sectors** (although ScanDisk cannot repair sectors, it can divert data away from those that are bad)

- On disks where DriveSpace has been used to compress files, volume header, volume file structure, compression structure or volume signature problems

There are two ways to run ScanDisk: a standard scan, which is good for routine maintenance, and a thorough scan, which gives you more control over the process.

Here's a quick way to run ScanDisk:

1. Double-click My Computer to open it.

2. Right-click the icon of the disk you want to assess and repair.

3. Choose the Properties option from the menu.

4. Click Tools.

5. Click Check Now.

For a more specialized session with ScanDisk, you can also access it through the Start menu:

1. Select Programs, and then click Accessories.

2. Choose System Tools.

3. You have the option to choose one or more disks to be checked (hold down the Ctrl key and click drives to select more than one), and the type of test you would like performed.

The standard mode performs a faster, logical test; the thorough mode checks media as well. The standard test is the one you should run routinely for normal disk maintenance. You should do a thorough test (surface scan) periodically, especially if you have reason to believe there are problems with the hard drive. A thorough test takes some time, and it's best not to continue working while the drives are being checked because if you happen to save anything to a hard drive while it is being checked, ScanDisk is forced to start over.

If you need a thorough test, but want to speed up the time it takes, you can click the Options button in the ScanDisk dialog box and choose from several surface scan options. Choosing to run the test on the system only speeds up the testing process. A system-only test goes quickly and lets you know about any catastrophic errors waiting in the wings. You can also choose to have the computer skip the write-testing portion of the program, and this shortens testing time as well.

Unless you check the Automatically Fix Errors checkbox, ScanDisk shows a dialog box every time it detects an error. This dialog box gives you the option to choose how to fix the problem or to ignore it.

For further ScanDisk options, click on the Advanced button in the ScanDisk dialog box. This dialog box offers you a number of choices:

- Display Summary and Log File option—This is where you can choose how you want ScanDisk to handle the results of its tests. Unless you instruct it otherwise, the default setting causes ScanDisk to display its results and record them in a log file called **scandisk.log**. It also replaces the previous results with those from the most current test. You can change the defaults by using these option buttons.

- Lost File Fragment—Here you have two options. If you choose Free, you are telling ScanDisk to simply free up any lost clusters. If you choose the Convert to Files option, Scan Disk organizes chains of lost clusters into new files and stores them in the root directory for that disk. You can then read them using Notepad. This gives you a choice to keep or delete information.

- Check Files for Invalid Filenames and/or Invalid Dates and Times—By default, ScanDisk makes sure that filenames are valid, which is an important function. It also verifies file dates and times, which is less crucial but may affect file sorting. To change either of these defaults, use the checkboxes in this section of the dialog box.

- Check Host Drive First—By default, ScanDisk checks the host drive first when it is testing compressed disks. This is a good strategy because errors in the host drive can affect other compressed data. It's a good idea to leave this default as-is, but you do have the option to change it.

- Cross-linked Files—Delete, Make Copies, and Ignore options.

If any of your software is copy protected, *do not* let ScanDisk repair bad sectors in hidden and system files. When ScanDisk sees these types of errors, it relocates the data to good sectors. This could fool the software into thinking that the program has been illegally copied, which could cause it to malfunction. To avoid this problem, go to the Surface Scan Options dialog box and choose the Do Not Repair Bad Sectors in Hidden and System Files check box.

Optimizing or defragmenting the hard disk

Suppose you are in the kitchen, about to bake a cake from scratch. It's a pretty complicated recipe, so you take a few moments to assemble all the ingredients before you start cooking. If you didn't do that, you'd waste time looking all over the place every time you needed a different element for your masterpiece. It would take you a lot longer to finish cooking. So the effort you take to organize everything before you start saves time and aggravation when you actually begin.

Defragmenting the hard disk, also called optimizing, is like preparing to bake a cake: It's the process by which the computer organizes data and groups it together by file. At this point, you might be wondering why a file's data isn't stored in the same place to begin with, since logically, it would seem that it should be. So let's talk about how Windows treats stored data.

When you begin to save files on a newly formatted disk, Windows is quite methodical and writes the data for each saved file in **contiguous** clusters right next to each other. It all starts out in perfect order, but as with most things, time and use take their toll. The first time you delete a file, the sequence begins to go awry. Windows starts using the available space, which is now broken into clusters of data with spaces between them, to store files—a little here and a little there as needed. This is okay for awhile, but left unchecked, Windows is like a chef who doesn't have all his ingredients on the kitchen counter—every time he needs another piece of the recipe, he has to stop and find it—and the disk becomes fragmented.

Eventually, as the disk becomes more and more fragmented, the drive's ability to read and access files slows down considerably. That's where **Disk Defragmenter** comes in. When you run Disk Defragmenter, it rearranges your data back into contiguous clusters. Running Disk Defragmenter regularly ensures that your ability to access and read files is as efficient as it can be.

Here's how you run Disk Defragmenter:

1. Open My Computer and right-click the disk you want to defragment.

2. Choose Properties.

3. Choose the Tools tab.

4. Click Defragment Now.

As Disk Defragmenter looks at the disk, it assesses whether things are in bad enough shape to need defragmenting. If the data seems relatively well organized, Disk Defragmenter tells you that you don't need to defragment immediately, but it allows you to go ahead with the process if you want to. When Disk Defragmenter starts the process of putting things back where they belong, you can click the Show Details button to see a display of the program's progress. If you want the process to move along faster, don't show details and don't use the disk while it's being defragmented.

Backing up data

I'm sure it hasn't escaped you that backing up files is a good idea. If you aren't acutely aware of it, sooner or later you will be. At some point, you'll be chugging along, blithely assuming that just because you saved a file, it'll always be there. Then fate will intervene in the form of a hard drive crash, or the one floppy disk that contains your entire life story will suddenly and stubbornly announce that it is unreadable, and that, as they say, will be that. After a brief mourning period, you'll recover and learn from bitter experience how important it is to make a backup copy. Happily, there are ways to avoid this unpleasant scenario.

To back up a file or drive means to make a copy of it somewhere else, so if the original goes bad, you can still refer to the copy. This means backing up files to a separate floppy disk, another disk drive such a ZIP, JAZ, or TRAVAN, or on **QIC** tapes (special quarter-inch cartridge tapes designed for data backup) or DAT tape.

Windows 95/98 includes a program for doing backups, called **Microsoft Backup**, that helps you perform these functions. It can show you how to back up files, and it can restore lost files by copying them from a backup set you have made. If you are copying large files onto floppies, you'll be happy to know that Microsoft Backup can split files between disks or tapes, so it's not a problem if your files are larger than the capacity of one disk. Backup simply asks you for another disk as needed.

There are two different types of backups:

- As the term implies, a **full backup** is a compete copy of all specified files. The term *full* doesn't necessarily mean you are copying all the files on the computer. It just means you are copying all the files in a set you have designated for backup, even ones that have not changed since you last made a backup copy.

- An **incremental backup** includes only copies of files that have changed since the last backup was made.

A combination of the two types of backups is recommended. You should generally perform a full backup weekly, and perform incremental backups daily.

It's a good idea to alternate between two separate backup media. For instance, if you are doing backups to a floppy disk, use two disks for that purpose and use them as follows: Make the first backup to one disk, and the next one to the second disk. Then revert to the first disk for the following backup. This way, if anything happens to the most recent backup, you still have the previous one, which although not completely current, is at least better than losing everything.

Let's run through a session with Microsoft Backup to see how it works:

1. From the Start menu choose Programs.

2. Choose Accessories, and then System Tools.

3. Choose Backup. You can now make the choice to copy to a tape, if that's your preferred medium, but first you need to format it. To locate this option, go to the Tools menu, where you see Format Tape. Large tapes may take more than an hour to format, so plan your work accordingly. Be aware that using the computer extensively while it is formatting a tape may cause the process to abort.

4. The next step in backing up files, no matter what medium you choose, is to go to the initial Backup screen and choose the files you want to copy. This is called creating a **file set**.

5. You will see what looks like an Explorer window: The left side contains drives and folders, and the right side displays folders and files. Use this window to select the folders and files to be copied.

6. Choose Settings, Options. The choices are self-explanatory for the most part; however, be aware that if you choose the advanced option Verifying Backup Data, Backup compares file copies with originals and reports any errors.

7. Click Next Step, and then tell the computer where you want the backup to be saved by clicking in the left side of the Backup window.

8. Click Start Backup and enter a name for the backup set.

Restoring data

Suppose the worst-case scenario occurs: Your hard drive crashes and all your files take an unscheduled trip to parts unknown. Fortunately, you had already followed the steps described earlier and made a full system backup. Now how do restore the system to its precrash state?

Here's what you do:

1. Start Backup and click the Restore tab in the Backup window.

2. Select the backup media from the left side. All the backup sets on that medium are then displayed on the right side.

3. Click the backup set you want.

4. Choose Settings, Options, and decide the location where you want the files restored. The other options are fairly obvious. Keep in mind that if you allow the backup to overwrite files, you will lose any changes made since the last backup. If the entire contents of the hard drive have been lost, this option doesn't apply, but if some original files exist, you can choose to overwrite older files only. This saves revisions made since the last backup.

5. When you're done choosing options, click OK.

6. Click Start Restore.

Comparing backup files to originals

If you chose to verify backup data when you made a backup, Microsoft Backup executed an in-depth comparison between the backup files and the originals. You could also have chosen not to have Backup perform that particular function, and saved quite a bit of time in the backup process. You always have the option to compare files yourself like. Here's how you do it:

1. Choose the Compare tab in the Backup window.

2. Choose the backup medium from the left side.

3. Choose the backup set for comparison in the right side.

4. Click Next Step.

5. Select the folders from the right and left sides that you want to verify.

6. Click Start Compare.

Scheduling disk maintenance

If you have **Microsoft Plus**, you can schedule regular automatic disk maintenance with the help of a Windows utility called System Agent. System Agent runs programs at preassigned times. You can schedule ScanDisk, Disk Defragmenter, and Microsoft Backup to run regularly, which keeps the system operating at its best and safeguards data. System Agent has these default settings:

- Hourly—It checks available disk space and warn you if it falls below a preset level.

- Daily—It checks hard drive integrity with ScanDisk, and defragments the drives.

- Monthly—It does a thorough ScanDisk test of the hard drives, including a full surface scan.

To access System Agent, follow these steps:

1. From the Start menu choose Programs.

2. Choose Accessories, System Tools.

3. Choose System Agent.

Concept Questions   *Semester 2, Unit 6, Lesson 28*

Demonstrate your knowledge of the concepts in this lesson by answering the following questions in the space provided.

1. Explain why it is important to optimize a system regularly.

2. Explain the difference between a full backup and an incremental backup

_____

_____

_____

_____

_____

_____

_____

_____

_____

_____

_____

_____

_____

_____

_____

_____

_____

_____

Vocabulary Exercise   *Semester 2, Unit 6, Lesson 28*

Name: _____

Date: _____   Class: _____

Define the following terms as completely as you can.

Disk Defragmenter

_____

_____

file set

_____

_____

full backup

_____

_____

incremental backup

_____

_____

Microsoft Backup

_____

_____

Microsoft Plus

_____

_____

optimize

_____

_____

ScanDisk

_____

_____

Focus Questions

Semester 2, Unit 6, Lesson 28

Name: _____

Date: _____   *Class:* _____

1. Describe the ways you can optimize file system performance.

_____

_____

_____

2. Describe the disk errors ScanDisk can repair or identify.

_____

_____

_____

3. Describe how you run ScanDisk.

_____

_____

_____

4. Describe how often you should run the standard mode of ScanDisk.

_____

_____

_____

5. Describe how often you should run a thorough test of ScanDisk.

_____

_____

_____

6. Describe the ScanDisk advanced options.

_____

_____

_____

7. Describe why you would not let ScanDisk repair bad sectors in hidden and system files.

_____

_____

_____

8. Describe how you run Microsoft Backup.

_____

_____

_____

9. Describe how you restore data.

_____

_____

_____

10. Describe how you compare backup files to the originals.

_____

_____

_____

SEMESTER 2, UNIT 6, LESSON 29
Troubleshooting the Windows 95/98 File System

You have learned how to optimize a system's performance by using ScanDisk, Disk Defragmenter, Microsoft Backup, and System Agent. All these programs are designed to help prevent problems from happening or catch them before they cause significant damage. In this lesson, you will discover how to troubleshoot other kinds of problems.

Windows 95/98 offers an additional set of options for troubleshooting the file system. Keep in mind that when you enable these particular options, you seriously degrade the system's performance, so it's a good idea to use them only when it is really necessary.

Here's how to access the file system troubleshooting options:

1. Open the Control Panel, and click the System option.

2. Access the Performance tab, and click the File System button.

3. Access the Troubleshooting tab.

You see a list of file system options (in this case they are referred to as *debugging switches*) to choose from, which are designed to help you sort out and fix problems in older programs that are not compatible with Windows 95/98.

File system options

The following is a list of options you see on the Troubleshooting tab, and what they mean:

- Disable New File Sharing and Locking Semantics—If you have an MS-DOS–based program that is having problems sharing under Windows 95/98, you can use this option to change the file sharing rules so sharing will happen more smoothly.

- Disable Long Name Preservation for Old Programs—If you have an important **legacy application** that is not compatible with long filenames, you can enable this option. It turns off the **tunneling** feature, which is designed to save long filenames even when the programs that open the files cannot read long filenames.

- Disable Protected-mode Hard Disk Interrupt Handling—If the hard drive is not handling **interrupts** correctly, it could be because Windows 95/98 is terminating them and bypassing the ROM protocol that handles them. If you enable this option, it allows the ROM routine to handle them. You should be aware that this slows down the system's performance considerably, so it should only be used temporarily.

- Disable Synchronous Buffer Commits—Allows uncommitted buffers to be written to the disk and returns control before verifying write completion.

- Disable All 32-Bit Protected-Mode Disk Drivers—If Windows 95/98 and the hard drive are experiencing compatibility programs, you can use this option to allow the system to stop using Windows protected-mode drivers and revert to using the older real-mode drivers. This causes the computer to run more slowly, but it helps with compatibility problems.

- Disable Write-Behind Caching for All Drives—If you are worried about frequent power outages, this option might be for you. Ordinarily, Windows saves data to the **cache** temporarily before sending it to the hard drive. This makes saving data go more quickly, but there is the slight risk of losing data if the power goes off before the system has saved it to disk. If this is a possibility, you can choose this option to send all saved data directly to the hard disk, which is very safe, but considerably slower.

Concept Questions   *Semester 2, Unit 6, Lesson 29*

Demonstrate your knowledge of the concepts in this lesson by answering the
following questions in the space provided.

1. Explain when troubleshooting should be done.

2. Explain what effect troubleshooting has on Windows 95/98.

_____

_____

_____

_____

_____

_____

_____

_____

_____

_____

_____

_____

_____

_____

_____

_____

_____

_____

Vocabulary Exercise   *Semester 2, Unit 6, Lesson 29*

Name: _____

Date: _____   *Class:* _____

Define the following terms as completely as you can.

cache

_____

_____

interrupt

_____

_____

legacy application

_____

_____

tunnel

_____

_____

Focus Questions

Semester 2, Unit 6, Lesson 29

Name: _____

Date: _____ *Class:* _____

1. Describe how you access the file system troubleshooting options.

_____

_____

_____

2. Describe how to disable new file sharing and locking.

_____

_____

_____

3. Describe how to disable long filename preservation for old programs.

_____

_____

_____

4. Describe disable protected-mode hard disk interrupt handling.

_____

_____

_____

5. Describe how to disable all 32-bit protected-mode disk drivers.

_____

_____

_____

6. Describe disable write-behind caching for all drives.

_____

_____

_____

SEMESTER 2, UNIT 6, LESSON 30
Unit 6 Exam

If you have access to the online Aries A+ curriculum, contact your instructor for the Assessment System URL. If you do not have access to the online curriculum, please continue to Unit 7.

SEMESTER 2, UNIT 7

- Lesson 31: Operating System Threads and Processes
- Lesson 32: Types of Applications and Their Operating Environments
- Lesson 33: Optimizing the Application Environment
- Lesson 34: Troubleshooting the Application Environment
- Lesson 35: Unit 7 Exam

SEMESTER 2, UNIT 7, LESSON 31
Operating System Threads and Processes

You have learned about troubleshooting the Windows 95/98 file system. Now you will learn about various applications and their environments. In this lesson you will learn about the roles of threads and processes, and about multitasking.

A **process** can be simply defined as data manipulation in a computer. In actual practice, a process ends up being much more complex than this because it involves an executable program, its own memory address space, system resources, and at least one thread. For example, the operating system considers an application running in the system to be a process.

The basic unit of operating system execution is the **thread**. Whenever a process is executed, the threads of a process work together to carry out the assigned code, check the system status, and gather the necessary resources. Switching from one thread to another within the same process is far less taxing than switching from one process to another, which would require changing the address context in addition to changing the thread context.

Unlike the active role of the thread, the process as a whole is passive. It's there to store the resources, including the threads, that make their home in the address space of the process. Whenever a thread is formed, one thread is created to execute initial coding, and a default is created for memory storage. Additional threads and resources may be added during the life of the process.

Multithreaded applications

Because a thread is the basic unit of application execution, logically a **multithreaded application** allows more than one thread to execute commands simultaneously. A number of Windows applications allow multiple threads for a process to enhance responsiveness, to aid background processing, and to simplify user interaction.

One example is a word processing application process. As the application begins to run, one thread responds to the keyboard, another performs spell-checking operations, and a third sends a document to the printer. In a sense multithreading allows a program to multitask within itself, appearing to separate itself into separate threads of execution.

Multitasking

Multitasking has been around for a while on mainframe computers. These large computers often have many terminals attached to them, and appear to give each terminal complete access to the machine. Mainframe computers allow users to submit programs to be carried out by the machine while the user works on something else.

Multitasking on a PC has taken a while to develop. In reality, a PC operating system allots time for each actively running process. As long as the pieces of time are small enough and the machine is not overloaded with programs, it gives the illusion that the programs are running simultaneously. No longer do PC users have to wait impatiently for one task to finish before going on to another program. Now office workers can perform several tasks at once on their PCs and don't have as many excuses to take water breaks—one of the few downsides of multitasking PCs.

The evolution of multitasking

Back in the dinosaur days of the PC, some computer users dreamed about multitasking while others wondered why anyone would want to do such a thing. Why would an individual ever want to perform multiple computer tasks simultaneously?

The early pioneering microprocessors certainly weren't engineered for multitasking. Early attempts made computers function so slowly and caused so many memory challenges that it seemed a fruitless endeavor. DOS came out in the early 1980s, but wasn't much of an improvement as far as multitasking was concerned, since it primarily loaded programs and accessed the file system.

However, you can't stop resourceful minds from creating new ways of operating a computer. Sure enough, popup applications such as **SideKick** came about, which could perform task switching, and other multitasking shells developed over DOS. Of course, the most widely used operating system to come out with multitasking capability was Windows.

In 1985 Microsoft's Windows 1.0 offered a rudimentary **nonpreemptive multitasking** function. Unlike the systems that use a clock to interrupt tasks in short intervals and start others, in this version a program would lie dormant in memory until it received a message, act on the message, and return control to Windows when finished. This much was possible with the 16-bit program, and at least it let you know when a program was busy by displaying a small icon—the infamous hourglass cursor.

Microsoft's first serious attempt to implement multitasking occurred in the mid-1980s, in collaboration with IBM with its OS/2 system and the **Presentation Manager (PM)**. OS/2 supported multitasking, but the PM could not function similarly because it could not deliver keyboard or mouse messages to another program while the previous program was working. With the development of multithreading, the dream of PC multitasking could become a reality.

Differences between preemptive and cooperative multitasking

If you're using a 16-bit Windows program such as Windows 3.x, you are going to be dealing with **cooperative multitasking**. Cooperative multitasking requires the various system processes to cooperate with one another. Windows expects system applications to periodically check a **queue** and proceed when no higher-priority tasks are waiting.

Applications seeking control send messages to the CPU, and these messages are placed in the queue. When an application with a lower priority checks the queue, it should relinquish control to the operating system, which passes control to the waiting application.

The main problem with cooperative multitasking is that different programs checked the queue at different times. It's like a basketball team that has several players who work well together and pass the ball between them, but one is a ball hog and wants to take most of the shots. The same thing happens in Windows 3.x: One application might check every other millisecond, and another might only check every 10 seconds or so. Although the CPU hog programs ran fast with cooperative multitasking, other programs ran slowly, and all programs ran in a stop-and-go fashion, like they were going over a washboard dirt road instead of a highway.

To exit the back roads of multitasking and get onto the highway, you leave the 16-bit Windows 3.x and move on to the 32-bit Windows 95, which uses preemptive multitasking. To *preempt* means to take control away from, so in this format, the operating system acts like a traffic cop. It times each application as it proceeds, and takes complete control if a higher-priority matter comes up. This same scheme has been in use for mainframe computers for years and was utilized in Windows NT before debuting in Windows 95.

Benefits of preemptive multitasking include the following:

- No queue checking, so less management code is needed.

- Fairer distribution of processing time for applications, allowing smoother operation.

- Performance enhancement using threads, allowing more work to get done.

This preemptive multitasking is only possible for 32-bit programs. It cannot perform magic and transform applications only coded for 16-bit systems into preemptive models. Instead, it reverts back to cooperative multitasking for those applications.

Concept Questions   *Semester 2, Unit 7, Lesson 31*

Demonstrate your knowledge of the concepts in this lesson by answering the following questions in the space provided.

1. Describe threads and processes, and their roles in Windows 95/98.

2. Describe preemptive multitasking and cooperative multitasking.

_____

_____

_____

_____

_____

_____

_____

_____

_____

_____

_____

_____

_____

_____

_____

_____

_____

_____

_____

_____

Vocabulary Exercise *Semester 2, Unit 7, Lesson 31*

Name: _____

Date: _____ Class: _____

Define the following terms as completely as you can.

cooperative multitasking

_____

_____

multitasking

_____

_____

multithreaded application

_____

_____

nonpreemptive multitasking

_____

_____

Presentation Manager (PM)

_____

_____

process

_____

_____

queue

_____

_____

SideKick

_____

_____

thread

_____

_____

Focus Questions

Semester 2, Unit 7, Lesson 31

Name: _____

Date: _____ *Class:* _____

1. Describe how multitasking has evolved, and describe nonpreemptive multitasking.

_____

_____

_____

2. Describe the differences between preemptive and cooperative multitasking.

_____

_____

_____

3. Describe the benefits of preemptive multitasking.

_____

_____

_____

4. Describe the similarities and differences of multithreading and multitasking.

_____

_____

_____

5. Describe the differences between process and thread functions.

_____

_____

_____

SEMESTER 2, UNIT 7, LESSON 32

Types of Applications and Their Operating Environments

Now that you are familiar with the multitasking functions of Windows 95/98, you will learn how various programs operate in the Windows 95/98 environments. Because Windows 95/98 is backward compatible, it will run Windows 3x programs and MS-DOS programs, along with other applications configured specifically for Windows 95/98.

MS-DOS–based programs

Many organizations have chosen Windows 95/98 as their operating system because it supports nearly all MS-DOS programs, so you need to know how to configure Windows 95/98 to support MS-DOS.

Unlike the Windows programs, which store their configurations in the Registry, MS-DOS programs store their configurations in a **program information file (PIF)**. PIFs are not created during installation, but are created whenever a listed MS-DOS program is run or viewed.

Unlike previous Windows programs, Windows 95 possesses no PIF Editor program. To configure a PIF application, right-click the executable file and click Properties. Any changes you make to the properties of an MS-DOS program are made in an existing PIF. If the file does not exist, a new PIF is created as soon as changes are made to the program's configuration; thus, a PIF is created automatically whenever you first run a DOS program. Any shortcut you make to an MS-DOS program automatically creates a PIF in whatever directory the shortcut was created. You can identify the PIF files easily in the MS-DOS directory. No matter how else they may disguise themselves, they always have a **.pif** extension.

When you begin an MS-DOS program, Windows 95 searches for a PIF in the directory that contains the file you are starting. If that fails, it searches the Windows PIF directory, and if there's no PIF there, it searches the path specified in the **autoexec.bat** file. If no PIF is found, Windows 95 searches the **apps.inf** file for a match.

Windows 95 is very persistent. If it doesn't find an entry for the application in the **apps.inf** file, it uses default settings for the application. If you have upgraded Windows 3.1 program to Windows 95, you will find a **_default.pif** file in the directory. Otherwise, you can create it by copying **dosprmpt.pif** to **_default.pif**.

One feature Windows 95 engineers worked very hard to create was to make sure Windows 95 users would not have to exit Windows to work out of DOS directly. Previous Windows versions allowed easy exit to DOS. Windows 95 makes it more difficult to leave the Windows program entirely, yet it allows the user to effectively work with DOS programs under its shell.

Windows 95/98 supports two different MS-DOS modes. One is a windowed environment that allows a DOS program to run alongside other programs in the system. The second mode allows exclusive control of the entire machine and its resources to a single MS-DOS task. Both of these modes operate under the watchful eye of the **virtual machine manager (VM manager)**.

The VM manager creates a virtual machine for each DOS program; thus, DOS programs may look and act like DOS programs, but really still function in the multitasking environment of Windows 95/98. You may recall from Lesson 31 that DOS programs were never designed to run in a multitasking environment, so the VM manager allows each DOS program to function as if it has exclusive use of the system since other machine functions have temporarily been shut down.

You might occasionally find programs that must run in MS-DOS mode, but this is rare. Most of the DOS programs do quite well running out of an MS-DOS window from the Windows 95 environment. Whenever you operate in MS-DOS mode, no other applications can be running and you must exit the program and restart Windows to proceed with any other programs.

Either way, the PIF is essential in making DOS programs work within Windows. There are ways to modify the PIF to suit your needs, and these are discussed fully later in the unit.

Characteristics of a 16-bit application in Windows 95

Although Windows 95/98 operates with 32 bits, it is backward compatible so it can run previous 16-bit Windows programs satisfactorily. To understand how Windows 95/98 accomplishes this, you need to return to the VM manager to create VMs to run the Windows 16-bit applications.

The biggest reason Windows 95/98 must handle 16-bit applications with the VM manager is due to the limitations of the Windows 16-bit multitasking function. As you have learned, 16-bit programs use cooperative multitasking. This type of multitasking relies on the applications to periodically check a message queue to see what other tasks are waiting within the system and either continue or relinquish control.

Due to its cooperative multitasking function, Windows 16-bit programs must share an address space, so the VM manager creates this environment for the Windows 16-bit programs to provide a single message queue for all its applications. Under this system, it is possible that all the Windows 16-bit programs are affected whenever one of them crashes.

When a Windows 16-bit application freezes up (and this is sure to happen sometime in your computer experience), press Ctrl + Alt + Del to let Windows 95 know that you want to end the application and recover a portion of the address space. Windows displays a list of the system applications, asking which one you want to end. Simply choose the offending application, and it is closed. This works in theory, but in practice, the whole machine might **hang** and require you to reboot, so don't panic when this happens.

Whole system crashes using Windows 16-bit applications should be less frequent under Windows 95 than under Windows 3x. Windows 16-bit applications actually run better on Windows 95 because Windows resources have been restructured so that they don't consume so much memory. Table 7-1 shows the improvements in running Windows 16-bit applications under Windows 95.

Table 7-1 *Improvements from Windows 3.1 to Windows 95 in running 16-bit applications*

System Resource	Windows 3.1 Limits	Windows 95 Limits
COM ports	4 ports	Unlimited
Device contexts	Approximately 175 contexts	16,000 contexts
Installed fonts	Approximately 250 fonts	1,000 fonts
Edit control data	64 KB	Unlimited
Listbox data	64 KB	Unlimited
Listbox items	8 KB	32 KB
Logical fonts	64 KB local heap	Approximately 750 fonts
LPT ports	4 ports	Unlimited
Menu handles	Approximately 299 handles	32 KB each
Physical objects	64 KB local heap	Unlimited
Regions	64 KB local heap	Unlimited
Timers	32 timers	Unlimited

Characteristics of a 32-bit application in Windows 95/98

Although Windows 95/98 will run 16-bit programs more effectively than they can run in previous Windows versions, Windows 95 was designed to take full advantage of 32-bit applications. The advantages of Windows 32-bit applications over Windows 16-bit applications are numerous and include the following:

- Preemptive multitasking

- Long filename support

- Separate message queues

- Memory protection

- The ability to use Windows 32-bit applications

The main advantage to using 32-bit applications is that they run faster and more smoothly using preemptive multitasking. Unlike Windows 16-bit applications, each 32-bit application can operate from a separate address and uses multithreading to speed up operations. Windows 32-bit applications that run under Windows NT should also run under Windows 95 as long as they aren't Windows NT–specific applications. When an application stops responding, press Ctrl + Alt + Del as you do with Windows 16-bit applications, and it should close without affecting other tasks.

To use Windows 95/98 most effectively, an application should be based on 32 bits, be OLE compliant to allow for data sharing, use Remote Procedure Call (RPC) if networked, and use Windows Sockets if networked. You will learn more about this in future lessons and will soon learn how to configure software to optimize MS-DOS programs, 16-bit programs, and 32-bit programs.

Concept Questions   *Semester 2, Unit 7, Lesson 32*

Demonstrate your knowledge of the concepts in this lesson by answering the
following questions in the space provided.

1. Explain the differences between MS-DOS, Windows 16-bit, and Windows 32-bit
programs.

2. Explain the characteristics of Windows 32-bit programs.

_____

_____

_____

_____

_____

_____

_____

_____

_____

_____

_____

_____

_____

_____

_____

_____

_____

_____

Vocabulary Exercise   *Semester 2, Unit 7, Lesson 32*

Name: _____

Date: _____   *Class:* _____

Define the following terms as completely as you can.

apps.inf

_____

_____

hung

_____

_____

PIF

_____

_____

VM manager

_____

_____

Focus Questions

Semester 2, Unit 7, Lesson 32

Name: _____

Date: _____   *Class:* _____

1. Describe the function of a PIF.

_____

_____

_____

2. Describe the two different modes that Windows 95/98 supports.

_____

_____

_____

3. Describe a virtual machine.

_____

_____

_____

4. Describe the characteristics of a 16-bit application in Windows 95.

_____

_____

_____

5. Describe what happens when a 16-bit application freezes.

_____

_____

_____

6. Describe the characteristics of a 32-bit application in Windows 95/98.

_____

_____

_____

7. Describe the characteristics an application should have to use Windows 95/98 most effectively.

_____

_____

_____

SEMESTER 2, UNIT 7, LESSON 33
Optimizing the Application Environment

You have learned how MS-DOS programs, 16-bit programs, and 32-bit programs work in a Windows 95 environment. In this lesson you will go a step further and learn how to modify the Windows environment for different types of applications so they will run most efficiently and effectively.

Optimizing an MS-DOS program in Windows 95

Although Windows 95 does a commendable job setting up a DOS environment, it also allows you to become the commanding general of your software and reconfigure the environment the way you want it.

First, you should decide whether you want to operate with a full screen display or a windowed display of DOS. Of course, in the full-screen mode you get the wide screen visual advantage, and some programs may run faster. You can always switch to a different program by pressing Alt + Tab for the Cool Switcher, by pressing Ctrl + Esc for the Start menu, or by switching back to a windowed display. Some possible benefits of working with a windowed display of DOS include easier switching between programs, the ability to view multiple programs simultaneously, the ability to copy from one program and paste in another, and the ability to access the program's property sheet.

Do you remember how DOS programs can only run in Windows with a PIF? You will now use the PIF to change the settings to match the needs of your programs. You can change the PIF in three ways:

- Right-click the icon for the executable file or the PIF itself, and choose Properties from the menu.

- While the DOS program is running, right-click the title bar for the program window, and choose Properties from the menu.

- If the program is not running, right-click its entry in a folder or Windows Explorer window, and choose Properties from the menu.

You will now see the Properties dialog box for the program. Any changes you make will be used the next time you boot up the program. Among the options you can modify are changing a program's title bar caption, adding command-line parameters, specifying a startup folder, specifying the name of a batch file, specifying a shortcut key, specifying the initial window state, keeping a program's final screen visible at close, changing a program's icon, preventing a program from knowing that it's running under Windows, and running a program in MS-DOS mode.

Font, Memory, Screen, and Miscellaneous tabs allow other MS-DOS reconfigurations. The Font tab lets you choose various display fonts to be used when running an MS-DOS program out of Windows 95, and the Memory tab lets you reallocate amounts of memory to various categories. The default settings should work for most programs, but you can change them if necessary. These memory categories are as follows:

- Conventional—Memory ranging from 0 KB to 640 KB

- Expanded (EMS)—Physical memory above 1024 KB that is mapped into 640 KB and 1024 KB range

- Extended (XMS)—Memory above 1024 KB

- DOS Protected-Mode—Extended memory managed by the DOS Protected Mode Interface (DPMI) specification

Besides selecting between full-screen and windowed display modes, you can change other variables from the Screen tab, such as specifying a 25-line, 43-line, or 50-line display; displaying or hiding the toolbar; remembering or forgetting window settings; turning off video ROM emulation; and turning off dynamic memory allocation.

The Miscellaneous tab allows you to disable the Windows screen saver, allow an MS-DOS–based program to run in the background, allow Windows to close an MS-DOS program, adjust the idle sensitivity, slow the paste function, disable Windows shortcut keys, and use mouse options such as Quick Edit.

Optimizing a 16-bit program in Windows 95/98

Because all 16-bit applications operate within the VM, you must change the conditions under which the VM was created if you want to change the environment. Also consider that this VM is created automatically whenever you start Windows 95/98, and any changes made to the system VM apply to all Windows programs. This means that there's not a whole lot you can do to change the Windows 95/98 environment to run Windows 16-bit applications besides adjusting parameters that can benefit your entire system. For example, you can adjust your video monitor performance or how you get to your hard disk, but you can't change the environment for a single Windows 16-bit program.

Try right-clicking on an icon of a Windows 16-bit application and select the Properties option. You see a dialog box that only allows you to change the file attributes—read only, hidden, and so on. One simple thing you can do to optimize a particular Windows 16-bit application is to specify a specific folder for the program to run from, and to create a shortcut to that folder. This might not seem like much, but it gives you speedier access to the program.

You will likely need to deal with a few Windows 16-bit programs during your computer career. Certain applications may not be updated yet, or the user may be attached to a particular application or not want to spend the money for an upgrade. A few tips for using Windows 16-bit programs are as follows:

- Create backup copies of **.ini** files on your Windows 95 software. A Windows 16-bit application is ignorant about the Registry and saves its information in the **.ini** files.

- Avoid editing **win.ini** and **system.ini** directly unless absolutely necessary. Because these files are updated automatically when you change the Registry, use the Control Panel to let Windows modify the **win.ini** and **system.ini** files.

- Avoid using 16-bit disk utilities designed for older versions of Windows. They could destroy the long filenames used by Windows 95/98.

Optimizing a 32-bit program in Windows 95/98

Windows 95/98 was specifically designed for 32-bit programs that allow applications to run in separate memory spaces and take full advantage of preemptive multitasking features. Applications designed specifically for Windows 95 display the Designed for Windows 95/98 logo. To qualify, applications must use Windows 32-bit APIs executable in the portable executable (PE) format; support Windows 95/98 GUI system metrics for sizing, system colors, right mouse button for context menus, use of Windows Setup guidelines; use long filenames; be aware of plug-and-play events; and run successfully on Windows NT 3.5 or later.

As far as optimizing a specific 32-bit program is concerned, there's not a whole lot you can do to change the environmental conditions because 32-bit programs also operate within the same VM system as the 16-bit programs. Thus, any changes you make to the system VM apply to these programs as well. Besides, the 32-bit protected-mode coding of Windows 95/98 already includes three new self-tuning features to optimize performance: dynamic sizing of the cache, automatic selection of virtual memory disk space, and automatic setup adjustments for optimal performance.

You can generally allow Windows 95/98 to configure optimal settings for applications and to manage virtual memory effectively, but you can do a few things to keep the hard disk in order:

- Leave ample space for the virtual memory.

- Clear the Recycle Bin to avoid using too much space.

- Run ScanDisk and Disk Defragmenter regularly.

- Check for any device conflicts.

- Look out for any MS-DOS programs that are using too much memory.

- Eliminate any real mode (MS-DOS) drivers.

You can also adjust your desktop, create shortcuts, and reorganize the file system. When problems occur, you need to do some troubleshooting, so you will learn some details on this in the next lesson.

Concept Questions

Semester 2, Unit 7, Lesson 33

Demonstrate your knowledge of the concepts in this lesson by answering the following questions in the space provided.

1. Explain the benefits of optimizing the Windows 95/98 application environment for MS-DOS and 16-bit and 32-bit programs.

2. Explain the similarities and differences in the way Windows 16-bit programs and Windows 32-bit programs operate.

_____

_____

_____

_____

_____

_____

_____

_____

_____

_____

_____

_____

_____

_____

_____

_____

_____

_____

Vocabulary Exercise   *Semester 2, Unit 7, Lesson 33*

Name: _____

Date: _____   *Class:* _____

Define the following terms as completely as you can.

system.ini

_____

_____

VM

_____

_____

win.ini

_____

_____

Focus Questions   *Semester 2, Unit 7, Lesson 33*

Name: _____

Date: _____   *Class:* _____

1. Describe how you can quickly switch to a different program.

_____

_____

_____

2. Describe how you can quickly access the Start menu.

_____

_____

_____

3. Describe some of the advantages of working with a windowed display.

_____

_____

_____

4. Describe how you can change the PIF.

_____

_____

_____

5. Describe some options you can change the next time a program boots.

_____

_____

_____

6. Describe some options you can modify in the Properties dialog box for a program.

_____

_____

_____

7. Describe the default memory range for conventional memory.

_____

_____

_____

8. Describe the default memory range for expanded memory.

_____

_____

_____

9. Describe the default memory range for extended memory.

_____

_____

_____

10. Describe the variables you can change from the Screen tab.

_____

_____

_____

11. Describe what you can change with the Miscellaneous tab.

_____

_____

_____

12. Describe how you optimize a 16-bit program in Windows 95/98.

_____

_____

_____

13. What are some tips for working with Windows 16-bit programs?

_____

_____

_____

14. Describe how you tell if an application has been designed specifically for Windows 95.

_____

_____

_____

15. Describe how you optimize a 32-bit program in Windows 95/95.

_____

_____

_____

16. Describe some self-tuning features that optimize performance.

_____

_____

_____

17. Describe what you can do to optimize performance.

_____

_____

_____

SEMESTER 2, UNIT 7, LESSON 34
Troubleshooting the Application Environment

You have learned how various software programs work in the Windows 95/98 environment ideally. Because we don't live in a Utopia (even in the virtual world), problems crop up occasionally. In this lesson you will learn how to troubleshoot and handle many of these problems.

Troubleshooting application problems

Just as the U.S. government developed a civil defense system after World War II, complete with shelters, emergency broadcast programs, education programs, and warning signals to protect its citizens from nuclear attack, Microsoft has developed a system to prevent damage to its Windows 95/98 program. However, it's much more effective than the old civil defense program and promises to be an ongoing process.

Whenever a program in the Windows 95/98 environment attempts to violate the system's integrity (for example, overwriting a protected memory address), Windows 95/98 immediately stops the offending program before it does any damage by immediately sending a **general protection fault (GPF)** message. This message tells which application caused the problem and lists the module name and reference number. These problems can be resolved by communicating this information to the application vendor.

Common GPFs include the following:

- Memory fault caused by invalid memory reference.

- Application tried to use a memory address currently being used by another application.

- Error code returned by a system API.

Exactly what happens at this point depends on what else is running in the program's virtual machine (VM). In each case, however, you should record the error message information and choose OK to terminate the offending application. If an MS-DOS program receives a GPF message that its program failed, you terminate the program along with its VM as soon as you rid the screen of the message. This occurs because DOS programs act as if they have exclusive use of the computer system, so they always run inside a dedicated VM. Thus, when you kill the DOS program, you kill the VM.

As you have learned, Windows 16-bit–based programs operate differently from DOS programs in that they share a single address space in the system VM. Because the system VM also contains Windows 32-bit–based programs along with core operating system programs, the system traps the offending program to prevent contamination to the other programs that share the same address. Most of the time this works, but on rare occasions a badly written Windows 16-bit program can cause other Windows 16-bit programs to fail as well.

Windows 32-bit–based programs do not require the same trapping technique that Windows 16-bit programs require because each Windows 32-bit program has its own separate address space within the system VM. Thus, a failing Windows 32-bit program does not affect other programs and is simply terminated as soon as you move on from the GPF message.

Hung applications

If you've worked with computers for any time at all and accessed various programs, at some time you've come across a program that seems to take forever to load. You've probably stared at that irritating hourglass for an extended time and watched the messages at the bottom of the screen; sometimes you've seen the message queue go blank and found the program unresponsive. The screen often appears different, the keyboard may lock up, and the mouse may not work. What you have here is a **hung** application.

Terminating a stalled program

The easiest way to get out of offending Windows 16-bit and Windows 32-bit programs is to press **Ctrl +Alt + Del** to call up the Close Program menu. From this menu select End Task to terminate the application.

You need to follow a different procedure to terminate a hung DOS application, but it's also a simple procedure:

1. Switch back to Windows 95/98.

2. Display the properties sheet for the application.

3. Select Terminate for the application.

Common application errors

The following are some common application errors:

- The Start menu directory is corrupted or deleted—The following procedure creates a new Start menu folder.

  1. Click the Start button and click Shut Down.

  2. Click Restart the Computer.

  If the same error message appears after this procedure, delete the Start menu directory in My Computer or Windows Explorer and repeat the procedure.

- You cannot create a shortcut—This happens when the Start menu is corrupted or deleted and when you attempt to drag an icon to the Start menu. To correct this, repair the Start menu by following the above directions.

- A disk utility cannot write to a disk—Windows 95/98 does not support direct disk writes from MS-DOS or Windows 3.1 utilities.

- You can't print from an application—You can bypass this by sending printer output to a file and then dragging that file to a printer.

- The taskbar is hidden—To display the taskbar, minimize the application or manually resize the application's window. To display the Start menu, press Ctrl + Esc.

- An application on a compressed drive lacks enough memory to run—You might need to run this in MS-DOS mode because applications requiring maximum memory should not be run on compressed drives.

- Running an MS-DOS–based application causes Windows 95 to stall during startup—To restore Windows 95/98, shut down and restart the computer and press F8 when the Starting Windows 95/98 screen appears. From the Startup menu select the option Previous Version of MS-DOS, and remove the following lines in **autoexec.bat** by typing **rem** in front of them:

  cd c:\windows\command
  call c:\windows\command\<trouble application file >
  c:\windows\win.com/wx

  Also remove a line in **config.sys** by typing **rem:rem dos=single**.

- Text on menus and other screen elements is truncated—This can occur when users customize screen fonts. To correct this problem, right-click the desktop and click Properties. Choose the Appearance tab and click Windows Standard in the Scheme list.

- Strange colors and patterns appear on the desktop—This is a very common situation when working with young people who can be very creative with backgrounds and wallpaper. To correct this problem, remove the application from the **startup** folder or remove its entry in the **win.ini** file, or obtain a version of the application designed for Windows 95/98.

- You need to rebuild the Programs menu—You can rebuild inadvertently deleted components from the Programs menu by renaming **setup.old** to **setup.ini**. Then click the Start menu, click Run, and type **grpconv-s** in the Open box.

- Setup program cannot create shortcuts—Because of the differences between preemptive and cooperative multitasking, some Windows 3.1 programs may not be allowed to create shortcuts. In this case you can manually add folders and shortcuts to the Programs menu.

- You need to save a Notepad or WordPad file using an unassociated filename extension—To save a file using a filename extension that is not in the Registry, use quotation marks around the filename. Notepad and Wordpad default extensions are **.txt** and **.doc**, respectively.

Removing applications

Sometimes troublesome applications should just be removed from the system. The way you do this depends on the type of program you are removing.

MS-DOS programs are usually fairly easy since a simple folder deletion does the trick. The only other thing to check is clearing any DOS shortcuts off the desktop

Windows 16-bit programs are the most difficult to remove because Windows software almost merges with the operating system. The Windows 16-bit software may affect the following areas:

- INI files for the application in the **windows** folder

- Windows INI files (**win.ini**, **system.ini**, and **progman.ini**)

- Dynamic link library (DLL) files that may be in the **windows** folder

- Program groups

To remove Windows 16-bit software, follow these steps:

1. Delete the folder(s) containing the application.

2. Remove any shortcuts.

3. Check the INI files in the **windows** folder to determine whether any were unique to the application. If so, copy the file to a floppy first so you can restore it, if needed. Then delete the file.

4. Examine the technical documentation to see if it lists DLL files, and remove them if they exist. Definitely make a copy first because DLL files can be shared by other applications.

Windows 98 troubleshooting tools

A number of special troubleshooting tools are installed during the setup of Windows 98 (see Table 7-2).

Table 7-2   *Windows 98 troubleshooting tools*

Program	Filename
Dr. Watson	**drwatson.exe**
Automatic Skip Drive Agent	**aso.exems_dos**
Report Tool	**dosrep.exe**
Microsoft System Recovery	**pcrestor.exe**
Microsoft Backup	**msbackup.exe**
Maintenance Wizard	**tuneup.exe**
Microsoft System Information	**msinfo32.exe**
Scheduling Tasks	**mstask.exe**
System Configuration Utility	**msconfig.exe**
Windows Report Tool	**winrep.exe**

In order to use the Windows 98 troubleshooting tools effectively, you must do the following:

1. Keep your system running.
2. Isolate the problem.
3. Do diagnostic work to locate the application problem.
4. Fix the application problem.
5. Seek further assistance.

Using Dr. Watson as the primary troubleshooting tool

You can use Dr. Watson as the default to create the log and to correct traps that the application might fall into. You can run a minimized Dr. Watson in the Taskbar.

To start Dr. Watson, follow these steps:

1. Click Start.

2. Select Run.

3. Click Dr. Watson.

4. Click OK.

To start a log file, follow these steps:

1. Double-click on the Dr. Watson taskbar or the Dr. Watson icon.

2. Gather information about the system, and respond to the Dr. Watson dialog box.

To view the advanced tabs in Dr. Watson, follow these steps:

1. Start Dr. Watson.

2. Click Option, View, and Advanced View.

3. Under Advanced View you can get information about the following system components: diagnostics, the system, tasks, startup, the kernel driver, users' drivers, and 16-bit modules.

Concept Questions   *Semester 2, Unit 7, Lesson 34*

Demonstrate your knowledge of the concepts in this lesson by answering the following questions in the space provided.

1. Explain how Windows 95 protects itself from having its system integrity threatened.

2. Explain how MS-DOS, Windows 16-bit, and Windows 32-bit function with VMs.

_____

_____

_____

_____

_____

_____

_____

_____

_____

_____

_____

_____

_____

_____

_____

_____

_____

_____

Vocabulary Exercise   *Semester 2, Unit 7, Lesson 34*

Name: _____

Date: _____   *Class:* _____

Define the following terms as completely as you can.

Ctrl + Alt + Del

_____

_____

GPF

_____

_____

hung

_____

_____

Focus Questions   *Semester 2, Unit 7, Lesson 34*

Name: _____

Date: _____   *Class:* _____

1. Describe some common GPFs.

_____

_____

_____

2. Describe how Windows 16-bit–based programs differ from DOS programs in operation with regard to VMs.

_____

_____

_____

3. Describe what happens to other programs if a Windows 32-bit–based program fails.

_____

_____

_____

4. Describe how you terminate a stalled program.

_____

_____

_____

5. Describe how you create a new Start menu folder.

_____

_____

_____

6. Describe what happens when you cannot create a shortcut.

_____

_____

_____

7. Describe what happens when a disk utility cannot write to a disk.

_____

_____

_____

8. Describe what you can do if you cannot print from an application.

_____

_____

_____

9. Describe what you can do if an application on a compressed drive lacks enough memory to run.

_____

_____

_____

10. Describe what you can do if an MS-DOS application causes Windows 95 to stall during startup.

_____

_____

_____

11. Describe what you do if the text on menus and other screen elements is truncated.

_____

_____

_____

12. Describe what you can do if strange colors and patterns appear on the desktop.

_____

_____

_____

13. Describe what happens when the Setup program cannot create a shortcut.

_____

_____

_____

14. Describe how you remove MS-DOS programs.

_____

_____

_____

15. Describe how you remove Windows 16-bit programs.

_____

_____

_____

16. Describe some troubleshooting tools installed during the setup of Windows 98.

_____

_____

_____

17. Describe how you start Dr. Watson.

_____

_____

_____

18. Describe how you start a log file in Dr. Watson.

_____

_____

_____

19. Describe what information is available in the Advanced tab in Dr. Watson.

_____

_____

_____

SEMESTER 2, UNIT 7, LESSON 35
Unit 7 Exam

If you have access to the online Aries A+ curriculum, contact your instructor for the Assessment System URL. If you do not have access to the online curriculum, please continue to Unit 8.

SEMESTER 2, UNIT 8

- Lesson 36: Windows 98
- Lesson 37: Setting Up Local Printers
- Lesson 38: The Windows 95 Printing System
- Lesson 39: Mobile PC/Laptop Computers and Printing with Windows 95/98
- Lesson 40: Unit 8 Exam

SEMESTER 2, UNIT 8, LESSON 36
Windows 98

Now that you're familiar with the Windows 95/98 operating system, we'll take a closer look at new features in Windows 98. With all the fuss the Department of Justice was making about this version of Windows, you might have expected something along the nature of a comet plunging toward Earth. Instead, we find a program that essentially upgrades the Windows 95 program and follows **Bill Gates**'s vision in his book *The Road Ahead* by continuing to develop a more user-friendly product.

Comparing Windows 98 and Windows 95

Originally Microsoft was only intending a minor upgrade to be released in the middle of 1997, but delays and legal challenges to release certain features of its upgrade forced the company to unleash its latest version a year later, in summer 1998.

At first glance Windows 98 looks very much like Windows 95, and it functions in much the same way. Switching from Windows 95 to Windows 98 doesn't require a user to make radical adjustments, as in the transition from Windows 3.x to Windows 95. People already familiar with Windows 95 and Windows Internet Explorer feel especially comfortable because the Windows 98 GUI essentially looks like a hybrid of these two interfaces.

Windows 98 provides some useful advancements over Windows 95 that we'll detail later in this lesson. Windows 98 has sharper icons, is less buggy, loads more quickly, and even cleans up after itself. However, the consensus so far on this program is that it operates pretty much like its predecessor.

Major new features of Windows 98

There are some notable improvements in Windows 98. The claim that Windows 98 emphasizes the Internet is like saying, "The summers are hot in Phoenix." The new interface design of Windows 98 is the most obvious change from older Windows systems. Designers worked very hard to customize its GUI and other features for Internet users. The following sections list the major modifications in Windows 98.

True Web integration

One of the biggest enhancements to Windows 98 is its Web integration, including the following:

- Integration of the Web browser and Windows Explorer—Windows 98 does this so effectively that users will think they have logged on to the Internet from the first screen, and they can navigate their files and folders just like Web pages. Windows 98 even has programs to help the user create and maintain Web pages. You can connect to local drives, network drives, Web sites, and FTP sites all in one window. Note that with Windows 98 you can still use Netscape as your Internet browser, although you have to search through the GUI for it. You can also download Netscape easily from the Internet itself—just ignore any "illegal" warnings you may see.

- Improved TCP/IP—You get a steadier, more reliable connection to the Internet and a slightly faster loading time.

- **Onscreen Channel Guide** that leads you to major Web sites—The guide can also deliver content to a user's computer on a regular schedule.

Sleeker help system

The old help popups have been replaced by a more intuitive, HTML-based interface. Also, the Back button functions exactly as it does in a browser. You can access Microsoft's online support database directly if you're connected to the Internet.

Web TV for Windows support

In *The Road Ahead* Bill Gates discusses having computers that are as user friendly as televisions. **Web TV** support should come as no surprise.

More reliable and efficient Setup process

Computer technicians will love this feature. With a few clicks and commands, the technician can take an extended break as Windows 98 goes about its business configuring the system. The install screen is also more informative.

Multiple monitor support

Windows 98 can support up to nine monitors simultaneously. Graphics people and Web designers may do cartwheels over this feature because they can now have an array of whole monitor displays of separate windows. Of course, Mac and UNIX users have already been using this multiple monitor feature for years.

More advanced multimedia device support

With the deluge of entertainment media, Microsoft is doing its part to support consumer demand by providing huge upgrades in this area. For some people, one of the following features will be sufficient reason to upgrade to Windows 98, although many of the features have already been included with the OSR2.x versions of Windows 95:

- USB—A speedy port for jacking in cameras, scanners, and joysticks that do not require a degree in rocket science to use.

- Improved power management features.

- The Intel MMX multimedia extension.

- **DVD**—The recent and coming trend in movie viewing.

Other new features of Windows 98

The following are some other features of Windows 98:

- Larger FAT files—Even though it's not immediately visible, one of Windows 98's best improvements occurs in the File Allocation Table (FAT). The new FAT conversion utility allows you to convert a FAT16 hard drive to FAT32. Plus, the upgraded FAT allows you pack more data into smaller spaces, so the user may realize a 20% to 30% increase in usable disk space. Another benefit for future upgraders is the fact that Windows NT 2000 also supports this utility.

- Maintenance Wizard—Users who have a hard time remembering when to change their oil and service their cars will enjoy this feature, which essentially tunes up the PC automatically.

- Other new and upgraded system maintenance utilities—Windows 98 offers many of these, including System Recovery, TweakUI, System Information, System Configuration Tool, Version Conflict Manager, System File Checker, Automatic Skip Driver Agent, Dr. Watson, Registry Checker, Backup tool, Scheduled Tasks, Disk Defragmenter, and Disk Cleanup.

- Automatic backup—Windows 98 makes multiple backups of the Registry and automatically restores it if a problem is detected.

- Faster bootup and shutdown—These are now accomplished in seconds.

Windows 95 features eliminated for Windows 98

A number of programs were added to Windows 98, very little was deleted. Because Microsoft is working hard to blur the distinctions between its software and the Internet, Microsoft Fax is no longer included, as Windows 98 is moving toward an integrated e-mail/fax system. However, Windows 98 leaves the Microsoft Fax function in place if you are upgrading from Windows 95.

Upgrading to Windows 98

Upgrading to Windows 98 from other Microsoft systems is easier than the day you went from a tricycle to a bicycle. You will be amazed how easy upgrading to Windows 98 is, especially if you have Windows 95 installed, but you can also upgrade easily from MS-DOS and Windows 3.x systems.

Before you start the upgrade, one standard operating procedure in all cases is to back up all your important data. Next, make sure your computer system can handle all the Windows 98 hardware requirements, which are significantly greater than requirements of previous operating systems and include the following:

- A minimum of at least a 100-MHz Pentium PC

- 20 MB to 295 MB disk space—100 MB more than is needed for Windows 95

- At least 16 MB RAM, and preferably 32 MB (note that RAM is inexpensive. so this is a good place to exceed the requirements)

- A CD-ROM or DVD-ROM drive

- A VGA or better monitor with a graphics card

By following the software manual instructions, you should have a fully functioning Windows 98 machine within 90 minutes (though you should allot 3 hours in case you encounter any challenges). And keep in mind that if you don't like what you get with Windows 98, it is easy to reinstall Windows 95.

When Windows 95 burst on the scene, it was a huge leap forward from the 16-bit Windows 3.x system, and it soon gained the largest share of the market. Windows 95 is likely to hold on to its market position since Windows 98 does not differ too much in its basic architecture. On the other hand, consumers wanting Windows will expect manufacturers to supply the latest version, so you can expect to encounter a number of both versions in the field, along with the newest Microsoft offering, Windows 2000.

Concept Questions   *Semester 2, Unit 8, Lesson 36*

Demonstrate your knowledge of the concepts in this lesson by answering the following questions in the space provided.

1. Explain the major improvements Microsoft has made in Windows 98.

2. Explain the similarities and differences of Windows 95 and Windows 98.

_____

_____

_____

_____

_____

_____

_____

_____

_____

_____

_____

_____

_____

_____

_____

_____

_____

_____

Vocabulary Exercise   *Semester 2, Unit 8, Lesson 36*

Name: _____

Date: _____   *Class:* _____

Define the following terms as completely as you can.

Bill Gates

_____

_____

DVD

_____

_____

Onscreen Channel Guide

_____

_____

Web TV

_____

_____

Focus Questions

Semester 2, Unit 8, Lesson 36

Name: _____

Date: _____   *Class:* _____

1. Describe how Windows 98 integrates with the Internet.

   _____

   _____

   _____

2. Describe how the help system changed with Windows 98.

   _____

   _____

   _____

3. Describe how the setup process changed with Windows 98.

   _____

   _____

   _____

4. Describe the features Windows 98 has with regard to multimedia support.

   _____

   _____

   _____

5. Describe some system maintenance utilities included with Windows 98.

   _____

   _____

   _____

6. Describe what Windows 95 features were eliminated for Windows 98.

_____

_____

_____

7. Describe what is necessary for upgrading to Windows 98.

_____

_____

_____

SEMESTER 2, UNIT 8, LESSON 37
Setting Up Local Printers

You have learned about the differences between Windows 95 and Windows 98. In this lesson you will learn how to install, configure, and manage local printers on Windows 95/98 systems.

Printer installation

A **local printer** is a printer that is connected directly to a computer, as opposed to being connected to a network. Windows 95/98 contains all kinds of standard options designed to make things easier than they were in previous Windows versions. The Print Manager feature common to earlier versions has been replaced by the **Printer folder**, which provides the same options in a more accessible format.

Although Windows printer installation features give you maximum flexibility, a printer might come with specific manufacturer-designed software created for that purpose. If that software exists, by all means use it because it will probably do the best job of installing its own printer drivers. When a printer is installed, all relevant information about it is stored in the Registry.

Windows 95/98 offers several ways to install a local printer:

- Plug-and-play printer detection

- The New Printer Wizard

- The Point and Print option

These methods are described in the following sections.

Plug-and-play printer detection

As the name implies, **plug-and-play** capability means that, essentially, you plug in your printer, and the computer does the rest. Windows 95/98 automatically installs the correct driver when the printer is installed or when the computer boots up. Windows accomplishes this by reading the printer's device ID and searching **INF files** (which are device information files) for a match. Printer manufacturers create and provide printer device–specific INF files that enable their products to communicate with the designated operating system. Windows searches for these files during the installation process.

If Windows finds the driver file it is searching for, it installs the needed printer support and resources. If Windows fails to find a suitable driver, you have the opportunity to search available files for a compatible driver. Windows suggests which of all the compatible drivers is the best one to use. When a compatible driver is found, you can ask Windows to install it, provide the driver from a CD or disk, or tell Windows not to install any drivers at this time.

The Add Printer Wizard

If a printer does not come with device-specific software or plug-and-play capability, the **Add Printer Wizard** can also take you through the process of installing printer support files. Here's how to use the Add Printer Wizard to install a local printer, assuming that you have an HP LaserJet 5MP printer you'd like to install:

1. Go to the Printers folder, and open the Add Printer icon. The Add Printer Wizard appears onscreen.

2. Choose Next, ensure that Local printer is selected, and then click Next again.

3. Look in the list of manufacturers for the company that made your printer, in this case, Hewlett Packard. You'll find it represented by the designation HP. Highlight your choice by clicking on it.

4. In the list of HP Printers, find HP LaserJet 5MP, highlight it, and click Next.

5. In the list of available ports, choose LPT1, and click Next.

6. Enter HP LaserJet 5MP (Local) in the Printer Name text box.

7. Choose Yes to make this printer the default for Windows 95/98, and then click Next.

8. Choose not to print a test page right now by clicking No, and then choose Finish.

At this point you see a dialog box informing you that the appropriate printer drivers and support files are being copied. (You might need to insert the Windows 95/98 CD.) An icon for the printer appears in the Printers folder when the process is complete.

The Point and Print option

Using the **Point and Print option**, you can install a local or network printer by supplying the proper printer information. There are several ways to access the Point and Print capability. You can use Network Neighborhood to open its print queue, or type the printer's pathname in the Run dialog box (which you reach through the Start menu). You can also activate Point and Print through the Add Printer Wizard. You choose a print server by pointing to it, and Windows 95 requests the appropriate printer information from the server.

You can retrieve various types of information during a Point and Print operation, depending on what you need:

• Printer driver files

• The server on which the needed driver files are stored

• For a local computer, printer model information (this tells the computer which driver to call up from the **windows** directory)

Configuring printer properties

When your printer is installed, you still have a few things to do before you use it. Now it's time to configure it. To configure a newly installed printer in Windows 95/98, open the My Computer window, and open the Printers folder. Open the Properties dialog box by right-clicking on the printer's icon. You see the General and Details tabs.

Although specific properties may vary depending on the printer you are using, you can adjust certain printer parameters—such as paper options, fonts, device options, and port—by clicking on the appropriate tabs.

Managing local printers

To manage a printer, go to the Printer folder and double-click the printer's icon. With this window open, you can perform a number of functions:

- Pause the printer

- Add documents to the local queue

- Pause a print job

- Cancel a print job

- Control a print job

The following sections describe these functions.

Pausing the printer

Double-click on the printer's icon to open its window. Open the pull-down Printer menu and click Pause Printing.

Adding documents to the local queue

With your printer window open, click Start, go to Find, and choose Files or Folders. A Find dialog box appears. Type in the name of the file(s) you want to add and click Find Now. If you aren't sure of the filename, but remember what kind of file it is, you can type, ***.doc**, for example, and Windows will search for Microsoft Word files and display them.

Select the files you want to print, and drag them to the top of the printer window. If you have chosen more than one file, a dialog box appears, allowing you to choose to print them all with one command. When you click Yes, the documents you have chosen to print show up in the printer window. If you want to change the order in which they appear, you can click and drag them to different positions in the window. Now you can close the Find dialog box.

Pausing a print job

In the printer window, right-click the queued job you want to pause, and then click Pause Printing.

Canceling a print job

In the printer window, right-click the queued job you want to cancel, and then click Cancel Printing.

Controlling a print job

Even after you've given the computer the Print command, you still have a short time in which to either pause or purge it. Short documents generally print in a few seconds, but with longer documents, you have time to open the printer window and pull down the Printer menu. You can choose Pause Printing or Purge Print Jobs. The Purge option cancels all pending print jobs.

Printer help

If, despite your best efforts, something goes awry while you are trying to print that important document, you can still get help. Go to the trusty Start menu, and choose Help. Double-click Troubleshooting, and choose the option If you have trouble printing. What follows is a short quiz to help you focus in on your particular printing problem.

Concept Questions   *Semester 2, Unit 8, Lesson 37*

Demonstrate your knowledge of the concepts in this lesson by answering the following questions in the space provided.

1. Explain how plug-and-play printer detection is accomplished.

2. Explain how you can access the Troubleshooting menu for advice about printing problems.

_____

_____

_____

_____

_____

_____

_____

_____

_____

_____

_____

_____

_____

_____

_____

_____

Vocabulary Exercise   *Semester 2, Unit 8, Lesson 37*

Name: _____

Date: _____   Class: _____

Define the following terms as completely as you can.

Add Printer Wizard

_____

_____

INF file

_____

_____

local printer

_____

_____

plug-and-play

_____

_____

Point and Print option

_____

_____

Printer folder

_____

_____

Focus Questions

Semester 2, Unit 8, Lesson 37

Name: _____

Date: _____ *Class:* _____

1. Describe where you configure a printer.

_____

_____

_____

2. Describe how you manage a local printer.

_____

_____

_____

3. Describe how you pause a printer.

_____

_____

_____

4. Describe how you change the order in which documents appear in the printer window.

_____

_____

_____

5. Describe how you pause a print job.

_____

_____

_____

6. Describe how you cancel a print job.

_____

_____

_____

7. Describe how you access help if you are having printing problems.

_____

_____

_____

SEMESTER 2, UNIT 8, LESSON 38
The Windows 95 Printing System

You have learned how to set up, configure, and manage a local printer. In this lesson you will learn about the print spooler and how to configure the Windows 95 printing system.

The print spooler

In Windows 95 printing is managed by special software called the **print spooler**. The word *spool* stands for *simultaneous peripheral operations online*, but it's unclear which actually came first, the name or the acronym. Think of a spool of thread: When the thread is wound on the spool, it is safely stored there until needed.

The print spooler performs amazing feats in order to deliver your documents, and has two primary responsibilities:

- It transmits files to the printer to be printed. The spooler does this by saving the data to a spool file that holds the print job as enhanced metafiles. It then converts the files so your printer is able to interpret it and produce a hard copy of what was onscreen.

- It manages a computerized three-ring circus of printers, drivers, print providers, monitors, ports, and data, hurtling through space on its way to be printed. It also juggles all the Registry information pertaining to printers.

Spool files

When you give a computer a print command, it sends the data to a spool file to be relayed to the printer. There are two kinds of spool files: **raw spool files** and **enhanced metafile format (EMF) spool files**

Raw spool files

In Windows 3.1 print commands generated raw spool files that were ready to be sent to the printer, but they sometimes took awhile to print. You couldn't use the computer while the spooler was sorting all this out, and it left users twiddling their thumbs, gazing forlornly at their monitors, attempting to meditate, or nervously pretending to read the paper. When Windows 95 came along, Microsoft tried to correct this, speeding things up with EMF.

EMF spool files

As users become more and more computer literate, an unnerving side effect often crops up in addition to their new-found knowledge: They begin to feel a gnawing sense of urgency about all computer-related activities. Somehow, their sense of time shifts, and the entire world seems to be moving in slow motion. Before long, they want everything to happen more quickly than is actually possible, and they get annoyed when it doesn't. How can you tell if this is happening to you? You'll know if you're one of the unfortunate multitudes if you can barely stand to wait while your e-mail downloads. Or if, waiting for a document to print, you give up in disgust and try to eat your entire lunch between the time you click OK and the moment the paper comes out of the printer. Don't be depressed if you're one of the millions affected by this technological epidemic because EMF spool files were made just for you.

When Windows 95 came out, EMF spooling was a big change. It became the method of choice for all print jobs except those sent to Postscript printers, which did not need it. The enhanced metafile format takes data that is sent to print, and stores all necessary information with the help of the **graphic device interface (GDI)**. The GDI, among other functions relating to graphics management, offers graphics support to printers and other devices. EMF spooling gives the computer a place to put the data, so it can get back to business. Thereafter, a process running in the background generates low-level printer language files.

When the printer data is spooled, the spooler can release the computer from its iron grip and let the user have it back, even if the requested files have not yet been printed. This means you are able to use the computer again more quickly than you could using the old raw spooler files, which sent data directly to the printer and made you wait longer. Downloading email might still drive you nuts, but you won't have to read the paper or grab a sandwich anymore while those print jobs are processing.

Spool file location

Spool files are stored in the ***win_root*\spool\printer** folder. Each print job has two files: a spool file (**.spl**) and a shadow file (**.shd**). Raw spool files contain the print job itself, whereas in EMF print jobs, an EMF file is generated for each page of the document and is stored in the **temp** folder. Shadow files allow you to resubmit the print job if it is interrupted. They contain the job owner's name, the name of the document, and the time it was submitted to print.

Configuring spooling options

When the computer takes spooled data and sends it to the printer, the process is called **despooling**. Windows 95 gives you three options:

- Start printing after the last page is spooled—This option reduces your total print time, but it takes longer before the computer returns control to you. This is because the spooler doesn't despool any part of the job until the entire print job has been spooled. (Remember that EMF printing creates a separate file for each page of the document before despooling begins.)

- Start printing after first page is spooled—This option requires more disk space and increases total print time, but it returns control of applications to you more quickly. EMF print jobs begins despooling as soon as the first page is spooled and new EMF pages are being generated.

- Print directly to the printer—This option can sometimes produce a printed document more quickly than other options, even though from the program's perspective it is the slowest way to print. Print jobs are sent directly to the printer, and no disk space is needed to spool files. The spooling and despooling processes are disabled, so there are no spool files at all.

Bidirectional printing support

A new printer can give you messages about the status of a print job, being out of paper, having a paper jam, and so on. You can get this information either through a little window on the printer itself or on the desktop.

This kind of printer is called a **bidirectional** printer because it receives information about print jobs so it can execute them, and it can also communicate with you, Windows 95, and any applications you are trying to print from. To make bidirectional printing work, you need a bidirectional printer, an IEEE 1284–compliant cable, and a properly configured bidirectional parallel port, either ECP or EPP. (You might need to reset your port to bidirectional if it is set in another mode by default.) Bidirectional printers can function efficiently, and applications have an easy time identifying them.

Configuring a Windows 95 printing system

Windows makes it easy to set a printer to fit your needs. To configure it, you need to access the printer's properties sheets, which you find by opening the Start menu and choosing Settings, Printers. When you right-click on the printer's icon, its properties sheet appears. Any changes you make here become default settings and affect all programs that use the printer from that point until you change them again.

The following sections describe the tabs in the properties sheet.

The General tab

The General tab is where you find basic printer options when you are sharing a printer with others on a network. You can choose from the following options:

- Comment—This option allows you to send a comment to another computer that is connected to a printer you are both sharing.

- Separator page—This option allows you to print a separator page between print jobs. The default is none, and the other choices are Simple and Full. Simple prints a blank separator page; Full prints a sheet containing information about the job.

- Print test page—This option tells the computer to print a test page. It tests whether the proper driver and ports are being used, lets you know what files the printer driver is using, and prints a logo.

The Details tab

The Details tab is divided into two parts and contains the following options:

- Print to the following port—This box shows the path to the current network printer. You can change the port by clicking the down arrow to display a menu of available ports. You can also add a port by clicking Add Port and typing the appropriate path. Use the Delete Port button to remove a port.

- Print using the following driver—You see your current driver displayed in this box. You can choose a new driver, if needed, by clicking the down arrow and choosing one from the menu. Or you can click the New Driver button.

- Capture printer port—Choose this option to open the Capture Printer Port dialog box, and enter the path to the network printer if it is not already displayed. Choose Reconnect at Logon, and OK. When you start up Windows again, you are automatically connected to the network printer.

- End capture—This option cancels the settings that connect you to the network printer. You have to recapture the printer if you want to use it again.

- Timeout settings—The Not Selected and Transmission Retry options specify how long Windows waits before it reports printer error messages. You should increase both of these settings if you have a slow printer.

- Spool settings—This button brings up the Spool Settings dialog box, which allows you to decide how a document will be sent to the printer. The Spool Data Format option allows you to choose between EMF and RAW spooling. EMF allows you to get back to work more quickly; if you have problems with EMF, choose RAW format, which may take longer to print but sends the file directly to the printer.

- Port settings—This option allows you to choose whether to spool print jobs that come from DOS applications and whether to test the port before printing.

The Sharing tab

When you are attached to a Windows 95 network, you can decide how much access you are willing to allow others to have to your printer. On the Sharing tab, if you specify Not Shared, other network members are not able to access your printer at all. If you specify Shared As, you can create a password, thereby restricting printer use to only those who have the password. In the Share Name text box, you need to type a name for your computer so the network recognizes it.

The Paper tab

On the Paper tab you can specify the following settings:

- Paper size—You can select letter, legal, executive, and A4, as well as various sizes of envelopes.

- Paper orientation—You can select portrait or landscape.

- Paper source—You can select tray or manual feed.

- Media choice—You can select paper or transparency (if your printer has this capability).

- Copies—You can select how many copies to print.

- Unprintable area—You can select the outside margin area (top, bottom, and sides) in which the printer cannot print.

- About—You can find printer and driver information.

- Restore details—Restores all paper options to their default settings.

The Graphics tab

Settings specified on the Graphics tab affect graphics only and have no effect on text. You can set the following parameters:

- Resolution—This setting is expressed in **dots per inch (dpi)**. Higher-resolution graphics are of higher quality, but take longer to print than lower-dpi images, which tend to be more grainy.

- Dithering—This option blends grays or colors to smooth out an image. The choices are None, Coarse, and Fine. If there are no shades of gray in the image you're printing, choose Line Art to create more definition. Choose Error Diffusion to sharpen photo edges.

- Intensity—The intensity range works like this: 0 is black, 200 is white, and the default is 100. Drag the lever to darken or lighten an image.

- Graphics Mode—You have a choice of raster or vector images. **Raster images** are comprised of dots (pixels), and **vector images** outline the graphic. Use vector for the sharpest images, and use raster as a backup if you have trouble printing as a vector image.

- Fonts Selecting—This option allows TrueType font options to be configured.

The Device tab

Whereas on the Graphics tab you can control the integrity of your images, the Device tab is where you can configure the printer to produce the highest-quality text possible. This tab gives you the following choices:

- Print Quality—A particular printer might have more specific documentation about its settings, but generally, you should use draft quality for proofs and normal for final documents.

- Printer Memory—This tells you how much RAM you have.

- Page Protection—This option allows the printer to use some extra memory space to accurately print pages that are more complex.

- Printer Memory Tracking—You can drag the lever between Conservative and Aggressive, to adjust the balance between the printer's available memory and its ability to print complex documents. If the tracking is too aggressive, the printer tries to print the document, but might fail to print because available memory has been exceeded. If tracking is too conservative, the driver might overestimate the amount of memory necessary to print a large printable page and not print it.

- Restore Defaults—This restores defaults to this tab and erases changes.

Concept Questions   *Semester 2, Unit 8, Lesson 38*

Demonstrate your knowledge of the concepts in this lesson by answering the following questions in the space provided.

1. Explain print spooling and how it functions.

2. Explain the difference between raw and EMF spool files.

_____

_____

_____

_____

_____

_____

_____

_____

_____

_____

_____

_____

_____

_____

_____

_____

_____

_____

_____

_____

Vocabulary Exercise   *Semester 2, Unit 8, Lesson 38*

Name: _____

Date: _____   *Class:* _____

Define the following terms as completely as you can.

bidirectional

_____

_____

despool

_____

_____

dpi

_____

_____

EMF spool file

_____

_____

GDI

_____

_____

print spooler

_____

_____

raster image

_____

_____

raw spool file

_____

_____

vector image

_____

_____

Focus Questions   *Semester 2, Unit 8, Lesson 38*

Name: _____

Date: _____   *Class:* _____

1. Describe where the spool file is located.

_____

_____

_____

2. Describe how you access the Printer Properties dialog box.

_____

_____

_____

3. Describe the options on the General tab.

_____

_____

_____

4. Describe the options on the Details tab.

_____

_____

_____

5. Describe the options on the Sharing tab.

_____

_____

_____

6. Describe the options on the Paper tab.

_____

_____

_____

7. Describe the options on the Graphics tab.

_____

_____

_____

8. Describe the options on the Device tab.

_____

_____

_____

_____

SEMESTER 2, UNIT 8, LESSON 39

Mobile PC/Laptop Computers and Printing with Windows 95/98

You have learned about print spooling and how to configure a Windows 95/98 printing system that is connected to a network. In this lesson you will learn about portable technology in the PC industry. Whereas the first portable computer was a 25-pound box from Compaq, and later models from IBM and Zenith were 12-pound laptops, current models of laptops weigh about 2.5 pounds and are made by a variety of manufacturers. You can also find very small portables called *palmtops*.

Portable computer components

The following are the basic components of a portable computer, some of which are discussed in detail in this lesson:

- Keyboard
- Point devices
- PCMCIA slot
- Display
- Hard drive light
- Battery indicator
- Headphone port
- Microphone port
- Speaker port
- Internal speaker
- Printer port
- External VGA port
- Modem port
- Serial port
- USB port
- P/S2 port

- Power input port

- Infrared port

Display panels

There are three types of display panels for portable computers, all of which are very sensitive and susceptible to damage:

- **Liquid crystal display (LCD)** panel—These have gas plasma and monochrome LCD panels that were introduced on the market in 1980. LCD displays used a lot of power and were phased out in the mid-1990s.

- **Passive-matrix LCD**—LCD images are formed by sending a signal through vertical and horizontal wires. When the two lines intersect, the crystal is charged but fades out gradually after the charge is withdrawn from the intersection. This causes ghost images onscreen. Some people prefer this over an active-matrix screen due to the added privacy it provides. Passive-matrix screens were introduced in the early 1990s but started to be phased out in the late 1990s.

- **Active-matrix LCD**—Taking the passive-matrix display technology and upgrading the line intersections at thin-film transistors (TFTs), active-matrix displays are the current screens on the market. The TFTs give an instantaneous and higher-quality signal to the crystal, forming clearer and sharper images without ghost images. On the downside, TFT displayers drain more power from the battery and cost a great deal more. Nearly all the laptops on the market today use TFTs.

Batteries

The main concern about batteries for portable computers today involves their longevity. There are three main types of laptop batteries currently on the market:

- **Nickel cadmium (NiCad)**—A rechargeable battery that is relatively inexpensive. One problem it has is the phenomenon of memory effect. NiCad batteries are the oldest technology in batteries.

- **Nickel metal hydride (NiMH)**—NiMH batteries eliminate the memory effect completely, but they are more expensive and have a shorter lifetime than NiCad batteries.

- **Lithium ion**—Newer technology found in most laptops, mobile phones, and other portable devices today. It provides a longer window for battery charging and contains no lithium metal. These batteries use the ions of lithium, pushing them back and forth on charging and discharging cycles.

AC adapters

Most portable power supplies are located outside the computer and are very durable.

Memory

Portable computer memory is based on the manufacturer's design, so most laptop users need to go to the original manufacturer to buy upgraded memory. A notable exception is a special memory house such as Kingston, which allows you to get various brand-name laptop memory, such as Toshiba, IBM, and Compaq. Until early 1988 most manufacturers were using EDO or SDRAM modules.

Docking stations and port replicators

As laptop computers become more powerful, convenient, and reliable, end users want more portability solutions, including the following:

- An external port for a printer

- A mouse and a monitor

- A port replicator

Users also want more flexibility in their portable computers, such as networking and various I/O devices such as docking stations.

Pointing devices

Portable computers have various pointing devices, including mouse devices, touchpads, trackballs, and glide points.

Deferred printing

Even if you and your laptop are far from home or the office, you can still spool print jobs, and the computer will hold them until you are able to connect to the printer again. This feature can also come in handy if the network printer is temporarily offline. With deferred printing, when you plug the laptop into the network, plug the mobile computer into its docking station, or regain access to the network printer, you are prompted to print the jobs you queued when you were off the network.

Configuring deferred printing

Deferred printing may be automatic for your portable computer if the necessary hardware profiles are in place. If this is not the case, you can configure it manually. Access the printer's menu by double-clicking its icon, and choose the Work Offline or Print Offline option. When the printer comes online, you will have to deselect this option again in order to print the queued documents. If there are no Work Offline or Print Offline options available, you can accomplish the same task by selecting Pause Print. Be sure not to turn off the spooling option, or you won't be able to make use of deferred printing. Don't be alarmed if you see the printer's name in gray instead of black in the Printers folder: It will look that way until you are connected to the printer again.

Printing from an MS-DOS–based program

When Windows 95 tries to print an MS-DOS–based document, it must use raw format and not EMF. MS-DOS applications don't make use of GDI to print, as EMF does. So even though these types of print jobs can use the Windows spooler to print, they take longer than it would for a Windows-based application to relinquish control.

In order for spooling to work, the printer must be installed to an LPT port, not a COM port. If you try to print via a COM port, Windows 95 is not able to tell the difference between an MS-DOS print job and other MS-DOS application–based information.

Concept Questions   *Semester 2, Unit 8, Lesson 39*

Demonstrate your knowledge of the concepts in this lesson by answering the following questions in the space provided.

1. Describe some of the components of laptops.

2. Explain deferred printing for mobile computers.

_____

_____

_____

_____

_____

_____

_____

_____

_____

_____

_____

_____

_____

_____

_____

_____

_____

_____

Vocabulary Exercise   *Semester 2, Unit 8, Lesson 39*

Name: _____

Date: _____   *Class:* _____

Define the following terms as completely as you can.

AC adapter

_____

_____

active-matrix LCD

_____

_____

LCD

_____

_____

lithium ion battery

_____

_____

NiCad battery

_____

_____

NiMH battery

_____

_____

passive-matrix LCD

_____

_____

Focus Questions   *Semester 2, Unit 8, Lesson 39*

Name: _____

Date: _____   *Class:* _____

1. Describe memory options for portable computers.

_____

_____

_____

2. Describe some pointing devices on portable computers.

_____

_____

_____

3. Describe some basic portable computer components.

_____

_____

_____

4. Describe how you configure deferred printing.

_____

_____

_____

5. Describe GDI, and explain its relation to the spooling process.

_____

_____

_____

6. When Windows 95 tries to print an MS-DOS–based document, what format must it use?

_____

_____

_____

SEMESTER 2, UNIT 8, LESSON 40
Unit 8 Exam

If you have access to the online Aries A+ curriculum, contact your instructor for the Assessment System URL. If you do not have access to the online curriculum, please continue to Unit 9.

SEMESTER 2, UNIT 9

- Lesson 41: Network Architecture and Configuration
- Lesson 42: Configuring a PC for Peer-to-Peer Networking
- Lesson 43: Using and Managing a PC on a Peer-to-Peer Network
- Lesson 44: Optimizing and Troubleshooting a Peer-to-Peer Network
- Lesson 45: Unit 9 Exam

SEMESTER 2, UNIT 9, LESSON 41
Network Architecture and Configuration

Now that you know how to configure software applications for individual machines, it is time to learn some basics about networking computers together. The next several lessons introduce basic concepts of networking; this lesson focuses on the network support architecture and configuring the network components.

Network architectures

Every network—whether it's a local-area network (LAN), a wide-area network (WAN), or a metropolitan-area network (MAN)—is likely to fall into one of the three most popular network architectures:

- **Ethernet** is the most popular network technology used today, and it is relatively fast and low in cost. Ethernet is flexible enough to handle a star or bus arrangement, and it can handle a variety of cable systems, including thick coaxial, thin coaxial, twisted pair, and optical fiber. When signals are transmitted over a long distance, an Ethernet network requires segmentation to avoid radical decreases in speed and reliability.

- A **Token Ring** network performs more reliably with its star formation but is more costly and complicated than an Ethernet network. It utilizes a **token-passing** mechanism for computer-to-computer communication.

- A **Fiber Distributed Data Interface (FDDI)** network claims the speed championship of the networking world as it primarily uses fiber-optic cable. An FDDI network can operate on unshielded twisted pair (UTP) cable, so it often serves as a **backbone** network. FDDI networks use a more sophisticated token-passing system than do Token Ring networks.

Windows 95/98 supported network architectures

It was a networking jungle in the 1970s, when manufacturers first began developing networking software and hardware, and essentially set their own proprietary standards. Fortunately, logic and sanity prevailed by the early 1980s, when these manufacturers began standardizing networking so that various networks could communicate with each other.

The two organizations primarily responsible for network standardization are the **International Organization for Standardization (ISO)** and the **Institute of Electrical and Electronic Engineers (IEEE)**. They determine the universally accepted standardized protocols for networking.

To identify and standardize the various levels of networking communication, the ISO developed a model called the **Open System Interconnect (OSI) model**, which defines a structured model for implementing network protocols. Table 9-1 shows the layers in the OSI model. Essentially, all communication occurring between layers is direct communication, and communication within the same layer is abstract and logical. You will continue to see references to the OSI model in later lessons and throughout your computer career, so you need to master this theoretical model.

Table 9-1   *The OSI model*

Layer	Definition/Function
Physical (Layer 7)	Not the physical network, but defines the way that data is transmitted over the physical media. The network architectures operate on this level, as does **Point-to-Point Protocol (PPP)**.
Data link (Layer 6)	Receives data from the network layer and presents it to the physical layer for transport; conversely, it packages data from the physical layer into frames to pass on to the network layer. The network architectures and PPP also operate at this level.
Network (Layer 5)	Translates addresses and finds the best route to send frames over an internetwork. It is the IP portion of **Transmission Control Protocol/Internet Protocol (TCP/IP)** and implements the IPX portion of **Internetwork Packet Exchange/Sequence Packet Exchange (IPX/SPX)**.
Transport (Layer 4)	Handles error detections and corrections. If the error is uncorrectable, retransmission is required. It is the TCP portion of the TCP/IP protocol and the SPX portion of the IPX/SPX protocol.
Session (Layer 3)	Establishes and maintains a session dialog between two nodes. Among protocols at this level are **Hypertext Transfer Protocol (HTTP)**, **File Transfer Protocol (FTP)**, **Simple Mail Transfer Protocol (SMTP)**, and **Network File System (NFS)**.
Presentation (Layer 2)	Receives requests for packets from the application layer and presents them to the session layer. Performs data reformatting, compressing, or encryption to enable communication between the application layer and session layer, or for data to be sent faster or more securely.
Application (Layer 1)	Responsible for interfacing with the application software using the network and for interfacing with actual computer programs. Common applications at this level include Web browsers, chat rooms, e-mail, FTP, Telnet, printer services, and network file services.

Installing and configuring a network adapter

Understanding theoretical networking protocols is one thing, but getting connected to a network takes some physical activity. A dialup connection can get a user online, but this type of connection pales compared to the type of connection possible through a network adapter (or network interface card [NIC]).

Before networking on a Windows 95/98 machine, you must configure the adapter card that will interface with the network. There's no real need to worry about networking support because Windows 95/98 supports the three main networking systems described earlier, as well as ARCnet and other wireless technologies. As long as this networking hardware is set up, you are ready to begin using the network as soon as you configure the adapter card.

Windows 95/98 can support up to four network adapters within a single computer. To install an adapter and to configure a computer properly, go to the Control Panel and use either the Add New Hardware option or the Configuration tab of the Network option. Supporting network cards is the **Network Device Interface Specification (NDIS)** version 3.1, an industry standard that provides independence between the network protocol(s) and the network adapter driver(s). Windows 95/98 also provides limited support for Open Datalink Interface (ODI), which is supported by Novell and Apple.

To install a Windows NT network adapter, check first to ensure that the adapter is compatible with Windows NT. The following are the basic steps you need to follow:

1. Set the dip switches or jumpers on the card to configure the IRQ and I/O base address used by the card. Install the card in the proper expansion slot.

2. After turning on the PC, go to the Control Panel and double-click Network.

3. Click the Adapters tab, and click Add.

4. Select the network adapter from the list or click Have Disk if the adapter is not listed.

5. Follow the directions in the dialog box, and when you are done, click OK, and you're set for networking.

Configuring and testing TCP/IP

Because most networks use TCP/IP, you need to get an IP address. You have two possible ways to get this address: automatically or by specifying an address assigned to the computer. Windows 95/98 can get a TCP/IP configuration automatically from **Dynamic Host Configuration Protocol (DHCP)** through a Windows NT Server computer or through any other computer running a DHCP Server service. With the automatic method, the Windows 95/98 machine gets an IP address, a subnet mask, and other optional parameters from a DHCP server during the system startup. Thus, correctly configured DHCP servers can issue unique IP addresses for every client request. There is also an assigned gateway to communicate beyond the LAN identified by the network ID. The gateway IP address is necessary for Internet use.

Another factor in using the Internet is using a **Windows Internet Name Service (WINS)** server to connect to other computers. You need to specify the WINS server that contains the Registry of your computer name and IP address; this server essentially acts as a network manager to enable remote subnets and computers to connect to the world. Without a WINS server the PC would have the massive job of keeping a database of computer name–to-address mappings to connect to other remote networks and computers.

Because TCP/IP is so complex, a number of testing and troubleshooting utilities exist to debug potential problems. The first step is to view your configuration. Go into MS-DOS and use the **winipcfg** program. This gives your TCP/IP configuration values—IP address, subnet mask, and default gateway. Then, send a **ping** command with an IP address, a host name, and a computer name to verify the connection. When a **ping** to a remote host fails, try a **ping** to the default gateway. If this also fails, the computer has in incorrectly configured IP address or subnet mask, or the default gateway is not available.

Network protocols for networking configurations

Deciding which network protocol to use depends a great on what kind of network you want. Windows 95/98 and Windows NT support multiple protocols, including the following:

- TCP/IP—For large networks that use routers, for networks connected to the Internet, and for veteran network administrators; it is the most sophisticated of the protocols.

- IPX—For large routed networks and networks connected to Novell NetWare file servers.

- **NetBEUI**—A revised version of NetBIOS for small nonrouted networks or workgroups.

- DLC—IBM's Token Ring protocol, which is not for networking with other PCs, but can be used to communicate with IBM mainframes or Hewlett-Packard JetDirect printers.

Network components

Before getting into details about configuring network components properly, you should become familiar with the various components, which are the following:

- Servers—The main computer that provides resources to other computers on the network. There are basically two types of servers: dedicated servers, which are assigned to perform applications and service for the network and nothing else, and non-dedicated servers, which are assigned to provide one or more network services yet allows user access.

- Clients—The network user, or the software program that communicates with the network operating system. An individual computer that uses this client software is a client computer or workstation.

- Network resources—These are items that can be used and shared on a network. Examples include printers and other peripherals, files, applications, and storage space.

Concept Questions   *Semester 2, Unit 9, Lesson 41*

Demonstrate your knowledge of the concepts in this lesson by answering the following questions in the space provided.

1. Explain the similarities and differences of the three basic network architectures.

2. Explain the networking roles of the ISO and IEEE.

_____

_____

_____

_____

_____

_____

_____

_____

_____

_____

_____

_____

_____

_____

_____

_____

_____

_____

Vocabulary Exercise   *Semester 2, Unit 9, Lesson 41*

Name: _____

Date: _____   *Class:* _____

Define the following terms as completely as you can.

backbone

_____

_____

DHCP

_____

_____

Ethernet

_____

_____

FDDI

_____

_____

FTP

_____

_____

HTTP

_____

_____

IEEE

_____

_____

IPX/SPX

_____

_____

ISO

_____

_____

NDIS

_____

_____

NFS

_____

_____

OSI model

_____

_____

PPP

_____

_____

SMTP

_____

_____

TCP/IP

_____

_____

token passing

_____

_____

Token Ring

_____

_____

WINS

_____

_____

Focus Questions   *Semester 2, Unit 9, Lesson 41*

Name: _____

Date: _____   *Class:* _____

1. Describe how Windows 95/98 supports different network architectures.

_____

_____

_____

2. Describe the OSI model and why it's important.

_____

_____

_____

3. Describe the layers of the OSI model.

_____

_____

_____

_____

_____

_____

_____

4. Describe how to install and configure a network adapter.

_____

_____

_____

5. Describe how to configure and test TCP/IP.

_____

_____

_____

6. Describe a gateway.

_____

_____

_____

7. Describe WINS.

_____

_____

_____

8. Describe how you choose the appropriate network protocol for a networking configuration.

_____

_____

_____

SEMESTER 2, UNIT 9, LESSON 42
Configuring a PC for Peer-to-Peer Networking

This lesson covers configuration and management of the file system, printer sharing, and user access utilities in peer-to-peer networks.

Advantages and disadvantages of peer-to-peer networks

IBM created the first **peer-to-peer network** software, PCLAN, which made it possible to share utility resources. No more copying files to disks and running them over to the one machine that could make hard copies—the infamous "sneaker nets." Additionally, file sharing could be accomplished by using identical PCs that function the same, without a single server—hence the term *peer-to-peer network*.

Because no single server takes charge of a peer-to-peer network, it is organized into workgroups with little security control and no central login process. Thus, you can use any of the network resources that are not restricted. So why do so many organizations use this type of network? There are some definite advantages:

- Cost-effectiveness—Less expense required for server hardware and software than with other types of networks.

- Ease of setup—No network administrator required.

- More resourceful—Multiple users can share resources, and it is more convenient than using floppy disks for transporting files.

- Independence—Machines do not rely on a server to provide resources.

There are also a few disadvantages of peer-to-peer networks:

- Decreased performance—The additional load of resource sharing degrades each computer's performance, which decreases the cost-effectiveness.

- File confusion—Lack of central control can make it difficult to find data.

- Lack of central control—Each user must administer his or her own computer, which makes large networks unwieldy.

- Security challenges—Security is often lacking, which can be dangerous.

- Ineffective with **application server**-based networks—Application servers are unable to adequately allocate the workload.

Despite the drawbacks, peer-to-peer networks are very popular, primarily due to their lower cost and ease of installation and configuration. Windows for Workgroups and LANtastic have made installation so easy that even a computer novice can do it. Another major plus for this type of network is that upgrading to a more complex network is fairly simple.

Configuring a computer to participate in a peer-to-peer network

How much do you want to spend on a network? Just like almost everything in life, you can invest varying amounts of money on hardware components for a peer-to-peer network. The challenge is finding the correct balance between desired features and costs.

Before selecting a NIC, you should consider your needs. What type of bandwidth will you require? Would 10 MBps suffice, or would 100 MBps be more suitable? This will affect your cabling needs.

Because the majority of network nodes are Ethernet varieties, selecting Ethernet would simplify matters. The two main cables to consider are 10Base2 and 10BaseT. Other alternatives would cause complications or cost far more than is required. As soon as you've selected the cabling, you can choose network cards with the proper connectors. You also need to be sure that the bus architecture of your machine—**industry standard architecture (ISA)**, **extended industry standard architecture (EISA)**, or **microchannel architecture (MCA)**—matches the NIC. After matching the cabling and network card properly, you are ready to configure the software.

Setting up a peer-to-peer network requires identifying the machine and setting its configurations. To begin the configuration process, go to the Control Panel, and double-click the Network icon. Then fill out the information on the three tabs:

- Identification—Add a computer name, a workgroup name, and a computer description.

- Configuration—Fill out four necessary aspects:

  Adapter—Your network card, which should already be installed.

  Protocol—Your method(s) of transferring data across the network. (Note that you can include more than one protocol.)

  Client—Software that facilitates access to other network machines and devices.

  Service—Includes special capabilities such as password verification, back up, and file sharing.

- **Access Control**—Enables others to use your machine in two aspects:

  File and Printer access—Simple clicks on the menu bar allow you to share files and a printer with the network.

  Type of access—**Share-level access** requires a password for each file or peripheral to be shared; to allow wide-open access, the password can be set as **nothing**. **User-level access** utilizes a master list of users who have unobstructed access to the network files and peripherals.

If the machine you are configuring will need to utilize a remote printer, first make sure that only the host computer has been set to share the printer. Then proceed to add the printer through the Add Printer icon in the Control Panel.

Managing the file system, printer sharing, and user access

When a machine is configured, you can easily reconfigure it by going into the Control Panel and changing the options. You can actually share an entire drive with the network, but this is not recommended; it is much safer to create a shared folder under the root directory and transfer files into it.

If you find that you need to access a remote machine's drive or folder often, you can reduce the required effort by either mapping the drive or by creating a shortcut. You can refer to previous lessons about managing your individual file program to straighten your own computer, but managing networked files takes a team effort. Communication is still the key element here, whether by email or by actual speaking and listening.

Mapping a network drive

This makes the remote machine's drive behave as if it is attached to your machine by assigning it a letter on your system, such as drive **f:**. Although it's not necessary for Windows 95/98 users, mapping can help keep the desktop better organized. To map a drive, click on the Map Network Drive option under the File menu and follow the directions.

Creating shortcuts

This is a really fast way to access a remote resource, and there are two methods to accomplish this:

- Drag a folder or drive from the remote machine's window to your desktop. Ignore the illegal warning dialog box and click Yes anyway.

- Highlight the resource name in the remote machine's window and choose File, Shortcut. Again you'll get a warning box that you can ignore; click Yes to proceed to the shortcut window. Accessing shared files is a simple matter of going into the Network Neighborhood and clicking the icon. The computer icons identify the names of the machines on the network. If you double-click on a computer icon, you see a window that presents all the shared drives and folders from that machine. Continue double-clicking the folders until you reach the desired file. Close the file just as you do one on your own machine, and the file is returned.

Concept Questions   *Semester 2, Unit 9, Lesson 42*

Demonstrate your knowledge of the concepts in this lesson by answering the following questions in the space provided.

1. Explain the characteristics of a peer-to-peer network.

2. Explain the similarities and differences of peer-to-peer networks and other networks.

_____

_____

_____

_____

_____

_____

_____

_____

_____

_____

_____

_____

_____

_____

_____

_____

_____

_____

Vocabulary Exercise   *Semester 2, Unit 9, Lesson 42*

Name: _____

Date: _____   Class: _____

Define the following terms as completely as you can.

access control

_____

_____

application server

_____

_____

EISA

_____

_____

ISA

_____

_____

MCA

_____

_____

peer-to-peer network

_____

_____

share-level access

_____

_____

user-level access

_____

_____

Focus Questions   *Semester 2, Unit 9, Lesson 42*

Name: _____

Date: _____   *Class:* _____

1. What do you need to consider before selecting a NIC?

_____

_____

_____

_____

2. Describe how you configure a computer to participate in a peer-to-peer network.

_____

_____

_____

_____

3. Describe how you manage the file system, printer sharing, and user accounts in a peer-to-peer network.

_____

_____

_____

_____

4. Describe how you map a network drive.

_____

_____

_____

_____

5. Describe how you can make network sharing of printers and files efficient.

_____

_____

_____

_____

SEMESTER 2, UNIT 9, LESSON 43
Using and Managing a PC on a Peer-to-Peer Network

You have learned how to configure a peer-to-peer network and a bit about file and printer management. This lesson delves more deeply into using shared files, printers, and resources.

Connecting to and utilizing another file system and printer

To utilize the file systems and printers of remote computers, you need to be thoroughly acquainted with the **Network Neighborhood**. The easiest way to stroll around the Network Neighborhood to see what resources are available is to double-click the Network Neighborhood icon and open its folder. You'll see all the other computers that make up the network. Simply double-click the various computers' icons to access their shared contents—folders, files, and printers.

By continuing to double-click your way through the folders, you will eventually be able to open the desired file, as long as you have been granted permission. Remember that a user can protect resources with either share-level access or user-level access. Depending on how the user has protected an item, you might be limited to only reading and copying a file; otherwise, you might have full access that allows you to view, modify, or delete the item.

Accessing printers works similarly. You can use a printer that is connected to your PC, and you can also use printers that are shared through the network, provided that the printer user has allowed appropriate access. Choose the remote printer you want to connect to from the dialog box, type the proper password if required, and you're ready to print from the remote printer.

Configuring the browse master

Even though all computers are by definition equal in a peer-to-peer network, one computer is designated as the **browse master**. The duties of the browse master include the following:

- Maintaining the browse list, which lists all the servers in the domain or workgroup and the domains on the network.

- Adds computers that send server announcements to the browse list.

- Returns lists of backup browsers to computers running Windows NT Server, Windows NT Workstation, Windows 95, Windows 98, and Windows for Workgroups.

- Broadcasts a Request Announcement datagram to force all servers to register when necessary.

- Forces an election whenever another computer claims to be the browse master.

By default the browse master is the first computer in a workgroup to enable file and printer sharing; however, you can manually configure a Windows 95/98 computer to always be the browse master. That could be very useful when a network computer is not used as a workstation very often, so it could function very much like a dedicated server.

Any network computer in a peer-to-peer system can act as the browse master, as long as it is configured correctly. To get to the browse master you must go to the Control Panel, select the Network icon, click the Configuration tab, and double-click the File and Printer Sharing icon. From here you have three possible settings:

- Enabled—This setting indicates that this computer is designated as the browse master. If in conflict with another machine, an election is held to decide which computer gains the browse master designation.

- Disabled—This setting indicates that this computer should never become the browse master. This setting would be appropriate for computers that have little free memory or operate slowly.

- Automatic—This is the default setting, and it indicates that this computer could become the browse master if the software program determines that this is necessary. If the designated browse master is shut down, and no enabled machine is available, an election is held to select the new temporary browse master from the eligible automatic computers.

A browse master election might occur when another machine claims to be the browse master, and an election always takes place under the following circumstances:

- A computer can't find its browse master upon system startup.

- A computer decides that a browse master Has disappeared.

- A computer running Windows NT Server (or any preferred browse master) joins the network.

When a server decides that a browse master election must take place, it sends an election datagram to the other browsers to compare eligibility. The highest-ranking browser wins the election. In the event of a tie, a set tiebreaker protocol ensures that only one browse master will rule the network at a time.

Configuring the computer for remote administration

To truly have access to all folders, files, and peripherals in a network requires administration status, and you can only gain this by having the remote administration enabled. Although a single PC is usually designated as the network's administrative machine, to be used for changing network configurations, sometimes there might be a reason to assign administration privileges to remote computers.

To enable remote administration, you once again need to return to the Control Panel, and then do the following:

1. Double-click Passwords.

2. From the Password Properties dialog box click the Remote Administration tab.

3. Select Enable Remote Administration for this server.

4. Type **admin** in the Password text box, and type **admin** in the Confirm Password box.

5. Click OK and close the Control Panel.

As soon as the administration is enabled, the remote administration creates two hidden shared folders:

- **admin$**—Provides access to the file system on the remote computer.

- **ipc$**—Provides an interprocess communication (IPC) channel between the two computers.

Managing and monitoring shared resources

After installing a functioning network, don't expect everything to run perfectly every day. Challenges are inevitable: Traffic will clog the system to a slow crawl at times, nonstandard software may corrupt network packets so the network can't handle the data, utilities that work fine on individual units might end up tying up other networked computers, and so on. You need to set up a management system to handle these challenges. Windows 95 provides three major utilities to help optimize network usage, standardize software, and monitor network conditions:

- **Netwatcher**—This tool shows the sharing status on clients and servers, lets users create shared resources, and lets users disable access to a shared resource.

- **System Monitor**—This tool allows you to observe a number of system behaviors that can point to potential and actual problems. Pull-down menus allow you to access various functions. By selecting Edit, Add, you can check on a variety of useful network parameters, including protocols, client and server machine behavior, and memory usage. System Monitor continues to show graphs for whatever item you add.

- **Network Backups**—How many times have you heard people tell you to back up your work? This is even more important when it comes to the network. So be sure to install the Network Backups software. A variety of software programs are available, and each has different properties that you can configure by highlighting the backup name and using the Properties button in the dialog box. From there you select the machine, device, protocol, and other necessary information to set up the backup.

Because none of these programs is set up automatically, you must install each of them from Add/Remove Programs in the Control Panel.

Concept Questions   *Semester 2, Unit 9, Lesson 43*

Demonstrate your knowledge of the concepts in this lesson by answering the following questions in the space provided.

1. Explain how to manage and monitor remote shared resources on Windows 95 computers in the peer-to-peer network.

2. Explain the roles of Netwatcher, System Monitor, and Network Backups.

_____

_____

_____

_____

_____

_____

_____

_____

_____

_____

_____

_____

_____

_____

_____

_____

_____

_____

Vocabulary Exercise   *Semester 2, Unit 9, Lesson 43*

Name: _____

Date: _____   Class: _____

Define the following terms as completely as you can.

browse master

_____

_____

Netwatcher

_____

_____

Network Backups

_____

_____

Network Neighborhood

_____

_____

System Monitor

_____

_____

Focus Questions   *Semester 2, Unit 9, Lesson 43*

Name: _____

Date: _____   *Class:* _____

1. Describe how you connect to and utilize another file system and printer.

_____

_____

_____

2. Describe how you configure the browse master.

_____

_____

_____

3. Describe which computer in a workgroup is the browse master.

_____

_____

_____

4. Describe possible browse master settings.

_____

_____

_____

5. Describe when a browse master election occur.

_____

_____

_____

6. Describe how you configure a computer for remote administration.

_____

_____

_____

7. Describe the two hidden shares created when remote administration is enabled.

_____

_____

_____

8. Describe how you manage and monitor shared resources.

_____

_____

_____

SEMESTER 2, UNIT 9, LESSON 44

Optimizing and Troubleshooting a Peer-to-Peer Network

It is important to get networks to function properly and solve problems when they don't work. In this lesson you will learn how to optimize a Windows 95/98 system for a network and troubleshoot some common networking problems.

Optimizing a Windows 95/98 operating system for networking performance

Generally, Windows 95/98 automatically adjusts to the user's network requirements, so a manual tune-up is rarely necessary. However, you can increase file sharing performance by changing some components:

- Use a 32-bit, protected-mode network client.

- Use the Windows 95/98 provided NDIS 3.1 adapter drivers.

- Install a 100-MBps network.

The following are some other methods of tweaking the system to get better file and printer sharing performance:

- Let Windows 95/98 determine the size of the swap file.

- Set the typical role of the computer to Network Server under the System icon in the Control Panel.

- Install high-performance network adapters.

- Disable rarely used network adapters.

- Ensure that the computer has enough memory (at least 64 MB).

- Install faster hard disks and/or disk controllers.

- Set the read-only attribute on shared files when possible on computers running File and Printer Sharing.

- Delete unnecessary protocols.

Because Windows 95/98 supports multiple **network adapters**, services, and protocols simultaneously, every network needs a way to interface with other network components—between adapters and protocols. This is called **binding**.

All possible bindings are enabled by default, but you might find that certain bindings are unnecessary on particular clients. Therefore, you can disable these settings to improve network performance slightly.

Common troubleshooting networking problems

Despite the fact that Windows 95/98 addresses a number of potential network problems with its configurations, you will still encounter some problems. Most network problems relate to one of three areas:

- The network card

- The **protocol stack**

- **Client software**

Troubleshooting a network card problem

A number of problems can arise when the network card isn't functioning correctly. Before going on to determine whether a network card cannot be found or whether it doesn't function properly, try the following:

- Make sure the NIC is properly fitted in the PC expansion slots.

- Check the connector. Ethernet networks especially have problems with connectors and cause the NIC to report problems when not connected properly.

- Make sure the NIC is compatible with the network system.

- Check other NICs in the same machine and remove them to ensure that conflicts do not exist between the cards.

- Record the configuration information.

- Make sure that the NIC's vendor and model number match those used in Windows 95/98.

- Make sure there is no conflict between the NIC and any sound cards or peripherals in the IRQ and **memory address** space.

After examining these preliminary checkpoints and determining that they are not the cause of the NIC malfunction, examine the following two main NIC problem areas: faulty parameters or protocol/service problems.

Troubleshooting faulty parameter problems

If there is an error message stating that the network adapter doesn't respond to the operating system's queries, you can fairly safely bet that the NIC's parameters are faulty. If this is the case, follow these steps:

1. Check the dialog box to see if the adapter is displayed. If not, you must be install it again by clicking the Add button.

2. Highlight the adapter name and click the Properties button.

3. Click the Resources tab.

4. Record the values for the NIC's IRQ and memory address.

5. Verify that the NIC settings match Windows 95/98's settings. If they don't, change the NIC's settings, or start Windows 95/98 and adjust the settings on the Resource screen.

6. If the NIC doesn't respond to the changes, remove it and reboot Windows 95/98. Usually this reprograms software-programmable cards.

7. If the NIC is still not working, see if the card works in another machine or under a different operating system. If it still doesn't work, you likely have a malfunctioning card.

Troubleshooting protocol/server problems

The second scenario for network cards that aren't functioning occurs when Windows 95/98 doesn't report any problems with the card itself when it boots. This indicates that the NIC answered the Windows 95/98 query properly, and you most likely have a protocol or service problem. Proceed as follows:

1. Verify that the NIC's IRQ and memory address are correct.

2. Make sure the protocol and the NIC match.

3. Check the network connections.

4. If the NIC still doesn't function, and it's not a protocol or service problem, contact the NIC manufacturer or dealer for a replacement or for more information.

Troubleshooting a network protocol problem

Protocol mismatches cause more failed network connections than any other problem. You need to check a number of Windows 95/98 spots for correct configuration, and you can start by following these steps:

1. Determine the network protocol you should be using.

2. Besides the configuration information found in the various properties sheets, check the applications to identify which protocol is necessary and set up the software accordingly.

3. Check the Network icon under the Control Panel for the protocol drivers. Even though more than one protocol can be used, you should check one at a time, beginning with the primary protocol. Highlight each protocol in the Network window and click the Properties button. Client for Microsoft Networks should be checked, along with file and printer sharing if they are to be used.

The following sections describe steps you can take to troubleshoot some individual protocols.

NetBEUI

If you are using NetBEUI, follow these steps:

1. Click the Advanced tab and make sure NetBEUI is be used as the default protocol.

2. If you didn't use the Windows 95/98 NetBEUI protocol drivers, or don't know which driver is loaded, try removing the driver and reloading it with the default Windows 95/98 NetBEUI protocol. You will have complications if you are using a non-Windows–compatible driver.

If the Properties information is correct, the protocol is loaded properly and the problem must lie somewhere else.

IPX/SPX

If you are using IPX/SPX, follow these steps:

1. Click on the Advanced page of the IPX/SPX Properties window and make sure NetBEUI is used as the default protocol.

2. If you didn't use the Windows 95 IPX/SPX protocol drivers or don't know which driver is loaded, try removing the driver and reloading it with the default Windows 95 NetBEUI protocol.

TCP/IP

Although peer-to-peer TCP/IP networks are possible, they are complex to configure because of the IP address requirements. If you are using TCP/IP and suspect that your problem might be related to TCP/IP, follow these steps:

1. Supply the IP address of the local machine, the IP address of the server if you use DHCP, and the subnet mask.

2. Check to see if you need to set WINS on the machine.

3. If necessary, supply the gateway IP address on the Gateway page.

4. If the machine is not sending information correctly, it may need DNS. If DNS is used on the network, provide the DNS server IP addresses on the DNS page.

5. On the Bindings page make sure that the binding for TCP/IP to the client software drivers is in place.

6. Use **ping** *ip_address* to test the TCP/IP configuration, starting with the IP address, then the gateway, and then DNS.

Troubleshooting the client software

Windows 95/98 provides client drivers that include the client software to connect to remote servers. Each driver has a properties sheet to indicate the servers and behavior the client should exhibit when connecting, so check these pages for analysis. If you have installed the software properly, there should be very little to concern you. The following are some steps you can take if you have problems:

1. Make sure the client is loaded properly and is active.

2. Check the protocol bindings to make sure the client and protocol are paired correctly. Use the Bindings page from the protocol properties sheet.

3. Check the client's properties sheet through the Networks window to make sure the server information is accurate.

Even though you've installed the network adapter in the client computer correctly and have configured the operating system to communicate with the card and the network, you might still have problems connecting to the network. The following is a brief overview of some other common problems you might face when connecting client computers to a network.

Ethernet troubleshooting

Ethernet troubleshooting involves checking the following:

- Cards—Check for unique MAC addresses, incorrect selection, and poor card connection.

- Cables—Check for a faulty terminator, a missing terminator, a missing T-connector, a break in the wire, electromagnetic interference, or an excessively long cable run. Solving the problem might be a simple matter of plugging in a connector or moving a cable that runs across a fluorescent light.

- Protocol—Check for IPX protocol compatibility with the four frame types that must match: Ethernet_802.2, Ethernet_802.3, Ethernet_SNAP, and Ethernet_II.

Token Ring troubleshooting

If you suspect that you are having Token Ring trouble, check for resource conflicts, internal errors, cabling problems, and speed configuration.

ARCnet troubleshooting

If you suspect that you are having **ARCnet** trouble, check NIC settings and cable connections.

FDDI troubleshooting

If you suspect that you are having FDDI trouble, check for problems in connectors, cabling, and communication delays.

Concept Questions   *Semester 2, Unit 9, Lesson 44*

Demonstrate your knowledge of the concepts in this lesson by answering the following questions in the space provided.

1. Explain how to optimize a Windows 95 operating system for networking performance.

2. Explain how to increase file sharing performance.

_____

_____

_____

_____

_____

_____

_____

_____

_____

_____

_____

_____

_____

_____

_____

_____

_____

Vocabulary Exercise *Semester 2, Unit 9, Lesson 44*

Name: _____

Date: _____ Class: _____

Define the following terms as completely as you can.

ARCnet

_____

_____

binding

_____

_____

client software

_____

_____

memory address

_____

_____

NetBEUI

_____

_____

network adapter

_____

_____

Focus Questions

Semester 2, Unit 9, Lesson 44

Name: _____

Date: _____ *Class:* _____

1. Describe some common troubleshooting steps for networking problems.

_____

_____

_____

2. Describe how you troubleshoot a network card problem.

_____

_____

_____

3. Describe how you troubleshoot a network protocol problem.

_____

_____

_____

4. Describe how you test a TCP/IP configuration.

_____

_____

_____

5. Describe how you troubleshoot client software.

_____

_____

_____

6. Describe how you troubleshoot client connections.

_____

_____

_____

SEMESTER 2, UNIT 9, LESSON 45
Unit 9 Exam

If you have access to the online Aries A+ curriculum, contact your instructor for the Assessment System URL. If you do not have access to the online curriculum, please continue to Unit 10.

SEMESTER 2, UNIT 10

- Lesson 46: Microsoft Networking Domain Models
- Lesson 47: Logging On and Utilizing Windows 95/98 Resources in the NT Domain
- Lesson 48: Sharing and Managing Windows 95/98 Resources in Windows NT Server
- Lesson 49: User Profiles, System Policies, and Common Windows Problems in a Windows NT Domain Network
- Lesson 50: Unit 10 Exam

SEMESTER 2, UNIT 10, LESSON 46
Microsoft Networking Domain Models

You have learned some peer-to-peer networking basics and have been introduced to optimizing and troubleshooting the network, primarily using Windows 95/98 because it is the most widely used operating system. Despite its popularity, Windows 95/98 does not claim to be the most robust system on the market, nor does it claim to be the ultimate software for networking. Many computer technicians and engineers prefer the operating system that Microsoft has specifically developed for networking—Windows NT. In this lesson you will learn the basic concepts behind Windows NT.

Networking models

After you decide that networking computers would be beneficial, you need to decide how to structure the network. There are three common models:

- **Workgroup model**—Also called a peer-to-peer network, this is a decentralized model in which each machine keeps track of its own account information. It has low administrative overhead, but requires extra administrative work and is most appropriate for small networks. **NT Workstation** can work under this model.

- **Client/server model**—A model in which administration is centralized at a server. Clients log on through the server and access resources associated with the server. To access resources from other servers, the main server must create new accounts for the client.

- **Domain model**—The ideal environment for Windows NT.

Trust relationships

Think about the relationships you've had. How much extra energy was spent in relationships in which there was no trust? On the other hand, trusting relationships are such a joy and comfort. Windows NT employs this principle to avoid the extra work and confusion caused by a client/server model, by using a **trust** to join two or more domains.

In a trust situation, users are not looked upon as hackers bent on evil, but as friends who are allowed access to resources in domains outside the one they are registered in. The user is located in a trusted, or **account**, domain, and the resource is located in a trusting, or **resource**, domain.

The essential technological concept here is that the user is trusted by the resource. The user does not have to develop a trusting relationship with the resource for it to work. On the other hand, users are unlikely to access resources that they don't trust—that's just the way most humans behave. When you have settled the trust issues, you can decide which domain model to use.

NT domain models

Microsoft supports four domain models:

- **Single master**

- **Master**

- **Multiple master**

- **Complete trust**

Before jumping to conclusions and choosing a domain model that might later cause administrative hassles, be sure to evaluate your networking needs carefully. The following are the main factors to consider:

- The number of accounts in the domain, including users, computers, or groups. A Windows NT domain can support up to 40,000 accounts.

- The geographical area of the domain.

- How users and resources will be defined in the domain.

A small organization seeking the simplest domain model to manage would be wise to consider the **single domain model** due to its highly centralized administration and its simplicity, since **trust relationships** are not necessary. A disadvantage would occur if you have a large **Security Accounts Manager (SAM)** database that would cause poor performance throughout the domain. Table 10-1 gives an overall view of the four NT domain models.

Table 10-1   *NT domain models*

Domain Model	**Number of Users**	**Accounts**	**Resources**
Single	Up to 40,000	Centralized	Centralized
Master	Up to 40,000	Centralized	Decentralized
Multiple Master	Unlimited	Centralized among Master Domains	Decentralized
Complete Trust	Unlimited	Decentralized	Decentralized

Concept Questions   *Semester 2, Unit 10, Lesson 46*

Demonstrate your knowledge of the concepts in this lesson by answering the following questions in the space provided.

1. Explain the basics of the Microsoft networking model.

2. Explain the four domain models.

_____

_____

_____

_____

_____

_____

_____

_____

_____

_____

_____

_____

_____

_____

_____

_____

_____

_____

Vocabulary Exercise   *Semester 2, Unit 10, Lesson 46*

Name: _____

Date: _____   *Class:* _____

Define the following terms as completely as you can.

account

_____

_____

client/server model

_____

_____

complete trust domain

_____

_____

master domain model

_____

_____

multiple master domain model

_____

_____

NT Workstation

_____

_____

resource

_____

_____

SAM

_____

_____

trust

_____

_____

trust relationship

_____

_____

Windows NT

_____

_____

workgroup model

_____

_____

Focus Questions   *Semester 2, Unit 10, Lesson 46*

Name: _____

Date: _____   *Class:* _____

1. What Microsoft operating system is designed specifically for networking?

_____

_____

_____

2. Describe an account domain.

_____

_____

_____

3. Describe a resource domain.

_____

_____

_____

4. Describe how many domains there are in a single domain model.

_____

_____

_____

5. Describe a SAM database.

_____

_____

_____

6. Describe the master domain model.

_____

_____

_____

7. Describe the multiple master domain model.

_____

_____

_____

8. Describe the complete trust domain model.

_____

_____

_____

SEMESTER 2, UNIT 10, LESSON 47

Logging On and Utilizing Windows 95/98 Resources in the NT Domain

You have learned about the four NT domain models and the trust relationship concept. Now you will learn about logging in and utilizing domain resources in a Windows NT network.

We all operate within comfort zones. We can relax with close family members and friends, socialize with friends, and work with acquaintances. Each set of relationships has its own parameters. There are also places associated with comfort zones. At home we can usually relax and be ourselves, and we often act differently at work, at school, or out on the street in public. Perhaps you can imagine an even more drastic change if you were suddenly thrust into a different environment: a Manhattan subway at 3 a.m., a San Quentin prison yard, a Marilyn Manson concert, or a beach in Maui. These could all be called domains.

In the computer world, domains most often parallel to a workplace environment with acquaintances and friends. In Windows NT a grouping of clients and servers that have a specific reference name and share a single security permissions database form a **domain**.

Like a workgroup, all the computers in a domain are displayed together in the domain's Network Neighborhood, but a domain differs greatly in its administration. Whereas each workgroup computer takes care of its own security and administration, a domain computer follows the same security and administration assigned to the **primary domain controller (PDC)**.

Joining a domain

To join a domain you must create a computer account in one of two ways:

- From the **domain controller**

- From an NT workstation

Using the domain controller to create an account requires a user who is a member of the Administrators group or one who has permission to add workstations to the domain. When you are in the domain controller, you use the Server Manager utility to add the computer account to the domain and do the following:

1. Select Computer—Add it to the Domain.

2. Click NT Workstation or Server and type **ntws2** in the computer name dialog box.

3. Click Close in the dialog box. The computer should be displayed through the Server Manager.

4. Proceed to the NTWS2 computer.

5.   Go to the Network icon through the Control Panel.

6.   On the Identification tab click Change.

7.   Under the Member of section click Domain and type the name of the domain. Then click OK.

8.   Click OK under the Welcome to the Domain box and click Close.

9.   The next prompt asks you to shut down and restart the computer to allow the new settings to take effect.

The other method of creating a computer account is from NT Workstation, which skips the preauthorization required from a domain controller. In this case, you need to know an administrative account and password in order to create the account through the Network icon on the Control Panel. Note that this method is less desirable because it creates security concerns by allowing the user an administrative name and password. Here's the basic process:

1.   Click Change on the Identification tab.

2.   Under the Member of section click Domain and type the name of the domain.

3.   Select the Create a Computer Account in the Domain box, and click OK under the administrator heading.

4.   Click OK under the Welcome to the Domain box and click Close.

5.   The next prompt will ask you to shut down and restart your computer to allow the new settings to take effect.

Logging on to a computer or domain

To log on to a Windows NT domain when you start Windows 95/98, you need to configure the Client for Microsoft Networks Properties dialog box. Simply select the Log on to Windows NT domain and type the name of the domain in the box.

Each time you start the computer, Windows NT prompts you to log on by pressing Ctrl + Alt + Delete. You can then use the Logon Information box to log on to a computer or to a domain. You have a number of options in this dialog box:

- User Name—Enter the user account name that was assigned by the administrator; otherwise, access will be denied.

- Password—Enter the assigned password for user account name, and remember that passwords are **case sensitive**.

- Domain—To log on to the domain, select the name of the domain. The domain's directory database is checked for validation. To log on to a computer, select the name of the computer—the computer's database is checked for validation.

- Logon Using Dial-up Networking—When the **Remote Access Service (RAS)** is installed, this option allows the user to log on to a remote network by using RAS.

- Shut Down—Closes all files, saves all operating system data, and prepares the computer to be safely shut off. Only authorized users are allowed to shut down NT Server.

Using the Windows NT Security dialog box

When a user is logged on, he or she can access the Windows NT Security dialog box by pressing Ctrl + Alt + Del. Following are the options:

- Lock Workstation—All applications remain running, and the computer is secure without logging off.

- Logoff—Logs off the current user while leaving NT services running.

- Shut Down—Closes all files and prepares the server/workstation to be turned off safely.

- Change Password—Allows user to change the user account password as long as the old password is known.

- Task Manager—Lists applications that are running, switches between applications, and stops applications that don't respond. It also displays process information and performance data.

- Cancel—Closes the dialog box.

Changing domain passwords

Windows NT maintains separate passwords for accessing Windows 95/98 and for using the NT domain. To change either password is a simple matter of going to the Passwords option under the Control Panel. You are offered a choice of changing either the Windows password or the Windows NT domain password by clicking the Change Other Passwords button.

Concept Questions   *Semester 2, Unit 10, Lesson 47*

Demonstrate your knowledge of the concepts in this lesson by answering the following questions in the space provided.

1. Explain how to utilize the resources on a Windows NT domain network.

2. Explain the similarities and differences of domains and workgroups.

_____

_____

_____

_____

_____

_____

_____

_____

_____

_____

_____

_____

_____

_____

_____

_____

_____

_____

Vocabulary Exercise   *Semester 2, Unit 10, Lesson 47*

Name: _____

Date: _____   Class: _____

Define the following terms as completely as you can.

case sensitive

_____

_____

domain

_____

_____

domain controller

_____

_____

PDC

_____

_____

RAS

_____

_____

Focus Questions   *Semester 2, Unit 10, Lesson 47*

Name: _____

Date: _____   Class: _____

1. Describe how you join a domain.

_____

_____

_____

2. Describe how to log on to a computer or domain.

_____

_____

_____

3. Each time you start the computer, Windows NT prompts you to log on. What do you need to press?

_____

_____

_____

4. Describe what is meant by case sensitive and why it is important.

_____

_____

_____

5. Describe whether passwords are case sensitive.

_____

_____

_____

6. Name the following options in the Windows NT security dialog box:

Option	Details
	All applications remain running, and the computer is secure without logging off.
	Logs off the current user while leaving NT services running.
	Closes all files and prepares the server/workstation to be turned off safely.
	Allows user to change the user account password as long as the old password is known.
	Lists applications that are running, switches between applications, and stops applications that don't respond. It also displays process information and performance data.
	Closes the dialog box.

7. Describe how you change domain passwords.

_____

_____

_____

Semester 2, Unit 10, Lesson 48

Sharing and Managing Windows 95/98 Resources in Windows NT Server

Now that you know how to join a Windows NT domain and utilize its resources, we will discuss sharing and managing Windows 95 resources in the Windows NT domain.

Connecting to a Windows NT–based server

You will find that a Windows 95/98 computer will be able to connect to any Windows NT Server machine and use its resources. You might not be able to do so easily though, because Windows NT protects itself from intrusion with user-level security.

As long as you have logged on to the Windows NT domain with a proper user account and password and you have sufficient permissions to access the Windows NT machine, you have access to NT resources.

If you are denied access, make sure you have followed proper procedures to add your computer to the network. You might need to install a client package for that network by accessing the Client for Microsoft Networks properties section. On that page, identify the domain name and click OK.

Printing from a Windows NT–based server

It can be frustrating to attempt to retrieve hard copy with an uncooperative printer. These frustrations should be minimal for Windows 95/98 users who can access a Windows NT–based printer. As long as you are connected properly, printing from a Windows NT printer should be as easy as printing from a Windows 95/98 printer.

After connecting to a network workgroup or domain, you can easily connect to shared printers. First, click Network Neighborhood and select a computer in your workgroup. To create a permanent connection to a network printer, you have two options:

- Make a **shadow** of the resource—To make a shadow, right-click the resource in the Network Neighborhood or Whole Network, and drag the icon to the desktop. A menu appears, asking whether you want to copy the object or make a shadow. By choosing the shadow, you have a connection to the actual object on the computer.

- Map a drive to the file or directory—To map a drive letter to a shared directory, select Tools and Map Network Drive in Windows Explorer. The drive letter strand appears.

To connect to a network printer, select the Add Printer icon in the Printers panel and let the Select Printer Wizard do its job. You are able to select a local or network printer, or browse the network to find a desired printer.

Networks are only as good as the resources that are shared. A Windows 95/98 machine can share its files and printers as long as you configure the computer properly. To do so, follow these steps:

1. Click the Network icon in the Control Panel.

2. In the Configuration tab, click the File and Print Sharing button.

3. Check the following two options:

   I want to be able to give others access to my files.

   I want to be able to allow others to print to my printers.

4. Click OK and close the Network window.

Enabling user-level security

Because you can choose only one **security provider** for a Windows 95/98 computer, choose wisely. For user-level security on a Windows NT network, you must choose a security provider from the domains and computers in the network. This provider maintains the list of users and groups to whom you can grant resource permissions.

A Windows 95/98 user-level security server follows a four-step process to pass an identification request through the network to its security provider:

1. A remote user passes a username and password to a Windows 95/98 user-level security server.

2. The security server asks its security provider to verify the identity and password of the remote user.

3. The security provider checks the username and password, and informs the Windows 95 server if the information is verified.

4. The Windows 95 user-level security server grants access to the verified remote user. Of course the user-level security only works if it is enabled. To enable the security, follow these steps:

   a. Click the Network icon in the Control Panel.

   b. Click the Access Control tab.

   c. Click the User-level access control option.

   d. Write the name of the security provider in the Obtain list of users and groups from box.

   e. Click the OK button and restart the computer.

Editing an access control list

Adding or removing users from user-level security requires interfacing with the **access control list (ACL)**. This list is stored in the Registry under **HKEY_LOCAL_MACHINE\security\access*drive**folder_name***. Editing the list is a simple matter of using the Add and Remove buttons. When adding users, the Add Users dialog box appears, with a list of groups and users available on the security provider. You can also assign permissions to trusted domains if the security provider is a Windows NT domain.

To save management headaches it's usually better to assign permissions to groups rather than to users, and to make sure to assign users to the appropriate groups. If the ACL assigns permissions to both the user and the group, the user's permissions overrides the group permissions. This quirk happens in Windows 95/98, but not in Windows NT.

If really tight security is not a concern, you can enable public access by granting permission to The World. This account grants access to any validated user on the security provider.

Assigning folder permissions

Permissions for folders can also be defined from the ACL, but they are complex. You can assign read-only, full access, and custom access rights. Although it is recommended that administrators grant either read-only or full security, other custom rights are available, as listed in Table 10-2.

Table 10-2 *Custom access rights*

Custom Access Right	Action Allowed
Read files	Read and open files in the folder.
Write files	Write to existing files in the folder.
Create files and folders	Create new files and subfolders in the folder.
Delete files	Delete existing files and subfolders.
Change file attributes	Rename files and subfolders. Modify file and subfolder attributes.
List files	View a list of files in the folder.
Change access control	Modify permissions (no Windows 95 utility is capable of doing this).

Explicit versus implicit permissions

Two subtle distinctions exist for user-level permissions with folders: explicit and implicit. Explicit permissions are granted to a user or group somewhere in the shared folder hierarchy, and implicit permissions are inherited from the explicit permissions assigned.

Any attempts you make to change permissions on a subfolder are greeted with the message "You have given users permissions, but have not explicitly shared this folder. Share folder now?" To create a new share, click Yes. Clicking No merely changes the explicit permissions. Managing ACLs within Windows NT when using an NTFS file system is significantly easier.

Concept Questions   *Semester 2, Unit 10, Lesson 48*

Demonstrate your knowledge of the concepts in this lesson by answering the following questions in the space provided.

1. Explain how to share Windows 95/98 resources with Windows NT domain users.

2. Explain how to manage Windows 95/98 resources within the Windows NT domain.

_____

_____

_____

_____

_____

_____

_____

_____

_____

_____

_____

_____

_____

_____

_____

_____

_____

_____

Vocabulary Exercise   *Semester 2, Unit 10, Lesson 48*

Name: _____

Date: _____   Class: _____

Define the following terms as completely as you can.

ACL

_____

_____

security provider

_____

_____

shadow

_____

_____

Focus Questions   *Semester 2, Unit 10, Lesson 48*

Name: _____

Date: _____   *Class:* _____

1. Describe how you connect to a Windows NT–based server.

_____

_____

_____

2. Describe how you print from a Windows NT–based server.

_____

_____

_____

3. Describe how you make a shadow.

_____

_____

_____

4. Describe how you map a drive letter.

_____

_____

_____

5. Describe how you connect to a network printer.

_____

_____

_____

6. Describe how a Windows 95/98 computer shares files and printers.

_____

_____

_____

7. Describe how you enable user-level security.

_____

_____

_____

8. Describe some permission levels for folders.

_____

_____

_____

9. What are explicit and implicit permissions?

_____

_____

_____

SEMESTER 2, UNIT 10, LESSON 49

User Profiles, System Policies, and Troubleshooting Common Windows Problems in a Windows NT Domain Network

You have learned about sharing and managing Windows 95/98 resources in the NT network. In this lesson, you learn more about the subject and examine user profiles, system policies and common troubleshooting problems.

The basics of the user profile and system policies

Just as you adjust an automobile's mirrors and seats to suit you, you also adjust a computer to suit your needs. The **user profile** contains configuration preferences and options, including Windows 95/98 settings, such as fonts, colors, and backgrounds; network settings; and application settings, such as recently opened documents and toolbar configurations.

The user profile includes all the settings in the **HKEY_CURRENT_USER** section of the Registry and might also include other configurations, such as shortcuts on the desktop or in the Network Neighborhood, and PIFs on the Start menu and in the Programs folder.

Local user profiles do not need a network server for their settings. These are stored only at the user's logon computer. This is the most appropriate solution in networks where multiple users share a Windows 95/98 computer. If you have a situation where a number of users log on to various computers, you should use roaming user profiles, which must be managed by a network server.

System policies supersede local user profiles, and as such can be used to offer unified working environments across a network. They are Registry settings that are automatically imposed when the user logs on. and they can apply to computers, users, and groups.

User profiles

Every time a network user logs on to a computer, Windows 95/98 searches the Registry to determine whether the user has a local profile and checks for the user profile on the server. If the user profile on the server is the most current, Windows 95/98 copies it to the local computer for the session and then loads the settings into the Registry. If no local user profile exists, Windows 95/98 copies the server version to the local computer. On the other hand, Windows 95/98 creates a new user profile with default settings on the local computer if no user profile is found at all.

When the user logs off, both the local and network copies of the user profile are automatically updated with current settings. If the same user logs on to more than one computer simultaneously, only the last logoff is saved, so that multiple profiles or hybrid profiles do not occur. Although this information outlines what happens with the user profiles, it leaves out some details about the process. When user profiles are enabled and a new user logs on and creates a new profile, Windows 95/98 creates a hidden folder called **\windows\profiles***user_name*, which contains the profile information shown in Table 10-3.

Table 10-3   *User profile information*

Item	What It Contains	When It Is Created
user.dat and **user.da0**	User-specific Registry settings. **user.da0** is a backup of the **user.dat** file.	Always
\desktop	Desktop shortcuts	Only when Include desktop icons and Network Neighborhood contents in user settings is selected in the Password Properties dialog box.
\nethood	Network Neighborhood shortcuts	Only when Include desktop icons and Network Neighborhood contents in user settings is selected in the Password Properties dialog box.
\recent	Shortcuts to recently accessed documents	Only when Include desktop icons and Network Neighborhood contents in user settings is selected in the Password Properties dialog box.
\Start Menu	The Programs folder on the Start menu	Only when Start Menu and Program groups in user settings is selected in the Password Properties dialog box.

A different kind of user profile is created when you use **roaming user profiles**. This **mandatory user profile** is never updated when a user logs off or shuts down a computer. Although it contains the same information as any user profile, the mandatory user profile contains a **user.dat** file in the Registry.

Setting up user profiles on a Windows NT network

As long as the computer is configured to use Client for Microsoft Networks, you can utilize user profiles with Windows 95/98 on a Windows NT network. Windows 95/98 doesn't use the Profiles directory on a Windows NT server, which records only Windows NT profiles.

To set up user profiles on a Windows NT network, follow these steps:

1. Make sure user profiles are enabled.

2. Under the Network option in the Control Panel, select Client for Microsoft Networks as the Primary Network Logon client.

3. Make sure each user has a home directory on a Windows NT network server.

When the user logs off, Windows 95/98 automatically updates the user profile in the user's assigned directory on the Windows NT network.

System policies

Serving as a powerful tool for controlling and managing resources and user accounts on networked computers, system policies can allow you to restrict what users can do from the desktop, restrict access of Control Panel options, customize the desktop layout, and configure network settings.

Before rushing to control every aspect of the network you should take some time to determine what profiles and policies would be most beneficial to your situation. Consider the following:

- Even mandatory profiles can be superceded for a current session.

- A policy prevents users from making changes.

- Mandatory profiles apply to user settings only, and system policies are more flexible and can control both user and computer settings.

- Mandatory profiles work only when the profile server is available, and system policies remain in effect at all times.

- You should use mandatory user profiles or system policies, but not both.

To check the system policy settings, examine the system policy file, which by default is called **config.pol**. A system policy file contains Registry settings that are loaded during the logon process and effect one of two areas:

- Desktop settings, stored in the **HKEY_CURRENT_USER** subtree.

- Logon and network access settings, stored in the **HKEY_LOCAL_MACHINE** subtree.

When a user logs on to a Windows 95 computer, the operating system looks for a policy file in one of three locations:

- The *win_root* folder on a single computer.

- The **netlogon** share of the domain that the user logs on to for networked computers, set to Client for Microsoft Networks.

- The **sys:public** directory on the NetWare server for networked computers, set to Client for NetWare Networks.

Installing and configuring the System Policy Editor

To install the **System Policy Editor** you need to access the administrator files from the **admin** directory on the Windows 95/98 CD. After doing so, follow these steps:

1. Double-click the Add/Remove Programs option in the Control Panel.

2. Click the Windows Setup tab in the dialog box.

3. Click Have Disk.

4. In the Install from Disk dialog box, click Browse, choose the **admin\apptools\poledit** directory, and click OK.

5. In the Have Disk dialog box, make sure System Policy Editor is checked, and click Install.

6. After the files have been copied, click OK.

To run the System Policy Editor, click Start, Run, type **poledit**, and click OK. To use group policies you must install the System Policy Editor on each Windows 95 machine. To set these group policies, follow the same procedure described above until you reach the Have Disk dialog box, where you need to check the Group Policies option and click the Install button.

Using the System Policy Editor

You have two choices for using the System Policy Editor: Registry mode and Policy File mode. Registry mode allows you to directly edit the Registry of the local or remote computer, and Policy File mode allows you to indirectly edit the Registry. This mode is indirect because you can create policy files for other computers that are only recognized by the Registry after a user has logged on.

To use the System Policy Editor in Registry mode, follow these steps:

1. Click the File menu.

2. Click Open Registry.

3. Double-click the appropriate User or Computer icon.

4. Shut down and restart the computer so that the changes take effect.

To use the System Policy Editor in Policy File mode, click the File menu and then click New or Open to open the policy file. When you edit settings in this mode, clicking a Registry option gives you three possible states:

- Checked—The policy is implemented immediately.

- Cleared—The policy is not implemented. If it was implemented previously, those settings are removed from the Registry.

- Grayed—The setting remains unchanged.

Implementing system policies on a network

If you've ever worked on a computer network, you realize that things can slow to a crawl at times, especially if the network hasn't been configured optimally. Potential for poor network performance exists if the system policies do not use load balancing. To avoid a potential network slowdown, you need to enable load balancing so that system policies are obtained from the logon server instead of from the PDC. To do so, follow these steps:

1. Check *computer_name*\network\update\remote update policy.

2. Select the Load-balancing setting.

Troubleshooting Windows NT interoperability and user profiles

Some of the most common troubleshooting situations relating to Windows NT interoperability with Windows 95 and user profiles are listed in Table 10-4.

Table 10-4 *Common Windows NT interoperability and user profiles troubleshooting situations*

Problem	Probable cause	Solution
When attempting to connect to a user-level share, you get the error message "Access to the specified device, path or file is denied."	You do not have an account on the security provider, or you entered the wrong username or password.	Create an account on the security provider, or retype your identification.

Problem	Probable cause	Solution
When attempting to connect to a user-level share, you get the error "*server**share* is not accessible. Access is denied."	Resource permissions have not been assigned to your user or group accounts.	Assign permissions to one of your groups or to your user account.
When attempting to connect to a user-level share, you get the error message "You must supply a password to make this connection."	Your account on the security provider doesn't match your local Windows password.	Enter the password for your account on the security provider.
When attempting to connect to a user-level share, you get the error message "There are currently no logon servers available to service the logon request."	A domain controller is not available to authenticate you.	You must wait until a domain controller is available.
Desktop shortcuts work on some computers but not on others.	The user has made a shortcut to an application on a remote machine.	Desktop shortcuts must be installed at the computer where the user is logged on.
User profiles are not available on a Windows NT Workstation computer.	A Windows 95 user is switching computers and using a roaming user profile.	Although both Windows NT Workstation and Windows 95 support roaming user profiles, their formats are incompatible and they do not **interoperate**.
Documents and folders on the desktop are not stored in the user profile.	Documents, programs, and folders are ignored in the Windows 95 user profiles.	Only shortcuts on the desktop are stored in the Windows 95 user profiles, unlike the Windows NT user profiles.
A user's briefcase reverts to an ordinary folder.	Briefcases created before user profiles are enabled are not saved in a user's profile.	Create a new briefcase after user profiles are enabled.

Troubleshooting system policies

When you encounter system policy problems, first verify the following:

- The related Registry key is correct in the policy template (**.adm**) file.

- The related policy is set properly in the policy (**.pol**) file.

- The related application actually uses the Registry key being changed.

- The policy file is located in the correct network location and is accessible from the Windows 95/98 computer.

- The username, group name, and computer name are correct for group policies, and the user is a member of the group.

Some specific problem areas are shown in Table 10-5.

Table 10-5 *Common system policy troubleshooting situations*

Problem	Cause	Solution
Cannot create or edit a system policy for groups.	Group policy support is not available by default for Windows 95 computers.	Add Group Policy through the Add/Remove Programs option in the Control Panel.
Group policies are not processed by all clients.	Group Policy must be installed on a Windows 95 computer to process them, unlike in Windows NT.	Add Group Policy through the Add/Remove Programs option in the Control Panel.
User policies are downloaded for Windows 95 users or for Windows NT users, but not for both.	The System Policy Editor files are not named the same and are not interoperable.	Create a user policy in both system policy files (**config.pol** and **ntconfig.pol**).

Concept Questions   *Semester 2, Unit 10, Lesson 49*

Demonstrate your knowledge of the concepts in this lesson by answering the following questions in the space provided.

1. Explain the similarities and differences of a local user profile and a roaming user profile.

2. Explain the characteristics and properties of a system policy and the System Policy Editor.

_____

_____

_____

_____

_____

_____

_____

_____

_____

_____

_____

_____

_____

_____

_____

_____

_____

_____

Vocabulary Exercise   *Semester 2, Unit 10, Lesson 49*

Name: _____

Date: _____   Class: _____

Define the following terms as completely as you can.

interoperate

_____

_____

mandatory user profile

_____

_____

roaming user profile

_____

_____

system policies

_____

_____

System Policy Editor

_____

_____

user profile

_____

_____

Focus Questions   *Semester 2, Unit 10, Lesson 49*

Name: _____

Date: _____   *Class:* _____

1. The user profile includes all the settings in what section of the Registry?

_____

_____

_____

2. Describe where local user profiles are stored.

_____

_____

_____

3. Describe how user profiles work.

_____

_____

_____

4. Describe how you set up user profiles on a Windows NT network.

_____

_____

_____

5. What is the name of the system policy file?

_____

_____

_____

6. Describe how you install the System Policy Editor.

_____

_____

_____

7. Describe how you execute the System Policy Editor.

_____

_____

_____

8. To avoid a potential network slowdown, what do you need to enable so that system policies are obtained from the logon server instead of from the PDC?

_____

_____

_____

9. Describe some common troubleshooting situations relating to Windows NT interoperability with Windows 95 and user profiles.

_____

_____

_____

10. Describe what you should do if you encounter system policy problems.

_____

_____

_____

Semester 2, Unit 10, Lesson 50
Unit 10 Exam

If you have access to the online Aries A+ curriculum, contact your instructor for the Assessment System URL. If you do not have access to the online curriculum, please continue to Unit 11.

SEMESTER 2, UNIT 11

- Lesson 51: Using Windows 95 on a Novell Network
- Lesson 52: Logging In and Using Novell Network Resources
- Lesson 53: Sharing and Managing Windows 95 Resources on a Novell Network
- Lesson 54: Troubleshooting Windows 95 on a Novell Network
- Lesson 55: Unit 11 Exam

SEMESTER 2, UNIT 11, LESSON 51
Using Windows 95 on a Novell Network

You have learned about Windows NT networks and how to troubleshoot problems. In this lesson, you'll learn about Novell networks and how they compare to Windows networks.

Network operating systems

Operating systems are the programs that manage individual PCs. A typical PC operating system keeps track of local file systems, computer memory, application program functions, peripheral device functions, and CPU scheduling of applications.

Networks also have their own operating systems—**network operating systems (NOSs)**—and their function is to keep track of stations, printers, bridges, routers and gateways. A NOS also manages resources, but on a much larger scale than a local operating system. A NOS manages remote file systems, server memory, shared application program functions, shared network devices, and server CPU scheduling of NOS processes.

There are two basic types of networks, and they interact in different ways. As you have learned, a peer-to-peer network is one in which each of the individual computers, or nodes, on the network is running the NOS. A client/server network is one in which there is a central server; the server holds applications and files that are accessed by all computers on the network. Client computers communicate with the server by using a subset of the NOS. **NetWare** 2.x and 3.x are examples of client/server network operating systems.

The operating system on each individual computer must also be compatible with the NOS in order for the network to function. NetWare is compatible with a number of workstation operating systems, including DOS, OS/2, UNIX, and Macintosh.

Novell NetWare

Novell networks and their accompanying NetWare software comprise the most widely used NOSs in use today. A NetWare NOS is the client/server type, having a central, powerful server interfacing with a host of individual client computers (also called *nodes*). Novell systems support DOS, Windows, OS/2 and Macintosh platforms, so even a very diverse office environment can benefit from a Novell network.

NetWare software has progressed through a number of incarnations until arriving at the current version. NetWare 2.x, an early version, ran on a 286 PC and could handle a 100-node network. NetWare 3.12, which is still available, supports 250 users. In 1993 NetWare introduced the 4.0 version, which could support 1,000 concurrent nodes, and in 1996, version 4.11 entered the scene, a combination of Novell Web Server and other components. The package was called IntranetWare, but still used the NetWare operating system. NetWare 5 supports Novell's IPX network protocol and IP protocol for use on the World Wide Web. It also offers Web server support, which enables NetWare to function successfully in a variety of network situations, including the Internet.

NetWare and Windows NT

NetWare and Windows NT are competitors in the business office networking market. They offer many of the same features, but NetWare centers on primarily network-related features, whereas Windows NT also offers other operating system options such as word processing. NetWare servers function as standalone servers; a Windows NT server could conceivably be used as a workstation while it was also operating as a server, although doing that would probably slow down the network considerably.

NetWare and Windows 95

As discussed earlier in this lesson, one of the platforms supported by NetWare is Windows 95, and because of the widespread use of Novell networks in offices, it's very likely that in a business environment you could encounter Windows 95 computers running on a NetWare system.

Windows 95 runs on NetWare workstations equipped with NetWare versions 2.15, 2.2, 3.x, and 4.x servers. Several networking client programs can facilitate this partnership and bridge the gap between NetWare and Windows: 32-bit, protected mode Microsoft **Client for NetWare Networks**; Novell NetWare 3.x real-mode networking client (NETX); and Novell NetWare 4.x real-mode networking client (VLM).

Each of these client programs has unique features and advantages, but Windows 95 brings its own features into play, regardless of which support software you choose. Features Windows 95 has that support NetWare networks include the following:

- Automatic setup of Windows 95 on workstations.

- System policies to enforce desktop and system settings on workstations.

- Total integration of network resources in Network Neighborhood.

- Password caching for network connections and user-level security, and pass-through validation to servers.

- Utilizing Point and Print to print via NetWare print queues.

Microsoft Client for NetWare Networks

Microsoft Client for NetWare Networks offers many advantages when used to interface between Windows 95 and a Novell Network. Because it uses 32-bit protocols, drivers, and supporting files, it uses no conventional memory space. It also has the ability to share workstation resources, such as a CD-ROM drive, as a network resource.

Microsoft Client can also support NetWare login scripts with NetWare versions 2.15, 2.2, 3.x, and 4.x servers. It automatically reconnects if a workstation loses its connection to the network, and then rebuilds the client environment, including connection status and printer connections. This feature protects the client if the server is down.

Microsoft Client also provides enhanced performance and additional networking features, such as the following:

- Client-side caching of network data and plug-and-play support

- Remote network access to NetWare networks

- User profiles for system configuration

- Long filenames on the local computer and on NetWare servers

For further detail on these and other NetWare/Windows 95 issues, consult the **Windows 95 Resource Kit**.

Novell NetWare clients

A Novell real-mode network client can by itself support Windows 95 nodes. Also, Windows 95 can use Client for Microsoft Networks in conjunction with NETX or VLM client. Windows 95 provides a number of features that support NetWare clients, including the following:

- Windows 95 networking support can use a diverse variety of network adapters, including Open Datalink Interface (ODI), Datapoint ARCnet, and IPX monolithic protocol stack (**ipx.com**).

- Windows 95 contains protocols to connect to other computers that use IPX/SPX protocol for Windows NT, Windows 95, and MS-DOS.

- NetWare services and commands operate normally on a Windows 95 system, without special configuration modifications.

The OSI model

The OSI model is a standard developed by the International Organization of Standardization that is used to compare different networking systems. Systems designed according to the OSI model are compatible. Prior to the creation of the OSI model, each of the major network software manufacturers had its own proprietary system, and network interconnectivity was almost unheard of. For instruction purposes, the OSI model illustrates clearly how network components relate to each other.

The OSI model contains seven layers, with the physical layer on the bottom. Control is passed through each level of the hierarchy until the interaction reaches the top layer, the application layer. The following are the layers in the OSI model:

- Layer 7 (Application)—At this layer, computer and user meet. This is where users view messages, and where data requests and responses take place.

- Layer 6 (Presentation)—This layer handles the way data is presented. It contains common syntax data that helps nodes convert data from one format to another so they can communicate with each other.

- Layer 5 (Session)—This layer uses the transport layer to manage session services. A *session* refers to the time a user is logged on to the network, and related file transfer.

- Layer 4 (Transport)—This layer enhances network-layer services and ensures the integrity of data across the network. It builds on the error-detection mechanisms in the lower layers. This layer is where error recovery takes place.

- Layer 3 (Network)—This layer builds on the node-to-node data link–layer connection and extends services across the network.

- Layer 2 (Data link)—This layer augments the routing capability of the physical layer and transmits data node-to-node.

- Layer 1 (Physical)—This layer transmits bits of information over a communication channel, and deals with mechanical and electrical interactions on the physical network.

A NOS contains three major aspects that relate to the OSI model:

- Network drivers

- Subnet protocols

- Application-layer protocols

The following sections describe these aspects.

Network drivers

A **network driver** is responsible for transmitting and receiving data over a network. It contains a data link protocol that controls the particular network adapter (such as Ethernet) that is being used on a specific network.

Subnet protocols

The network uses **subnet protocols** to send application and system messages networkwide. Because of their key role, subnet protocols determine the overall speed of the network: Fast subnet protocols yield fast NOSs, and vice versa. On the other hand, a subnet protocol that induces high-speed transmission on a LAN might be sluggish on a WAN.

Application-layer protocols

Application-layer protocols are used to communicate with subnet protocols and expedite NOS services. Application-layer protocols perform a variety of functions, including the following:

- Facilitating open file functions, such as opening and closing files, and reading and writing data blocks

- Compiling lists of directory entries

- Enabling high-level connection services

- Synchronizing operations

NetWare 4.x

NetWare 4.x made a significant leap over earlier NetWare versions, with the introduction of NetWare Directory Service (NDS), a global database service. It features a distributed database that can catalog information for all the shared resources on a network, without actually residing on any one server in the network. NDS effectively replaces the bindery services of earlier NetWare versions. The following are some of the benefits of NDS:

- It organizes the network logically.

- It requires a single login for the network.

- It offers global network management.

- It offers freedom from dependence on a physical location of resources.

The following sections describe these benefits in detail.

Logical organization of the network

NetWare 4.x gives the network administrator a logical view of the network that masks the complexity of the physical network and portrays network resources in an easily understood, accessible manner. In NetWare 4.x, network resources are represented by objects. Network administrators usually do not need to know the details of the layout of the actual network; what they need is a usable, graphic representation of the relationships between resources. NDS simplifies the network layout to make that possible.

Single login to the network

With the advantage of a single login to access the entire network, network use is streamlined and the user is spared having to log in to each server separately. The network administrator can still control access to network resources, so although a user might be able to see all network resources after login, not all may be accessible without administrator permission. This simplifies network login without sacrificing security.

Global network management

In earlier NetWare versions, network management functions needed to be performed on each individual server separately. With 4.x versions, global network management capability permits changing network resources from anywhere on the network. Also, the network administrator can delegate administrative responsibility to other network users.

Independence from a physical location of resources

NetWare 4.x helps networks be more flexible. In earlier NetWare versions, if a peripheral device such as a printer was moved to another server, the bindery representation of the peripheral had to be moved to that server as well. In NetWare 4.x, peripherals function no matter where they are placed. Changes to such network resources are made via NDS and can be accessed from anywhere on the network.

Improvements in the NetWare file system

The efficiency and speed of the file system have been improved in NetWare 4.x by using the following techniques:

- Improved block suballocation

- File system compression

- Data migration

The following sections describe these techniques in detail.

Block suballocation

NetWare 4.x allows disk storage allocation to be more flexible than in the past. Unused space can now be allocated instead of wasted, as in earlier versions. Disk block space was formerly allocated in large 4-KB chunks; if a 200-byte file was created on a 4-KB block, all of the block would have been allocated for that file, and the majority of the space would be unusable for any other purpose. In NetWare 4.x, space is allocated in 512-byte chunks, making it far less likely that unused space will accumulate.

File system compression

NetWare found that most networks underused the capacity of their processors by almost 50%. NetWare 4.x makes use of this untapped processor capability to perform file compression as a background task. (A *background task* is quietly performed behind the scenes while the computer goes on with its normal functions.)

Other file compression programs compress disk blocks when they are written, and decompress when they are opened, which slows down computer operation. Because NetWare 4.x makes this a background operation, file blocks that are being decompressed are available immediately, without waiting for the entire document to be completed. This compression feature also increases effective disk space. NetWare compresses files only when it determines that doing so will increase available space.

Data migration

Data migration is another feature that ensures more available disk space. By moving or migrating files to an offline storage medium and accessing them only as needed, the files remain accessible to the network but do not take up space on the server.

File system security and management

Users gain access to a NetWare 4.x network by logging in to the NetWare directory. Each network initially establishes a directory tree containing security parameters. The network administrator, who controls network management as needed, allocates individual user access and can assign different levels of user and administrator responsibility as needed.

Concept Questions   *Semester 2, Unit 11, Lesson 51*

Demonstrate your knowledge of the concepts in this lesson by answering the following questions in the space provided.

1. Explain the basics of Novell networks and how it differs from Windows NT.

2. Explain the basics of the interaction between Windows 95 and Novell NetWare networks.

_____

_____

_____

_____

_____

_____

_____

_____

_____

_____

_____

_____

_____

_____

_____

_____

_____

Vocabulary Exercise   *Semester 2, Unit 11, Lesson 51*

Name: _____

Date: _____   Class: _____

Define the following terms as completely as you can.

application-layer protocol

_____

_____

Client for NetWare Networks

_____

_____

NetWare

_____

_____

network driver

_____

_____

NOS

_____

_____

subnet protocol

_____

_____

Microsoft Windows 95 Resource Kit

Focus Questions *Semester 2, Unit 11, Lesson 51*

Name: _____

Date: _____ *Class:* _____

1. Describe the function of a NOS.

_____

_____

_____

2. Describe the type of client operating systems that Novell supports.

_____

_____

_____

3. Describe the versions of Novell NetWare.

_____

_____

_____

4. Describe the similarities and differences of NetWare and Windows NT.

_____

_____

_____

5. Describe some client programs for Windows 95 on a NetWare network.

_____

_____

_____

6. Describe some features that Windows 95 has to support NetWare networks.

_____

_____

_____

7. Describe Microsoft Client for NetWare Networks.

_____

_____

_____

8. Describe some features that Windows 95 provides in support of NetWare clients.

_____

_____

_____

9. Describe the OSI model.

_____

_____

_____

10. Describe some benefits of NDS.

_____

_____

_____

11. Describe the logical organization of the network of NetWare 4.x.

_____

_____

_____

12. Describe the advantage of requiring a single login to a network.

_____

_____

_____

13. Describe global network management.

_____

_____

_____

14. Describe some improvements to the NetWare file system.

_____

_____

_____

SEMESTER 2, UNIT 11, LESSON 52
Logging In and Using Novell Network Resources

In this lesson you will learn more about Novell software, and you will learn how to configure and log in to a Novell Network.

Installing and configuring the IPX/SPX-compatible protocol

The **IPX/SPX**-compatible protocol facilitates communication between Client for NetWare Networks and NetWare servers. It can also be used to communicate with computers running file and printer sharing for NetWare Networks. When you install Client for Microsoft Networks on a Windows 95 system, the IPX/SPX-compatible protocol is installed automatically. Windows 95 also sets frame type, network address, and other necessary settings. This protocol also works with Client for Microsoft Networks, interacting with computers running Windows for Workgroups 3.11 or Windows NT.

In some cases configuration might need to be done by hand. Follow these steps to configure the IPX/SPX-compatible protocol:

1. Open the Control Panel and choose the Network icon.

2. Double-click IPX/SPX compatible protocol. If you have more than one network adapter, you need to configure each adapter with its own settings.

3. Click the Advanced tab in the dialog box. A typical installation offers accurate default setting values. If you need to change settings, see the Microsoft Windows 95 Resource Kit for a table of properties and suggested values.

Installing Windows 95 source files on NetWare servers

It is possible to place Windows 95 master files on a NetWare server and use them as source files to install Windows 95 on NetWare workstations, or to run Windows 95 across a network as a shared application. In order to do this, you need to run a program called Server-based Setup (**netsetup.exe**), which comes on the Windows 95 CD. (For detailed instructions on how to set up Windows 95 source files on a NetWare server, refer to the Microsoft Windows 95 Resource Kit.)

Automating setup for NetWare workstations

You can configure automatic setup procedures for installing Windows 95 on workstations, by taking the following steps:

1. Create setup **scripts** to install Windows 95 on NetWare Network nodes. Scripts must specify network client and supporting components, plus define any other needed software.

2. Define user and computer configurations for scripts for specific workstations.

3. Create login scripts to automatically set up Windows 95 on workstations when users log on.

For a detailed description of this procedure, see the Microsoft Windows 95 Resource Kit.

Supporting long filenames on NetWare servers

Windows 95 supports long filenames in NetWare 3.x and 4.x. Filenames have a maximum length of 254 characters and follow the 8.3 convention on the first instance of the filename. For an in-depth explanation of how to enable long filenames, refer to the Microsoft Windows 95 Resource Kit.

Supporting pass-through securities for peer resource sharing

NetWare servers connected to Windows 95 nodes that provide file and printer sharing services for NetWare Networks need to be configured with a **windows_passthru** account. This account supports **pass-through** validation for user-level security for Windows 95 in this situation.

Placing profile and policy files on NetWare servers

On a NetWare network where the computers are configured to use Microsoft Client for NetWare Networks, you can use user profiles to create a standardized desktop for all network nodes. You can do this by placing the appropriate **user.man** file in the user's **mail** directory.

Installing Client for NetWare Networks

If you didn't install Client for NetWare Networks when you originally set up Windows 95, you can do it now by following these steps:

1. Access the Network option in the Control Panel.

2. If the computer has NETX or VLM already installed, select that NetWare Workstation Shell client from the installed components list and click Remove. Also select and remove IPXODI if it appears in the list.

3. Click Add and double-click Client in the Select Network Component dialog box.

4. In the Select Network Client dialog box, choose Microsoft from the Manufacturers list, and then choose Client for NetWare Networks from the Network Clients list.

5. Click OK, and then shut down the computer and restart it to enable changes to take effect.

Configuring Microsoft Client for NetWare Networks

Configuring Microsoft Client for NetWare Networks can include a number of setup processes, including configuring protected-mode NDIS network adapter drivers for Client for NetWare Networks, configuring Client for NetWare Networks with ODI network adapter drivers, and running NetWare utilities with Client for NetWare Networks. For detailed references and procedures, see the Microsoft Windows 95 Resource Kit.

Configuring logon for NetWare networks

If you are using Client for NetWare Networks, you log on once to gain access to Windows 95 and the entire network. To gain access, you need an account on the NetWare server, and with it a user name and password. To configure Client for NetWare Networks for network logon, it's necessary to establish whether Client for NetWare Networks is the primary network logon client. This means that the following criteria have been met:

- User profiles and system policies will be downloaded from NetWare servers.

- Users will be prompted to log on to a NetWare server when Windows 95 starts.

- You need to specify a preferred server, which Windows 95 uses to validate logon passwords and usernames.

Follow these steps to configure network logon:

1. Find the Network option in the Control Panel, and choose Client for NetWare Networks in the Primary Network Logon box.

2. In the installed components list, double-click Client for NetWare Networks.

3. Set the values for configuration options in Client for NetWare Networks properties:

Preferred Server—Assigns the NetWare server that will appear in the network logon dialog box.

First Network Drive—Assigns the first drive letter you choose to designate the first network connection.

Enable Logon Script Processing—Designates the computer to process NetWare login scripts when users log on.

Printing to NetWare print servers

A Windows 95 computer can connect to a NetWare server and store printer driver files in the NetWare bindery. You need Supervisory privileges on the server in order to configure the NetWare printer server, and the computer must be using Client for NetWare Networks. When you request it, NetWare server automatically copies the printer drivers to a specified path on the computer.

Concept Questions   *Semester 2, Unit 11, Lesson 52*

Demonstrate your knowledge of the concepts in this lesson by answering the following questions in the space provided.

1. Explain the function of the IPX/SPX-compatible protocol.

2. Explain what function running the program Server-based Setup would accomplish.

_____

_____

_____

_____

_____

_____

_____

_____

_____

_____

_____

_____

_____

_____

_____

_____

_____

_____

Vocabulary Exercise   *Semester 2, Unit 11, Lesson 52*

Name: _____

Date: _____   Class: _____

Define the following terms as completely as you can.

IPX/SPX

_____

_____

pass-through security

_____

_____

script

_____

_____

Focus Questions   *Semester 2, Unit 11, Lesson 52*

Name: _____

Date: _____   *Class:* _____

1. Describe how you configure IPX/SPX.

_____

_____

_____

2. Describe how you install Windows 95 source files.

_____

_____

_____

3. Describe how you configure automatic setup procedures for installing Windows 95.

_____

_____

_____

4. Describe how you place profile and policy files on a NetWare server.

_____

_____

_____

5. Describe how you install Client for NetWare Networks.

_____

_____

_____

6. Describe how you configure logon for NetWare networks.

_____

_____

_____

SEMESTER 2, UNIT 11, LESSON 53
Sharing and Managing Windows 95 Resources on a Novell Network

In today's computer world you could very well be logged in to both a Windows NT server and a Novell NetWare server, while you are connected to a shared printer and sharing files. The network could be as small as two computers sharing files and a single printer, or as large as a full-blown network for a giant corporation. Or your computer setup could fit somewhere in between. In this lesson you will learn about sharing and managing resources on a NetWare network.

Installing and configuring file and printer sharing

Networking files and devices such as printers occurs primarily for efficiency and for economic reasons. It would be pointless to buy a printer for every PC on the network when PCs can share resources.

Although the principles for installing and configuring remain the same as the ones you learned for Windows NT, a few sharing details differ for Novell NetWare. These differences occur partly because NetWare uses dedicated servers and partly because Novell and Microsoft are competing for the networking market. For Windows machines to use file and printer sharing for NetWare Networks, the following must be true:

- The computer must use Client for NetWare Networks instead of Novell-supplied software.

- The network must use only user-level security.

- The IPX/SPX-compatible protocol must be installed.

- The service must avoid computers that are SMB-based file and printer sharing machines for Microsoft networks.

- There must be a **windows_passthru** account (without a password) on the NetWare server used as the **security provider** if you want pass-through validation.

After installing file and printer sharing for NetWare networks, you need to configure the method that computers on the network can use to find the computer. You have two browsing options:

- Workgroup advertising, which uses the same broadcast method as do workgroups on Microsoft networks.

- SAP (Service Advertising Protocol) advertising, which is also used by Novell NetWare 2.15+, 3.x, and 4.x servers. You must enable this option to share resources with computers running NETX or VLM.

For more extensive details on this and other Windows 95 and Novell NetWare issues, refer to the Microsoft Windows 95 Resource Kit.

Sharing resources with user-level security

Simple as it sounds, there would be no networking without sharing. The more sharing that occurs, the more **connectivity** there is. Although the future promises more connectivity, currently Novell networks require user-level security to function. You can always add more users to the list of trusted users with resource access to a NetWare server. Simply add the users to the NetWare pass-through security provider. When you add a new user to the Sharing properties of the shared resource, the user will have access to the peer server that controls the resource.

To make sure all users have the required server access, make sure that one NetWare server on the network has the accounts for all users or all servers, and then set that server as the security provider for every computer that has file and printer sharing for NetWare networks. File and printer sharing for NetWare networks allows access to printers and files on the basis of user membership. This requires the name of the server to retrieve the network usernames. For NetWare versions 2.15 and 3.x servers, all the information for users, groups, passwords, and access rights is stored in a server database called the **bindery**. NetWare 4.x servers are configured differently and use bindery emulation to give the appearance of a bindery. Windows 95 can use the bindery of one NetWare server.

The file and printer sharing for NetWare Networks permissions are basically the same as the permissions granted in File and Printer Sharing for Microsoft Networks. They just use slightly different terminology, as illustrated in Table 11-1.

Table 11-1   *File and printer sharing permissions*

Windows 95	NetWare
Read files	Read
Write to files	Write
Create files	Create
Delete files	Erase
Change file attributes	Modify
List files	File scan
Change access control	Access control

In large companies with multiple NetWare servers for different departments, problems can occur when the list of accounts differs between NetWare servers. If you keep getting messages stating that the pass-through server has not been specified, change it so that one NetWare server appropriately has all the accounts, and set that server as the security provider.

Setting up a user profile on a NetWare network

As long as the computer is configured to use Microsoft Client for NetWare Networks, you can utilize user profiles with Windows 95 on a NetWare network. Whenever a new user account is created on a NetWare server, a subdirectory of the **mail** directory is automatically created for the user. This is where Windows 95 stores user profiles.

To set up user profiles for a Novell NetWare network make sure

- User profiles are enabled on each computer.

- The Client for NetWare Networks is selected as the Primary Network Logon client in the Network option in the Control Panel.

- Each user has an established **mail** directory.

Setup for automatic downloading of system policies

By default Windows 95 automatically downloads system policies that are running on NetWare networks. Policies for client computers using NETX or VLM must be downloaded manually. If you want to download a NetWare network policy file and set up automatic downloading, do the following:

1. Under the Network option in Control Panel, make sure that Microsoft Client for NetWare Networks is selected as the Primary Network Logon client, and that a preferred server is selected in the properties for the network client.

2. Create the policy file to be downloaded, and save it to *preferred_server*\sys\public\config.pol.

Concept Questions   *Semester 2, Unit 11, Lesson 53*

Demonstrate your knowledge of the concepts in this lesson by answering the following questions in the space provided.

1. Explain the differences and similarities in installing file and printer sharing on Windows NT with NetWare.

2. Explain the differences and similarities for workgroup advertising and SAP advertising.

_____

_____

_____

_____

_____

_____

_____

_____

_____

_____

_____

_____

_____

_____

_____

_____

Vocabulary Exercise   *Semester 2, Unit 11, Lesson 53*

Name: _____

Date: _____   *Class:* _____

Define the following terms as completely as you can.

bindery

_____

_____

connectivity

_____

_____

security provider

_____

_____

Focus Questions   *Semester 2, Unit 11, Lesson 53*

Name: _____

Date: _____   *Class:* _____

1. Describe what is required for a Windows computer to use file and printer sharing on a NetWare network.

_____

_____

_____

2. Describe how you share resources with user-level security.

_____

_____

_____

3. Describe how you set up a user profile on a NetWare network.

_____

_____

_____

4. Describe how you set up automatic downloading of system policies.

_____

_____

_____

SEMESTER 2, UNIT 11, LESSON 54
Troubleshooting Windows 95 on a Novell Network

You have learned a bit about sharing and managing Windows 95 resources in a Novell NetWare network. What happens when problems come up in this type of network? That's what we'll examine in this lesson.

Troubleshooting NetWare interoperability

One slight oversight can cause a Windows 95 machine to fail to communicate on a NetWare network. Table 11-2 lists some examples of common **interoperability** problems.

Table 11-2 *NetWare interoperability challenges*

Problem	Probable Cause	Solution
Windows 95 user attaches to a NetWare server as a guest to receive an account, but cannot use the new account to connect to the NetWare server.	When attaching as a guest, you have the option to save the guest username and password in the password list. When you reattach to that server, the username and password for that server are applied to the password list.	To update a password list with new account information, right-click the server's icon and click Attach as. Enter new credentials, and check the list box Save this password in your password.
The user cannot access resources on a Windows 95 server running file and printer sharing for NetWare networks.	The security provider is unavailable.	The security provider must be present to authenticate logon requests.
The logon script does not execute completely.	**Terminate and stay resident (TSR)** programs and NetWare 4.x–specific commands are not processed by the Windows 95 logon script processor.	Load the TSRs in **autoexec.bat** or **winstart.bat** instead.
NetWare Supervisor cannot administer the server by running **sys.con** on a Windows 95–based computer.	**sys.con** was called up through Network Neighborhood or by direct UNC command.	Many NetWare utilities work only when run from a mapped drive, or when a mapped drive is in the search path.

Troubleshooting Microsoft Client for NetWare Networks

A few problems can occur while you are installing, configuring, or using Microsoft Client for NetWare Networks. Before getting to specific situations, make sure that the version of **netware.drv** is at least 2 KB. If it is much larger than that, remove Client for NetWare Networks in the Network option of the Control Panel and reinstall it. Common problems and solutions are listed in Table 11-3.

Table 11-3   *Common Microsoft Client for NetWare Networks problems and solutions*

Problem	Solution
No network is available after Windows 95 starts.	Try the following: • Verify that Client for NetWare Networks is installed. • Use the Network option in Control Panel to view a list of installed clients, protocols, and services. • Verify that the IPX/SPX-compatible protocol is in the list of installed components.
The login script does not run.	Make sure that the correct preferred server is set and that Enable Login Script Processing is checked in the properties for Client for NetWare Networks.
NetWare servers can't be found.	Make sure you are in the right frame type for the server: • Verify the frame type set in the advanced properties for the IPX/SPX-compatible protocol in the Network option in the Control Panel. • Switch the setting from Auto to the specific frame type used on the server. Make sure that the bindery set for the server directory includes the Windows 95 users who should have server access. Try one of the following: • To view and set the bindery context on NetWare 4.x servers, load the **servman** NetWare loadable module. • View and set the **set bindery context** parameter. • Type **set** at the command prompt to view the **set** parameters.

Problem	Solution
Every logon requires a Windows 95 password and a NetWare password.	Make the passwords the same for both the NetWare server and Windows 95.
Access to NetWare servers is denied.	Because Client for NetWare Networks uses the credentials provided for preferred server authentication to access other NetWare servers, make sure the credentials on all the NetWare servers is identical by using the Novell **setpass** command at the command prompt.

Troubleshooting Windows 95 using Novell NetWare clients

Before you do any other troubleshooting, make sure that the **netware.drv** file version 3.03.94.280 or later for VLM as well as version 2.02 or later for NETX are present. If necessary, restore this file from the Novell-supplied installation source. Some general preventive measures include the following:

- Check the version numbers of all NetWare workstation components, including IPX, NETX, VLM, LSL, IPXODI, and the ODI driver files. Make sure the latest versions are in use.

- Check for multiple copies of the NetWare files. Remove all but the most recent copies.

- Make sure IPXODI is binding to the network adapter by running the NetWare **never** utility, using the same settings as **net.cfg** and the same link driver name. If IPXODI is not bound to the network adapter, change the entries in **net.cfg** to correct the problem.

- For monolithic configurations, make sure the configuration does not use the **/o#** switch on **ipx.com** or the **config option=** statement in **shell.cfg**.

- If the user is running a shared copy of Windows 95, make sure the home directory and the shared Windows directory are the first two items in the path.

Some specific common troubleshooting items are listed in Table 11-4. For additional help with troubleshooting consult the Windows 95 Resource Kit and other sources that are discussed in Unit 14.

Table 11-4 *Common troubleshooting items for Windows 95 using Novell NetWare clients*

Error Message	Solution
Setup requires Novell Workstation Shell Installation Program.	Follow the instructions contained in "VLM Technical Notes" in the Windows 95 Resource Kit.
Cannot attach to the NetWare file server after installing Windows 95.	Verify the frame type used by the NetWare server, and if necessary, manually edit **net.cpg** so that the correct frame type is first in the link driver section.
Cannot see other computers running Windows 95 or NetWare server.	Try the following: • Determine the frame type at the site and verify that it is listed as **net.cfg**. • Verify that the correct **net.cfg** is being processed by **lsl.com**. • Verify that **net.cfg** has the correct settings for the network adapter, and restore this file from a correct backup version or edit it with the correct settings if necessary. • Verify that you are running the current version of the Novell-supplied ODI drivers and support files. • Make sure both client computers are running the same protocol, and if they are on different sides of a router, make sure that both computers are using the IPX/SPX-compatible protocol.
Cannot access the login drive after installing Windows 95.	It is not necessary to log on to NetWare server by using the drive letter F. The NetWare login drive is the next drive letter available after the **LastDrive=** statement in the Registry.
Doesn't run after installing VLM support under Windows 95.	Make sure the VLM client has been installed by using the Network option in the Control Panel.
Windows directory contains **nwsysvol\login\login.exe**.	This prevents the computer from incorrectly responding as the preferred server for other NetWare clients. See **win95rk.hlp** for information.

Concept Questions   *Semester 2, Unit 11, Lesson 54*

Demonstrate your knowledge of the concepts in this lesson by answering the following questions in the space provided.

1. Explain how to troubleshoot for NetWare interoperability with Windows 95.

2. Explain action you should take first when troubleshooting Windows 95 using Novell NetWare Client.

_____

_____

_____

_____

_____

_____

_____

_____

_____

_____

_____

_____

_____

_____

_____

_____

_____

Vocabulary Exercise   *Semester 2, Unit 11, Lesson 54*

Name: _____

Date: _____   *Class:* _____

Define the following terms as completely as you can.

interoperability

_____

_____

TSR

_____

_____

Focus Questions

Semester 2, Unit 11, Lesson 54

Name: _____

Date: _____   *Class:* _____

1. Describe how to troubleshoot for NetWare interoperability with Windows 95.

_____

_____

_____

_____

2. Describe common troubleshooting problems and solutions when installing, configuring, or using Microsoft Client for NetWare Networks.

_____

_____

_____

_____

3. Describe common troubleshooting problems and solutions when using Novell NetWare Client.

_____

_____

_____

_____

SEMESTER 2, UNIT 11, LESSON 55
Unit 11 Exam

If you have access to the online Aries A+ curriculum, contact your instructor for the Assessment System URL. If you do not have access to the online curriculum, please continue to Unit 12.

SEMESTER 2, UNIT 12

- Lesson 56: Modems and Dial-up Networking
- Lesson 57: Dial-up Networking Servers and Services
- Lesson 58: Dial-up Networking and the Internet
- Lesson 59: Troubleshooting Dial-up Networking
- Lesson 60: Unit 12 Exam

SEMESTER 2, UNIT 12, LESSON 56
Modems and Dial-up Networking

You have learned about troubleshooting in a Novell network. In this lesson, you will learn about that amazing little device that is your gateway to the Internet: the modem. You'll also learn how to use a modem to connect with the world of cyberspace.

Modems

You've probably used a **modem** before, and heard the irritating howl it lets out as it connects to an **Internet service provider (ISP)**. The word *modem* is an abbreviation, a blend of the terms **modulation** and **demodulation**, which is a description of what happens to the computer's data when it is converted from digital to analog form for transfer and vice versa.

Modems are designed to send computer data over ordinary phone lines (the appropriate technojargon is POTS, for plain old telephone system). They convert (or modulate) digital computer signals into analog signals the phone line can recognize. At the other end, another modem demodulates the modem's signal back into the 1s and 0s of binary computer language, and this is how computers talk to each other on the phone. Because the data signal is translated into audible tones, you could even say the computer is singing when you use it.

Part of what a modem is doing when it makes noises is negotiating parameters, such as speed of data transmission, with the modem on the other end. This process is called **handshaking**, and it happens at the beginning of every connection between modems.

You have several choices as to what type of modem you use. An external modem is a small device about the size of a paperback novel that connects to a serial COM port on the back of the computer. Internal modems are usually preinstalled and preconfigured in newer computers. If you install an internal modem yourself, configuring it can be a bit tricky, and can involve disabling COM ports and choosing IRQ settings.

If you have a laptop, you can buy a **Personal Computer Memory Card International Association (PCMCIA)** modem, a device a little larger than a credit card, and plug it into a slot on the side of your laptop. In Windows 95 you can plug or unplug a PCMCIA modem while the computer is on without causing any damage, a feature that makes this type of modem very convenient.

Connecting a modem

If you have an internal or a PCMCIA modem, the necessary connections to the computer are made when it is installed, and you only need to connect it to a telephone line. If you have an external modem, you need to physically connect it to the computer, a phone line, and a power source. There are phone jacks and a power connection on the back of the modem for this purpose.

First, make sure the computer is shut off, and then take a look at the connections on the back. You probably have several serial or COM ports on the back of the PC, and the mouse is no doubt occupying one of them. You plug the modem into another one, using either a 9-pin or 25-pin connector.

Run a line from the phone jack on the wall and plug it into the IN jack on the modem (this jack may be labeled LINE or WALL instead). If you need this line when the modem is not in use, you can plug the phone into the OUT jack (also called PHONE or TEL on some units). This way when you're not using the modem, you are able to use the phone as usual.

The modem should also have a power cord, which plugs in to a power outlet and in to the back of the modem.

Setting up a modem

When the internal, external, or PCMCIA modem is properly connected, it's time to install Windows **telephony application programming interface (TAPI)** support. TAPI is the Windows 95 protocol for modem configuration. Upon installation, Windows 95 is able to configure modems that are already hooked up to the computer. If you are installing a modem on an existing Windows 95 system, you need to set up the modem as follows:

1. Select Start, Settings, Control Panel. (Or you can double-click the My Computer icon to find the Control Panel folder.)

2. Open the Modems icon. The Install New Modem Wizard helps you set up the necessary support for the modem. In most cases, Windows 95 figures out what kind of modem you have and does the setup automatically. In the event that Windows can't recognize the modem, the Modem Wizard allows you to choose a modem from a list. The Don't detect my modem checkbox exists for this purpose, so you, instead of Windows, can decide what modem configuration the computer should use.

3. To allow Windows 95 to continue with the normal setup process, click Next. Windows systematically tests each serial (COM) port until it finds the one occupied by the modem. It then assesses the modem, checks it against the Windows internal database of modem types, and displays the modem's name in the Verify Modem window. If the choice Windows makes doesn't match the modem, you can click the Change button to search the list for a better choice. If you don't find one that matches, you can either choose Standard, which works in most cases, or trust that the first choice Windows makes, although not a perfect match, is chosen because it is compatible with your modem. Windows 95 is usually able to determine the best possible match from among the available modem support options.

If you have a brand new modem, it might come with a CD or floppy containing new and updated drivers. To install these drivers, click the Have Disk button in the Install New Modem window.

When you set up the modem for the first time, you are asked to enter information about the default location—that is, the country and area code from which you will be dialing when you go online. If you need to dial a specific number to access an outside line from your office, such as 9, you can enter this information, and it will be automatically used every time you dial out on the modem. You can also store calling card numbers that will be automatically accessed for each call.

ISDN adapters

An **Integrated Services Digital Network (ISDN)** adapter serves the same function as a modem, but operates in a different way. An **ISDN adapter** uses a high-speed, digital signal with a special digital phone line. ISDN adapters can communicate only with each other, and can transmit data at much faster speeds than POTS lines. They do not modulate and demodulate as modems do because they do not have to contend with the analog signal found on regular telephone lines. Like regular modems, they can be internal or external.

Dial-up networking

When you have completed the modem setup, you're ready for the next phase in the quest to connect to the Internet: installing **dial-up networking**. You've learned about other types of networks in which computers are connected to each other using a network adapter. This allows computers in the same office or even the same building to send data back and forth and access shared printers.

Dial-up networking is another way for computers to talk to each other, but in this case the connection to the network is a phone line and the adapter is a modem. Dial-up networking opens up a myriad of possibilities because it offers the potential to connect with any other computer in the world that has modem capability and access to a telephone line.

When you access the Internet, information comes to you when the computer and the ISP's computer connect via modem. When you send email, the message goes out to another computer, where it is stored until the recipient retrieves it. People use dial-up networking to shop, check their bank balances, talk to friends and family, read the news, find information on the weather, and look for work. It's a connection to the rest of the world through a computer.

Dial-up networking setup

Before you begin to use Windows 95's Dial-Up Networking features, you need to make sure it's activated and ready for use. Follow these steps:

1. Open the Start menu, and choose Settings. Open the Control Panel.

2. Double-click the Add/Remove Programs icon, and open the Add/Remove Programs Properties Window.

3. Access the Windows Setup tab.

4. Double-click the Communications option, and the Dial-Up Networking box appears. Click this box, and the dial-up networking component is added to your system.

You can verify that installation is successful by opening the My Computer icon on the desktop. If all went well, a folder called Dial-Up Networking appears there.

Making a dial-up connections

Now you need to access the Dial-Up Networking folder and give the computer some information. Select the Start menu, and choose Programs, Accessories. Then choose Dial-Up Networking. (You can also access this folder by opening the My Computer icon.)

In the Dial-Up Networking folder there is a Make New Connection icon. Double-clicking this starts the Make New Connection Wizard. Click Next to proceed. A window appears, and you can enter connection settings. You need to type the name of the connection in the space provided. The name should describe the connection, such as the name of the ISP. In the Select a Modem box, you have the opportunity to choose the modem you'll use to make the connection (Windows allows you to have more than one modem connected to a computer, but most of us only have one.) If you have just one modem connected to your system, simply click Next to continue.

The next window asks you to type in the modem phone number, complete with area code, for the ISP. The country code box gives you the opportunity to include an international dialing country code if you are calling from outside the United States. Click Next, and the wizard lets you know that you have completed the setup process. Click Finish to close the session with Connection Wizard. Remember that you can go through this process multiple times and create several connections if your ISP has more than one modem number, or if you have more than one ISP. Your new connections(s) shows up as an icon in the Dial-Up Networking window.

After all this, you must be feeling pretty ready to blaze off into cyberspace and explore the Internet. You're not quite ready, but setup for all these connections only needs to be done once, and after that, getting on line will be a breeze, as long as your ISP's modem line isn't busy. Go to the Dial-Up Networking window, and double-click the icon for your connection.

You are prompted to enter the username and password assigned by the ISP. If you don't want to be prompted to enter the password every time you log on, click the Save Password checkbox. If you have concerns about anyone else accessing the connection, leave this box unchecked and enter the password each time you use it. This way, no one except you and those with whom you share your password can log on to the ISP from the computer.

Dial-up servers

Your newly minted connection is now configured to allow you to click its dial-up icon and connect to the ISP's remote access server. Windows 95 provides support for a wide variety of protocols, such as the following:

- Windows 95 Dial-Up Server

- Windows NT 3.1 or higher

- Windows NT Workstation

- Windows for Workgroups 3.11

- Microsoft LANManager

- NetWare Connect

- Shiva LANRover and other dial-up routers

- Any UNIX server that supports Serial Line Internet Protocol (SLIP) or Point-to-Point Protocol (PPP)

Explicit and implicit connections

Now that you've learned how to create new dial-up connections, you should know that they can be started in one of two ways: explicit or implicit.

Explicit connections, like the one to your ISP, are started by double-clicking on the icon in the Dial-Up Networking folder.

Implicit connections are not available physically on the network. When you try to connect, you get a message asking you to use Dial-Up Networking to connect. Here are some examples of attempted actions that cause a computer to try to make an implicit connection:

- Attempting to use a persistent, mapped network drive connection

- Attempting to double-click a shortcut to a remote file or printer

- Attempting to print to a remote printer

To disable implicit connections, click Settings in the Connections menu. Look in the Settings dialog box, and select Do not prompt to use Dial-Up Networking.

Dial-up adapters

A **dial-up adapter** works with the Windows 95 communications device driver. It prevents the network from detecting that a modem is being used instead of a network adapter. The dial-up adapter is automatically activated via the Dial-Up Networking folder when you select Connections from the menu bar and click Dial-Up Server for the first time. If you don't already have a modem installed the first time you do this, the computer prompts you to install one.

Concept Questions   *Semester 2, Unit 12, Lesson 56*

Demonstrate your knowledge of the concepts in this lesson by answering the
following questions in the space provided.

1. Explain the function of a modem.

2. Explain the difference between an ISDN adapter and a modem.

_____

_____

_____

_____

_____

_____

_____

_____

_____

_____

_____

_____

_____

_____

_____

_____

_____

Vocabulary Exercise   *Semester 2, Unit 12, Lesson 56*

Name: _____

Date: _____   *Class:* _____

Define the following terms as completely as you can.

demodulation

_____

_____

dial-up adapter

_____

_____

dial-up networking

_____

_____

handshake

_____

_____

ISDN

_____

_____

ISDN adapter

_____

_____

ISP

_____

_____

handshaking

_____

_____

modem

_____

_____

modulation

_____

_____

PCMCIA

_____

_____

TAPI

_____

_____

Focus Questions   *Semester 2, Unit 12, Lesson 56*

Name: _____

Date: _____   *Class:* _____

1. Describe how are modems connected.

_____

_____

_____

_____

2. Describe how you set up a modem.

_____

_____

_____

_____

3. Describe how you configure dial-up networking.

_____

_____

_____

_____

4. Describe how you configure a dial-up connection.

_____

_____

_____

_____

5. Describe what happens when you are making a connection.

_____

_____

_____

_____

6. Describe explicit and implicit connections.

_____

_____

_____

_____

SEMESTER 2, UNIT 12, LESSON 57
Dial-up Networking Servers and Services

You have learned about modems and how to use Windows 95 to create a connection to the Internet. In this lesson, you'll learn about how to set up a PC to function as a dial-up networking server.

Installing Windows 95 Dial-Up Networking Server

To use a computer as a server, you need to configure the Windows feature Dial-Up Networking Server. Dial-Up Networking Server was not included in the original release of Windows 95. To use this feature, you need Windows 95 OSR2, Windows 95 ISDN Accelerator Pack, or Microsoft Plus.

Configuring Windows 95 Dial-Up Networking Server

Open the Dial-Up Networking folder and find Dial-Up Server on the Connections menu. Here you can access the Dial-Up Server dialog box. Click Allow Caller Access. (If needed, you can opt here to change the call-in password for clients by clicking Change Password.)

Next, choose the type of server you are using by clicking the Server Type button. Users of Windows 95, Windows NT, Windows for Workgroups 3.11, Workgroup Add-on for MS-DOS, and LANManager can dial in by using **Point-to-Point Protocol (PPP)** or **Remote Access Server (RAS)** protocols. If you select Default instead of specifying a line protocol, you allow the modems on both ends of the connection to negotiate the best common protocol. As soon as you click OK, the server is ready to accept calls.

Configuring Windows NT Dial-Up Server

Unlike Windows 95 dial-up servers, Windows NT servers can support TCP/IP instead of PPP. To configure Windows NT for this:

1. Open the Connections Properties dialog box, and click the Server button.

2. Click the Settings button.

Unlike Windows 95, which must use a server-assigned IP address, Windows NT can assign the address itself, or relay the address request to a Dynamic Host Configuration Protocol (DHCP) server. You can specify an IP address. Windows NT, unlike Windows 95, is able to assign name server addresses by exchanging information with a DHCP server. You can also specify addresses.

Windows 95, Windows 95 OSR2, and Windows NT servers support callback security. This feature protects the server by disconnecting remote users immediately after their calls are authenticated, and then dials them back at a specified phone number.

Server security

There are two kinds of security available in Windows:

- With share-level security, passwords are designated for shared folders or disk drives, and they are managed by a network administrator. The administrator can make changes to shared resources on the computer and anywhere else on the network. Network passwords for share-level security are usually stored on the administrator's computer.

- In the case of user-level security, which can only be used on Windows NT or NetWare servers, you and the network administrator can control who has access to your resources. The list of users who have access is stored on the computer.

The network administrator, who has remote authority over the computer, can allow other users to access the computer or the network. The complete list of users is kept on the Windows NT or NetWare server, including those who have access at the network administrator level.

It is recommended that you choose one type of security and use it exclusively, and not switch back and forth between the two types.

Follow these steps to set up security:

1. Open the Control Panel and double-click the Network icon.

2. Open the Access Control tab, and you see the Network Access Control properties sheet.

3. Choose either share-level or user-level access.

4. In User-level access, specify which server should hold the list of users.

5. Click OK, and then restart the computer so that the security settings take effect.

Virtual private networking

Virtual private networking (VPN) is a means by which secure networks can be created on and accessed over the World Wide Web. It's a way for private companies and organizations to use the Internet as if it were a secure, in-house network, while allowing worldwide access only to a select few who have been given permission to see privileged information.

The protocol that makes this network-within-a-network concept possible is called **tunneling protocol**. This protocol ensures privacy within an extremely public communications structure by encrypting data and network addresses on both ends of the transmission. Windows NT has **Point-to-Point Tunneling Protocol (PPTP)** built in for creating and using VPNs.

Concept Questions   *Semester 2, Unit 12, Lesson 57*

Demonstrate your knowledge of the concepts in this lesson by answering the following questions in the space provided.

1. Explain the protocols used by the Windows 95 Dial-Up Networking Server.

2. Explain the protocols used by the Windows NT Dial-Up Server.

_____

_____

_____

_____

_____

_____

_____

_____

_____

_____

_____

_____

_____

_____

_____

_____

_____

_____

_____

Vocabulary Exercise   *Semester 2, Unit 12, Lesson 57*

Name: _____

Date: _____   Class: _____

Define the following terms as completely as you can.

PPP

_____

_____

PPTP

_____

_____

RAS

_____

_____

tunneling protocol

_____

_____

VPN

_____

_____

Focus Questions   *Semester 2, Unit 12, Lesson 57*

Name: _____

Date: _____   *Class:* _____

1. Describe what is needed to install Windows 95 Dial-Up Networking Server.

_____

_____

_____

_____

2. Describe how you configure Windows 95 Dial-Up Networking Server.

_____

_____

_____

_____

3. Describe how you configure Windows NT Dial-Up Server.

_____

_____

_____

_____

4. Describe the two kinds of security available in Windows.

_____

_____

_____

_____

5. Describe how you set up security.

_____

_____

_____

_____

SEMESTER 2, UNIT 12, LESSON 58
Dial-up Networking and the Internet

You have learned about Windows 95 and Windows NT Dial-Up Server. In this lesson you will learn more about the Internet and your Internet connection. As you have learned, Windows uses dial-up networking to connect users to ISPs. Windows uses different connection protocols, depending on which system the ISP uses. If the ISP is using Windows NT to run its servers, you use Point-to-Point Protocol (PPP) to connect. If it uses UNIX, you can use PPP or **Serial Line Internet Protocol (SLIP)**.

SLIP

SLIP is compatible with UNIX servers and has been in existence longer than PPP. Being an older protocol, it is less secure, slower, and not as sturdy as PPP. It is also not capable of error correction/detection and gets passwords as clear text.

Installing SLIP and CSLIP

If a computer is running the original release of Windows 95, you have to install SLIP or CSLIP (a version of SLIP that offers IP header compression), which you can find in the Windows 95 Resource Kit, Microsoft Plus, or the **admin\nettools\slip** folder on the Windows 95 CD.

Scripting

SLIP servers initially ask you to enter your username and password by hand. Dial-up networking gives you the option to automate this action by using a script. If you install SLIP by using the Windows 95 Resource Kit or Microsoft Plus, scripting is installed automatically. You also have the capability to create and edit scripts, in the Accessories folder, where you find an option called Dial-Up Scripting.

The Internet

The **Internet** began in the 1960s, when the U.S. Department of Defense created a computerized communications network (called ARPANET, for Advanced Research Project Agency Network) to make research information available to scientists nationwide. Then in the 1980s, The National Science Foundation linked colleges and other research institutions in an improved, faster network linked to major computing centers around the United States.

The current World Wide Web is a diverse collection of large networks owned by big corporations. They interface with many smaller business, academic, and government systems, which in turn connect to privately owned service providers. The result is more than 12 million users on 100,000 interconnected networks in more than 100 countries. For you, the user, it means access to a mind-boggling amount of free information, through a simple connection to an ISP.

Network access points

Several major connection points in the United States join all the ISPs together, making it possible for a computer user somewhere where in the Pacific Northwest to contact another user in the Texas panhandle. Called **network access points (NAPs)**, these connection points are networks that provide services and support most well-known protocols. Regional NAPs are interconnected to the point that one entire NAP could interrupt service temporarily without hampering the rest of the Internet.

Some current NAPs are

- The Chicago NAP, operated by Ameritech

- The New York NAP, operated by Sprint

- The San Francisco NAP, operated by PacBell

- The Washington, DC, NAP, operated by WorldCom, and also called MAE East

- MAE West, in California's Silicon Valley, operated by WorldCom

- Big East, operated by ICS Network Systems

ISPs

You have learned how to configure a computer and modem to go online. Now you need someone to connect to, so you can open the door to the world of the Web. Who do you call? An ISP.

There are so many companies to choose from that if you don't already have a provider in mind, a quick browse through the local newspaper or yellow pages should yield several ads for Internet connections. You should be able to get online and have an email account for about $20 per month. Unless you live in an extremely rural area, the call your modem makes to the ISP will be a local call, so costs there will be minimal as well.

You can go with a small, independent provider, or sign up with a large national service such as America Online or CompuServe, both of which offer their own proprietary services in addition to Internet access. Whatever ISP you choose, it will be your connection to a regional NAP, and then the Internet universe will be at your command.

Intranets

Perhaps you've heard the term **intranet**, which sounds almost like Internet, but whose meaning is a bit different. Remember back to when you learned about how prefixes affect the meanings of words; *inter-* means *between*, and *intra-* means *within*. That's why intercoms work between rooms, and intravenous medication is circulated within the body.

Following that drift, the Internet should be a network that works between organizations, and an intranet should be a network that functions within one—and this is exactly the case. So, if you work for a company that has its own network for sending information from one office to another within the organization, that system is an intranet.

The Microsoft Internet strategy

Microsoft has long-term goals in place to ensure that its products meet the needs of a growing Internet market. In the future, look for more Internet capabilities in Microsoft products and services as the company seeks to assist organizations and other end users in meeting their technological needs. Microsoft will focus on three important areas:

- Leveraging Internet connectivity with distributed applications

- Creating, enhancing, and adopting Internet standards for data transmission and retrieval

- Joining forces within the computer industry to enhance the quality and scope of Internet services

Windows 95 on the Internet and intranets

Windows 95 has built-in features designed to support both private intranet use and Internet capability, such as the following:

- TCP/IP connectivity

- RAS to connect to ISPs

- Internet Explorer, used to access the Web, File Transfer Protocol (FTP), and Gopher resources

- Internet Mail and News

- Microsoft NetMeeting, useful for exchanging messages with Internet users and newsgroups

- Personal Web Server, used for publishing Web and FTP resources

In the event that your copy of Windows 95 does not include all these resources, you can access the Microsoft Web site at **www.microsoft.com/ic/** and download Internet Explorer, Internet Mail and News, NetMeeting, and Personal Web Server, free of charge.

TCP/IP

TCP/IP is an acronym that describes the two protocols which work together to allow Windows 95 and the Internet to communicate. All the computers on the Internet use TCP/IP as their common language.

TCP stands for *Transmission Control Protocol*. As its name implies, this protocol controls transmission by coordinating with IP to prepare packets of data for transfer over the Internet, and coordinates them at the other end of the transfer, so that everything ends up in the proper place.

IP stands for *Internet Protocol*, the basis for all Internet communication. Your computer, like every other computer online, has its own IP address that distinguishes it from any other.

Installing and configuring TCP/IP

If you want to connect to the Internet, you need to install TCP/IP. If it wasn't installed when you installed Windows 95, you can install it by following these steps:

1. Open the Control Panel.

2. Double-click on the Network icon, and then click the Add button.

3. You see the dialog box Select Network Component Type. Double-click Protocol.

4. In the Select Network Protocol dialog box is a Manufacturers List. Click Microsoft.

5. In the Network Protocols list, click Microsoft TCP/IP. Click OK.

6. You need to verify that TCP/IP is bound to the Microsoft dial-up adapter or a network adapter. You do this by scrolling through the list of network components in the Network window of the Control Panel. If you see an arrow next to TCP/IP that points to the dial-up adapter or to another network adapter, all is well.

Configuring a TCP/IP connection

It's time to set up your TCP/IP connection. Go into the Control Panel and open the Network dialog box. This opens the TCP/IP properties sheet. You have a number of tabs to choose from. Start with IP Address. If you click the option Obtain an IP address automatically, Windows obtains an IP address for you from a DHCP server.

If you want to install the information manually, click Specify an IP address and enter the necessary information (your IP address and subnet mask). The assumption here is that your ISP has assigned you this information. If this is not the case, allow Windows to obtain the settings for you.

DNS configuration

In order to use TCP/IP to connect to the Internet, the computer needs to be able to recognize **Domain Name System (DNS)** information. DNS's purpose is to convert computer and domain names into IP addresses, and organize them. An ISP might assign IP addresses for DNS servers and if so, it will be done automatically as needed. If your ISP does not do this, obtain the needed information from the ISP because you'll need it to configure each dial-up connection you create.

When you're done entering information, click OK, and you're done configuring TCP/IP settings. Restart the computer to initiate the changes you just made.

Browsing the Internet

Unless you've been living in a cave or under a rock for the past few years, you've probably at least heard about browsing the Web. It's fun, it can be addictive, and it's a way to access mountains of information on just about any topic, complete with videos and sound.

In order to surf the Web, you need a Web browser. This handy tool is a program that brings the Internet within reach and allows you to conduct searches; view text, graphics, and video; and hear sound via the computer. The first browser to use a GUI was Mosaic, and its ease of use changed the way people interacted with the Internet. Today, the most popular browsers are Netscape's Navigator and Microsoft's Internet Explorer, both of which make connecting to the Internet a virtually stress-free process.

Internet Explorer

Internet Explorer is included with Windows 95, but if you want to obtain a more recent version, you can visit the Microsoft Web site at **www.microsoft.com** and download what you need for free. You can also download Navigator for free at **www.netscape.com**.

To install and configure Internet Explorer, you use the Internet Connection Wizard, which takes you step-by-step through the setup process. The wizard sets up your dial-up adapter and dial-up networking connection with the ISP. If you don't have an ISP yet, the wizard calls the Microsoft Internet referral server and locates a local ISP. The Wizard then gives you the opportunity to sign up with an ISP. It also installs Internet Explorer and its components.

To install Microsoft Internet Explorer, follow these steps:

1. Open the Start menu, and click Run to open the Run dialog box.

2. Type **c:\labs\msie301m95** and click **OK**. The Microsoft Internet Explorer Setup window appears, and you see an end user license agreement. Read the agreement and click Yes. The installation begins.

3. When the installation is complete, you see a dialog box asking if you want to choose optional Internet components to install. Click Yes.

4. When the Optional Components dialog box appears, click OK to install all available components.

5. An Installation Status dialog box appears, to inform you of the progress of component installation.

6. A Copying Files dialog box appears as required files are copied.

7. When the process is complete, click Yes to restart the computer and finalize setup.

Accessing Internet Resources

Everything on the Internet has an address, called a **uniform resource locator (URL)**. If you already know the URL for the information you are seeking, you can simply type it in, press Enter, and go there. If you don't know the URL, you can use a **search engine** to help find the site.

URLs follow a certain syntax. When you understand it, you can tell a great deal about where a document came from by deciphering its address. Here are the parts of URL syntax (for the purpose of illustration, let's say use the URL example **http://www.bleep.com**):

* **Access method**—This initial part of the URL shows the protocol used by the server. All Web sites have URLs that starts with **http** because that's the standard protocol for the Web.

* Host name—The second section of the URL is the domain name, usually expressed in the form of **www.bleep.com**. The **www** is the host name of the Web server, **bleep** is the site name, and **.com** indicates that the site is located in the Internet's commercial domain.

* Locators—Locators may come after the host name, indicating a specific location within the site. In the sample address **http://www.bleep.com/index.html**, **index.html** indicates that the specific location within the bleep site is the index page.

Controlling access to inappropriate content

The Internet offers access to an incredible variety of information, which represents a challenge for parents and other individuals who want to be able to control the information that is accessible through their computers. To meet this challenge, Microsoft offers the Content Advisor feature, which provides a way to block information users consider objectionable, material that under ordinary circumstances is just as accessible on the Internet as the daily news.

To access Content Advisor, open Explorer and open the View menu. Select Internet Options, and then choose the Content tab. When the Content box comes up, you see the Content Advisor option at the top. Clicking Enable allows you to set the restrictions that meet your needs.

Next, a dialog box asks you to create and confirm your supervisor password. After you have activated it, only those who know the password are able to alter settings. After you enter the password, you progress to the next dialog box, where you have three sections:

- Ratings—You can configure ratings in four categories: language, nudity, sex, and violence, and limit each one (by dragging the slide bar) according to a 0–5 rating scale, with 0 being the most restrictive. The ratings system used by Internet Explorer was developed by the Recreational Software Advisory Council (RSAC).

- General—This tab is designed to determine access to sites that have not been rated. Parents can choose to restrict access to all unrated sites, or to allow viewers with a password to view restricted content. You can also use this tab to change the supervisor password.

- Advanced—This tab is used to add other rating systems to your Web browser.

Personal Web Server

Personal Web Server is a Windows feature that allows you to publish Web pages and exchange files by using FTP. With Personal Web Server, you can turn any Windows 95 computer into a Web server. Personal Web Server comes with the NT 4.0 Option pack and OSR2, but is also designed to be used with Windows 95. You can also go to **www.microsoft.com/ie** and download it.

Personal Web Server features include the following:

- HTTP service

- FTP service

- ISAPI and CGI scripts

- Pass-through security to Windows NT and Novell NetWare, as long as a file and print sharing service is installed and configured for user-level access control

- Secure Sockets Layer (SSL) protocol

- Remote administration using Internet Explorer or another browser

Installing and administering Personal Web Server

Here's how you install Personal Web Server:

1. From the Start menu click Run to open the Run dialog box.

2. Type **c:\labs\pws10a** and click OK.

3. When the setup process is complete, click Yes to restart the computer.

4. Your default home page is **c:\webshare\wwwroot\default.htm**.

Here's how you use Personal Web Server:

1. Open the Start menu, and choose Run.

2. Enter **http://*your_computer*** and click OK. Internet Explorer opens, showing the home page.

3. Close Internet Explorer.

Here's how you administer Personal Web Server:

1. Go to the Control Panel and open the Personal Web Server icon.

2. Go to the Administration tab and choose the Administration button.

3. Right-click the Personal Web Server icon, and click Administer.

Securing Personal Web Server

Personal Web Server's authentication protocol is based on the security protocol used by Windows NT. It enables you to set permissions on the folders you publish on Web pages, just as you would in a user-level security situation on a network. If your version of Windows 95 does not support file and print sharing for Microsoft networks or NetWare networks, Personal Web Server uses a local user database to administer user-level security.

Concept Questions   *Semester 2, Unit 12, Lesson 58*

Demonstrate your knowledge of the concepts in this lesson by answering the following questions in the space provided.

1. Explain the origin of the Internet.

2. Explain the difference between the Internet and an intranet.

_____

_____

_____

_____

_____

_____

_____

_____

_____

_____

_____

_____

_____

_____

_____

_____

_____

_____

Vocabulary Exercise   *Semester 2, Unit 12, Lesson 58*

Name: _____

Date: _____   Class: _____

Define the following terms as completely as you can.

access method

_____

_____

DNS

_____

_____

Internet

_____

_____

intranet

_____

_____

NAP

_____

_____

search engine

_____

_____

SLIP

_____

_____

URL

_____

_____

Focus Questions   *Semester 2, Unit 12, Lesson 58*

Name: _____

Date: _____   *Class:* _____

1. Describe what protocols allow you use to connect to an ISP.

_____

_____

_____

2. Describe scripting with SLIP.

_____

_____

_____

3. Describe ISP options.

_____

_____

_____

4. Describe some built-in features of Windows 95 that support both intranets and the Internet.

_____

_____

_____

5. Describe how you install TCP/IP

_____

_____

_____

6. Describe how you configure TCP/IP.

_____

_____

_____

7. Describe what you need in order to browse the Internet.

_____

_____

_____

8. Describe some popular Internet browsers.

_____

_____

_____

9. Describe how you install Microsoft Internet Explorer.

_____

_____

_____

10. Describe what is meant by the host name.

_____

_____

_____

11. Describe what is meant by a locator.

_____

_____

_____

12. Describe the Content Advisor.

_____

_____

_____

13. Describe what is meant by Personal Web Server.

_____

_____

_____

14. Describe how you install and administer Personal Web Server.

_____

_____

_____

15. Describe how you secure Personal Web Server.

_____

_____

_____

SEMESTER 2, UNIT 12, LESSON 59
Troubleshooting Dial-up Networking

You have learned more about the Internet and the protocols and software that make it possible for you to browse and use its resources. In this lesson you'll learn about how to fix common problems that occur in dial-up networking.

You've followed all the directions, installed all the options, responded dutifully to requests from endless dialog boxes, and clicked on a multitude of buttons, all because we told you that when it was over it would really be over, and you'd never have to do it again. Now, the moment is finally here for you to fire up your modem, but it doesn't work. Don't panic. Into each computer user's life a little static must fall, and challenges are just part of the game. It's time to enter the wonderful world of troubleshooting.

Modem problems

All of a sudden your modem's dial-up connection doesn't work. What do you do? Look to the Modem Diagnostics program to save the day. Go to the Control Panel and select the Modems option. Look in the Diagnostics tab for the More Info button, and click it to run the diagnostics program. What it does is check out the modem to see if it is properly connected and receiving data. If the modem is functioning properly, but is still not connecting, the problem could be in one of three areas:

- The connection settings

- The connection program

- The modem on the other end of the transmission

You can also use the **modemlog.txt** file to troubleshoot modem problems. You can use it to record a log file of all AT commands from TAPI programs sent to your modem, as well as the results.

Dial-up networking problems

Windows 95/98 contains built-in support for connecting to an ISP, using PPP or SLIP. You get SLIP support with the CD-ROM version of Windows 95/98, with the CD-ROM Extras for Windows 95 upgrade, and with the Internet Jumpstart Kit that comes with Microsoft Plus for Windows 95.

If you are having problems with dial-up networking, remember that you have an additional resource at your fingertips: Windows online help. Another good resource is Microsoft's **Windows 95 Resource Kit**. Also, you can talk with live people by calling your ISP technical support line, and most likely someone there will walk you through the solution.

Before calling for help, you should first check to make sure you have installed your dial-up TCP connection correctly. For starters you need a PPP or SLIP account with an ISP. You need the following information from the ISP: Your username, password, and local access phone number; the host and domain name; the DNS server IP address; and the authentication technique. Next, you can check Table 12-1 for some common problems and suggested ways to handle them.

Table 12-1   *Common dial-up networking problems*

Problem	Solution
You try to access the dial-up networking server, and the computer tells you the username is not valid.	Check the properties sheet in the dial-up server and make sure the username is on the list of users permitted access. To set up dial-up networking server to allow caller access options, open the Dial-Up Networking folder, click the Connections menu, and choose Dial-Up Server. In Properties, choose Allow Caller Access, and look for the username to make sure it appears in the list. The name appears only if you are using user-level security for the server.
When making a dial-up connection, you are unable to access remote NetWare servers.	When you make the connection, disable file and printer sharing service for NetWare networks.
You are unable to compress software.	Check settings for both the server type and software compression. To verify settings, open the Dial-Up Networking folder and access the Connections menu. Click Dial-Up Server. Choose the Server Type button, and check to see if the proper type of dial-up server has been selected. Make sure that the Enable Software Compression option is selected.
Your modem dials, but cannot seem to connect.	Verify modem configuration, and correct it if needed. Verify the access code, area code, and country code. If these are all correct, try choosing Generic Modem Drivers. Check to see that cables are connected firmly. See if the COM port configuration is correct by accessing Device Manager.

Problem	Solution
The dial-up networking server is not responding to incoming calls.	Disable the Allow Caller Access option and shut down the computer. Then turn the computer off completely to reset the COM port. If you have an external modem, turn it off. Then restart the computer and reconfigure dial-up networking. If this process fails to correct the problem, disable Allow Caller Access, and find out whether your modem software can manually answer a call. Verify that all external modem connections are correct and firmly connected. In the case of internal modems with nonstandard IRQ selections, have Device Manager check IRQ settings for the COM port and revise as needed. Another option is to choose Generic Modem Drivers on the dial-up server.
You connect to your ISP, but have problems running email.	Whenever you configure Winsock applications such as Internet Explorer, Navigator, or Eudora, you must be sure to specify the correct server name, which you get from the ISP. The server types are POP, SMTP, and NNTP.
You've forgotten your password.	Disable Allow Caller Access and shut down and restart Windows 95. Delete the **rna.pwl** file, and then restart dial-up networking. Note that when you first connect to the dial-up networking server, you get an error message saying that the password file for your modem is missing or corrupt. You also see this message if you have any null modem devices.
You keep getting DNS errors or not found messages	If your DNS server is not correctly specified, you cannot resolve other computers by name. So if you can access an IP address with a numeric code, but not with its alphabetical name, you likely have a DNS problem. Because most ISPs support dynamically assigning DNS addresses when you log in to the server, the DNS entry should be blank. Otherwise, check with the ISP to find out what the DNS server address should be.

Concept Questions   *Semester 2, Unit 12, Lesson 59*

Demonstrate your knowledge of the concepts in this lesson by answering the following questions in the space provided.

1. Explain the function of the Modem Diagnostics option.

2. Explain what to do if you forget your password.

_____

_____

_____

_____

_____

_____

_____

_____

_____

_____

_____

_____

_____

_____

_____

_____

Vocabulary Exercise   *Semester 2, Unit 12, Lesson 59*

Name: _____

Date: _____   *Class:* _____

Define the following terms as completely as you can.

modemlog.txt

_____

_____

Windows 95 Resource Kit

_____

_____

Focus Questions   *Semester 2, Unit 12, Lesson 59*

Name: _____

Date: _____   *Class:* _____

1. Describe what you do if the modem's dial-up connection does not work.

_____

_____

_____

2. Describe possible problems with a modem's dial-up connection.

_____

_____

_____

3. Describe some resources to help troubleshoot dial-up networking problems.

_____

_____

_____

4. Describe what you do if the computer tells you the username is not valid when you try to access dial-up networking.

_____

_____

_____

5. Describe what you do if you are unable to remotely access the NetWare server when making a dial-up connection.

_____

_____

_____

6. Describe what you do if you are unable to compress software.

_____

_____

_____

7. Describe what you do if the modem dials but cannot seem to connect.

_____

_____

_____

8. Describe what you do if the dial-up networking server is not responding to incoming calls.

_____

_____

_____

9. Describe what you do if you keep getting DNS errors or not found messages.

_____

_____

_____

SEMESTER 2, UNIT 12, LESSON 60
Unit 12 Exam

If you have access to the online Aries A+ curriculum, contact your instructor for the Assessment System URL. If you do not have access to the online curriculum, please continue to Unit 13.

SEMESTER 2, UNIT 13

- Lesson 61: The Basics of Boot Files in Windows 95
- Lesson 62: The Basics of Initialization Files in Windows 95
- Lesson 63: The Boot and Initialization Process
- Lesson 64: Troubleshooting the Boot Process and Initialization
- Lesson 65: Unit 13 Exam

SEMESTER 2, UNIT 13, LESSON 61
The Basics of Boot Files in Windows 95

You have learned about the Internet and dial-up networking. Now you'll learn about a procedure that clears the memory, **loads** the operating system, and gets the computer ready for action. This, of course, is the **boot**. The term *boot*, short for *bootstrap*, refers to the initial startup of the computer. It does not refer to software applications. For example, you can boot a Windows 95 machine and load a Photoshop program, but you cannot boot Photoshop.

Files required to boot Windows 95

If you've been using computers for any period of time, you have used two different kinds of boots: a cold boot and a warm boot. Whereas a **cold boot** happens each time you start a computer from scratch, a **warm boot** occurs whenever you use a reset button or press Ctrl + Alt + Del. Warm boots are less stressful for the hardware components because the hard drive and other components don't stop and startup again. However, certain components such as modems and faxes require a cold boot for resetting.

Both cold boots and warm boots require specific files, or your computer would never function. Among the hundreds of files in the *win_dir* folder, the files that significantly affect booting Windows 95 include the following:

- **io.sys**—Boots into real-mode Windows 95, and loads real-mode drivers and **terminate and stay resident (TSRs)**.

- **msdos.sys**—Controls the boot process for compatibility with applications that require this file before installation. This file is marked hidden, system, and read-only.

- **config.sys**—Sets and specifies system environment factors, and loads real-mode drivers and TSRs. This file is optional.

- **autoexec.bat**—Sets and specifies commands to be executed in real-mode before protected-mode Windows 95 initializes. This file is optional.

- **win.com**—Initiates the Windows 95 load phases.

The Windows 95 booting process

The average computer user turns on the power and is completely satisfied when the computer boots up and works. This user's usual problem-solving ventures consist of shutting down the computer and rebooting it, and this solves the majority of the user's computer problems. As a computer technician, you need to know much more than the average computer user, especially about the booting process. The following distinct phases occur when you boot a Windows 95 machine:

- BIOS bootstrap

- Master boot record (MBR) and boot sector

- Real-mode boot

- Real-mode configuration

- Protected-mode load

The following sections describe these phases in detail.

BIOS bootstrap

This preboot phase is handled by the computer's BIOS, and includes the following steps:

1. A CheckScan test is performed.

2. A power-on self-test (POST) is performed.

3. The plug-and-play devices are identified and configured.

4. A bootable partition is located.

5. The MBR and the partition table are loaded.

6. The MBR program is executed.

MBR and boot sector

Programs on the hard disk handle this preboot phase, which includes the following steps:

1. The MBR program determines the location of the bootable partition on the hard disk and passes control to the boot sector in that partition.

2. The disk boot program finds the location of the root directory and copies **io.sys** from the root directory into memory.

Real-mode boot

When **io.sys** is loaded into memory, the real booting action begins. Windows does the following:

1. Loads a FAT file system in order to load additional operating system components. Remember that Windows 95 must support its 32-bit applications, Windows 3.x 16-bit applications, and DOS applications.

2. Loads an updated version of DOS because Intel processors initialize in real mode and because most DOS programs run in real mode.

3. Reads **msdos.sys**, which is a hidden, read-only file on the boot drive, for boot configuration parameters.

4. Displays the Starting Windows screen and pauses briefly for function keys.

5. Loads and displays the bitmap stored in **logo.sys**, if it exists. If it doesn't exist, Windows 95 can get a copy of the default image from **io.sys**.

6. Loads **drvspace.bin** to support compressed drives (if **dblspace.ini** is present).

7. Performs an integrity check on **system.dat**.

8. Loads **system.dat** if present. If it is not present, loads a backup of **system.dat**.

9. Initiates double-buffering for SCSI controllers if necessary.

10. Selects a hardware profile from the Registry, based on the detected hardware.

11. Reads and processes **config.sys** and **autoexec.bat**, if present. Note that the Windows 95 **io.sys** renders these two files unnecessary.

Real-mode configuration

Although **config.sys** and **autoexec.bat** are optional, **io.sys** processes these files if they exist. If no **config.sys** is present, Windows 95 automatically loads **himem.sys**, **ifship.sys**, and **server.exe**, and sets other variables. You should supply **config.sys** only if you want to override or add to the default settings.

Protected-mode load

As soon as **autoexec.bat** is run, **win.com** is executed automatically:

1. **win.com** loads **vmm32.vxd** and other virtual devices that are referenced in the Registry and in **system.ini**.

2. **win.com** changes the processor into protected mode and initializes the virtual device drivers.

3. The core Windows kernel, GDI, and user libraries are loaded, along with the Explorer shell and network support into a **virtual machine (VM)**.

4. Programs listed in **HKEY_LOCAL_MACHINE\software\microsoft\windows\currentversion\run once** are run.

5. The program list stored in this Registry key is deleted, and the boot process is complete, so that you have a working desktop.

Controlling the boot process

Controlling the boot process and getting an idea where problems exist is just one button away when you first see the Starting Windows screen. Simply press the F8 function key, and you see a Startup Menu screen. This same screen automatically appears at the beginning of a boot process if **io.sys** detects a previous boot failure or corrupted Registry.

While the actual contents of the startup menu may vary due to variations specified in the **msdos.sys** file and computer configurations, the following are the standard startup options:

- Normal—Starts Windows, loading all normal startup files and Registry values.

- Logged—Starts Windows normally, but takes much longer due to simultaneous log updating.

- Safe Mode—Starts Windows, using only the basic system drivers. It boots quickly because it bypasses the startup files. You can also start this option by pressing F5 or typing **win/d:m** at the command prompt.

- Safe Mode with Network Support—Starts Windows, bypassing startup files and using only basic system drivers, including basic networking. You can also start this option by pressing F6 or typing **win/d:m** at the command prompt.

- Step-By-Step Confirmation—Starts Windows, requiring you to confirm startup files line-by-line. You can also start this option by pressing F8 when the startup menu comes on the screen. Expect a long startup when you do this.

- Command Prompt Only—Starts the operating system, loading **himem.sys**, **ifship.sys**, **config.sys**, and **autoexec.bat**, but doesn't load the protected mode of Windows 95. You can also start this option by pressing F5.

- Safe Mode Command Prompt Only—Starts the operating system without loading **himem.sys**, **ifship.sys**, **config.sys**, and **autoexec.bat**, and does not load the protected mode of Windows 95. You can also start this option by pressing Alt + F5.

- Previous Version of MS-DOS—Starts the version of MS-DOS previously installed on the computer. You can also start this option by pressing F4.

Concept Questions   *Semester 2, Unit 13, Lesson 61*

Demonstrate your knowledge of the concepts in this lesson by answering the following questions in the space provided.

1. Explain the similarities and differences of cold boots and warm boots.

2. Explain the boot process.

_____

_____

_____

_____

_____

_____

_____

_____

_____

_____

_____

_____

_____

_____

_____

_____

_____

_____

_____

Vocabulary Exercise   *Semester 2, Unit 13, Lesson 61*

Name: _____

Date: _____ *Class:* _____

Define the following terms as completely as you can.

boot

_____

_____

cold boot

_____

_____

load

_____

_____

MBR

_____

_____

TSR

_____

_____

VM

_____

_____

warm boot

_____

_____

Focus Questions　　*Semester 2, Unit 13, Lesson 61*

Name: _____

Date: _____　　*Class:* _____

1. Describe the files that are needed to boot Windows 95.

_____

_____

_____

_____

2. Describe the Windows 95 boot process.

_____

_____

_____

_____

3. Describe how you access the startup menu screen.

_____

_____

_____

_____

SEMESTER 2, UNIT 13, LESSON 62
The Basics of Initialization Files in Windows 95

You are now ready to examine initialization files. Although the initialization process in Windows 95 works very much like that in Windows 3.x, you will learn about some significant differences between the two.

Files required to initialize Windows 95

When you run Windows 95 Setup to create a shared installation for a client computer, the client machine's directory stores the following information:

- **win.com**

- Appropriate **initialization (INI)** and **configuration files**

- The **Registry** for the shared installation, which consists of the **system.dat** and **user.dat** files

- Files that determine the desktop, the Start menu directories, and other programs

- The printing spool directory

The primary initialization files are **system.ini** and **win.ini**. However, Windows 95 has taken most of the configuration options from these two files and stored them in the Registry, so you need to examine the Registry to find most of these files.

The following **system.ini** options have relocated to the Registry in Windows 95:

- All network driver parameters

- The **lanabase=** parameter

The following **win.ini** options have relocated to the Registry in Windows 95:

- Font information

- Desktop information

Even though most of the configuration options have migrated to the Registry, there's still plenty of work for the **system.ini** and **win.ini** files to do. Some of these options are left behind for compatibility with applications written for older versions of Windows, and some new options have been added to the **system.ini** files. Table 13-1 shows the major additions.

Table 13-1   *Options added to **system.ini***

system.ini Section	Additional Options
Boot section	**comm.drv=comm.drv** **dibeng.drv=dibeng.dll** **gdi.exe=gdi.exe** **sound.drv=sound.drv** **user.exe=user.exe**
386Enh section	**device=*vshare** **device=*vcd** **device=*int13** **device=*dynapage**

DOS users and Windows 3.x users are familiar with using initialization files for startup configuration and for installing software because they have dealt with the INI files directly. These files function the same way in Windows 95, but fewer Windows 95 users are familiar with INI files because the Registry does the work for them.

To prevent users from making syntactical configuration errors, Windows 95 offers a more user-friendly Control Panel for installing and configuring devices and software. Any changes made through the Control Panel are recorded in the initialization files of the Registry.

The Windows 95 initialization process

When you set up Windows 95 or install software, it must interface properly with various hardware devices. Thus, device information files (**INF files**) provide information for installation. Whenever manufacturers create new hardware products, they must also create INF files to define the required files and resources. These INF files are formatted exactly like Windows 3.x INF files.

INF files are organized by hardware, and each type of device has its own section. The organization shown in Table 13-2 applies to each device section.

Table 13-2 *INF files*

INF File Section	Purpose and Function	Syntax
Version	Contains a simple header that identifies the INF and the type of device the INF supports.	**[Version] Signature="$Chicago$" Class=class name Provider=INF_creator LayoutFile=filename.inf**
Manufacturer and Manufacturer Name	Lists the manufacturers of the identified devices and all the models built by that manufacturer. At least one manufacturer is listed. Entries are displayed to generate correct Registry setting.	**[Manufacturer] manufacturer-name| %strings-key%=manufacturer-name-section [manufacturer-name] device-description=install-section-name, device-id [,compatible-device-id]...**
Install	Describes the device driver and physical attributes of the device. Includes names of all the Install sections that contain installation information.	**[install-section-name] LogConfig= log-config-section-name[,log-config-section-name]... Copyfiles=file-list-section[,file-list-section]... Renfiles=file-list-section[,file-list-section]... Delfiles=file-list-section[,file-list-section]... UpdateInis=update-ini-section[,update-ini-section]... UpdateIniFields=update-inifields-section[,update-inifields-section]... AddReg=add-Registry-section[,add-Registry-section]... DelReg=del-Registry-section[,del-Registry-section]... Ini2Reg=ini-to-Registry-section[,ini-to-Registry-section]... UpdateCfgSys=update-config-section UpdateAutoBat=update-autoexec-section Reboot | Restart**

INF File Section	Purpose and Function	Syntax
ClassInstall	An optional section that defines a new class for the device.	**[ClassInstall]** **Copyfiles=file-list-section[,file-list-section]…** **AddReg=add-Registry-section[,add-Registry-section]…** **Renfiles=file-list-section[,file-list-section]** **Delfiles=file-list-section[,file-list-section]…** **UpdateInis=update-ini-section[,update-ini-section]…** **UpdateIniFields=update-inifields-section[,update-inifield-sections]…** **AddReg=add-Registry-section[,add-Registry-section]…** **DelReg=del-Registry-section[,del-Registry-section]…**
Strings	Specifies all localized strings used in the INF file.	**[Strings]** **strings-key=value**

Concept Questions   *Semester 2, Unit 13, Lesson 62*

Demonstrate your knowledge of the concepts in this lesson by answering the following questions in the space provided.

1. Explain the Windows 95 initialization process.

2. Explain the similarities and differences in how **system.ini** and **win.ini** files are handled by Windows 3.x and Windows 95.

_____

_____

_____

_____

_____

_____

_____

_____

_____

_____

_____

_____

_____

_____

_____

_____

_____

_____

Vocabulary Exercise   *Semester 2, Unit 13, Lesson 62*

Name: _____

Date: _____   *Class:* _____

Define the following terms as completely as you can.

configuration

_____

_____

INF files

_____

_____

initialization

_____

_____

Registry

_____

_____

system.ini

_____

_____

win.ini

_____

_____

Focus Questions   *Semester 2, Unit 13, Lesson 62*

Name: _____

Date: _____   *Class:* _____

1. Describe the primary initialization files.

_____

_____

_____

_____

2. Describe what information a Windows 95 client stores when first setting it up.

_____

_____

_____

_____

3. Describe the major INF files that are affected by new software installation, and describe each INF file's function.

_____

_____

_____

_____

SEMESTER 2, UNIT 13, LESSON 63
The Boot and Initialization Process

You have a five-minute break—just enough time to run to the restroom and check your e-mail—so you race to your computer and start it up. As the time ticks away you hear buzzing, whirring, and clicking, and finally the Starting Windows 95 screen pops up. Then you wait some more for the desktop to appear, just as your time is almost up. This scenario describes one of the few times that the average user thinks about the boot process, but the technician must know more about the boot process than the average user. This lesson focuses on the boot and initialization process itself.

The BIOS bootstrap

The reason the computer takes so long to boot is that it must read through a series of lists and relearn everything it once knew. Much of this read-only process takes place in the BIOS.

Because Microsoft worked with several hardware manufacturers (Intel, Compaq, and Phoenix Technologies) to develop a standard BIOS specification, most of the machines you see have a plug-and-play BIOS. However, you occasionally encounter a machine with a legacy BIOS. In legacy computers, the BIOS enables all devices on the ISA bus. Thus, a plug-and-play ISA card with an option ROM must start up when the computer is turned on, with the option ROM enabled. A plug-and-play BIOS goes through a fairly complex process:

1. It accesses nonvolatile RAM.

2. It determines which plug-and-play PCI or ISA cards should be enabled.

3. It determines where the option ROMs should be mapped.

4. It determines what IRC, I/O, DMA, and other assignments are to be given to the PCI or ISA cards.

5. It programs the plug-and-play cards before the POST.

6. It disables cards that do not have configurations in the BIOS.

7. It configures all devices on the motherboard.

MBR and boot sector

After completing the POST, the computer begins looking for the operating system to tell it what to do. Typically, it first looks for the disk drive, and then turns to the boot sector of the hard drive if it finds nothing in the disk drive. The Windows 95 boot sector begins running the **io.sys** program in read-only mode, checking the **msdos.sys** file, and checking for the **config.sys** and **autoexec.bat** files to follow their instructions or move on to the Registry. At this point booting begins in earnest, as the **io.sys** is loaded into memory.

Real-mode boot

Real-mode booting begins as soon as **io.sys** is loaded into its memory location in the Registry. The Windows 95 Registry contains every file that contains information about the system's configuration. Windows 95 settings, hardware information, and other program information reside in either the **user.dat** or **system.dat** files in the Registry.

The **user.dat** file is more personal than the **system.dat** file. Whereas the **user.dat** file contains passwords, desktop preferences, and start menu preferences, the **system.dat** file contains information about IRQs, hardware devices, and internal Windows 95 settings. Remember that any changes you make to the Registry are permanent. There's minimal danger of misconfigurations occurring during the boot because the **user.dat** and **system.dat** files are backed up whenever you close Windows 95.

Real-mode configuration

Windows 95 uses the **io.sys** file as its real-mode operating system file. It replaces the MS-DOS system files (**io.sys** and **msdos.sys**) necessary for Windows 3.x booting, and contains all the information necessary to start Windows 95 in real mode. Even though the **config.sys** and **autoexec.bat** files are unnecessary for starting Windows 95, they are preserved for backward compatibility for Windows 3.x and MS-DOS users. You should find the following drivers by default in the **io.sys** file if they do not already exist on the hard drive: **himem.sys**, **ifshlp.sys**, **setver.exe**, and **dblspace.bin** or **drvspace.bin**.

Protected-mode load

Microsoft recommends using 32-bit **protected-mode drivers** when possible. Configuration information from these drivers is stored in the Registry instead of in **config.sys** or other files. Previously, Windows 95 loaded the following necessary elements for protected mode:

- **win.com**—Controls the initial checks and loading of key Windows 95 components.

- **vmm32.vxd**—Creates the VMs and initiates VxD loading.

- **system.ini**—Checked for differences from the Registry entries.

After the VxDs are loaded, **vmm32.vxd** switches the processor to operate in protected mode, and the final phase of the booting process can begin.

Fairly quickly, the plug-and-play information previously compiled is processed, the GUI loads, a password screen may appear, and the Startup file runs. The Windows 95 system is now ready for e-mailing, word processing, and other traditional computer operations.

Concept Questions   *Semester 2, Unit 13, Lesson 63*

Demonstrate your knowledge of the concepts in this lesson by answering the following questions in the space provided.

1. Explain the boot process.

2. Explain the initialization process.

_____

_____

_____

_____

_____

_____

_____

_____

_____

_____

_____

_____

_____

_____

_____

_____

_____

_____

_____

Vocabulary Exercise   *Semester 2, Unit 13, Lesson 63*

Name: _____

Date: _____   *Class:* _____

Define the following terms as completely as you can.

protected-mode driver

_____

_____

real-mode boot

_____

_____

Focus Questions   *Semester 2, Unit 13, Lesson 63*

Name: _____

Date: _____   *Class:* _____

1. Describe the process of a plug-and-play BIOS.

_____

_____

_____

_____

2. Describe where and how the computer looks for an operating system.

_____

_____

_____

_____

3. Describe what drivers are provided by default in the **io.sys** file.

_____

_____

_____

_____

4. Compare the bootstrap process of a plug-and-play BIOS with that of a legacy BIOS.

_____

_____

_____

_____

5. Describe the preboot process.

_____

_____

_____

_____

6. Describe the real-mode boot process.

_____

_____

_____

_____

7. Describe the protected-mode boot process.

_____

_____

_____

_____

SEMESTER 2, UNIT 13, LESSON 64
Troubleshooting the Boot Process and Initialization

Now that you are familiar with the basic boot process and its initialization files, you need to know how to do some troubleshooting. A number of users have discovered that rebooting a machine will solve many computer problems. Ironically, the boot process is often the phase when the computer is most unstable and prone to problems. Wise technicians need to focus on this area to be successful troubleshooters.

Troubleshooting during the boot process

As long as a machine beeps just once, everything is going fine. More than one beep indicates that you've got trouble. The computer actually does all it can to help diagnose and solve its problems when you boot with its beeping signals during the POST and Windows Startup screen. Table 13-3 lists the POST beep signals and what they mean.

Table 13-3   *Common POST beep codes and problems*

POST Beep Code	Problem
No beep	Power supply problem
Repeated short beep	Power supply problem
One short beep with nothing onscreen	Video card failure
One short beep with video present but no booting	Floppy drive problem
Two short beeps	Configuration error
One long beep followed by one short beep	System board failure
Continuous beeps	Power supply problem or stuck keyboard

If you see an error message onscreen during the boot, at least you know the video display monitor is working. Table 13-4 lists some errors messages that can occur during the POST and what they mean.

Table 13-4   *POST error messages and diagnoses*

Error Message	Diagnosis
Code in the 100s	System board error
Code in the 200s	RAM error
Code in the 300s	Keyboard error
Code in the 500s	Video controller error
Code in the 600s	Floppy drive error
Code in the 700s	Computer processor error
Code in the 900s	Parallel port error
Code in the 1100s and 1200s	System board error
Code in the 1300s	Game controller or joystick error
Code in the 1700s	Hard drive error
Code in the 6000s	SCSI device or network card error
Code in the 7300s	Floppy drive error

Troubleshooting the boot process

You have learned how to diagnose some problems that prevent a computer program from booting up. Checking the power sources and doing a cold boot can often solve problems as well. What about situations in which the actual boot process has a problem? For that you need to check the files that actually affect the boot process, such as **msdos.sys**, **win.com**, and **bootlog.txt**.

The hidden, read-only file **msdos.sys** contains paths used to locate other Windows files, including the important Registry files. Although it was created primarily for application compatibility, it does support an **[Options]** section, which you can add to customize the startup process. Table 13-5 demonstrates some of the **[Options]** section descriptions and defaults that you can customize.

Table 13-5 [Options] *section descriptions and defaults*

Section	Description	Default
BootDelay=n	Sets initial startup delay to *n* seconds.	2 (note that 0 disables delay)
BootFailSafe=	Enables Safe Mode for system startup.	0 (disabled)
BootGUI=	Enables automatic graphical startup into Windows 95.	1 (enabled)
BootMenu=	Enables automatic display of the Startup menu, so that the user doesn't need to press F8 to see it.	0 (disabled)
BootMulti=	Enables dual booting.	0 (disabled)
BootWin=	Enables Windows 95 as the default operating system. Only useful with MS-DOS 5 or 6.x.	1 (enabled)
BootWarn=	Enables the safe-mode startup warning after a failed boot or corrupt Registry is found.	1 (enabled)

When you need to isolate an error condition, try using the **/d** switch with **win.com** to start Windows 95 from the command prompt. If Windows 95 does not start correctly, use the following switches with the **/d** switch:

- **F**—Turns off 32-bit disk access. Try this if disk problems or stalling occur.

- **M**—Starts Windows 95 in safe mode.

- **N**—Starts Windows 95 in safe mode with networking.

- **S**—Specifies that Windows should not use ROM address space between F000:0000 and 1 MB for a break point. Try this if Windows 95 stalls during startup.

- **V**—Specifies that the ROM routine will handle interrupts from the hard disk controller. Try this if Windows 95 stalls during startup or during disk operations.

- **X**—Excludes the adapter area from the memory range that Windows scans for unused space. Try this if you suspect an upper memory conflict.

When you really want to get specific about the boot process, examine **bootlog.txt**, which contains a step-by-step record of the Windows 95 boot process. The first time you successfully boot Windows 95, **bootlog.txt** is automatically created in the root directory, with each step logged as it occurs. The next time you boot Windows 95, the **bootlog.txt** file is renamed **bootlog.prv**, and a new **bootlog.txt** file is created. After the third boot, the **bootlog.txt** file is only created when you choose the Logged option from the startup menu.

The **bootlog.txt** files can diagnose boot problems, such as the following:

- Driver load failures—Because the first part of the **bootlog.txt** records whether drivers were successfully loaded, a failure in this first section can indicate that the driver was not found.

- Driver initialization failures—System drivers are recorded under the heading **syscritinit**, and no file I/O is allowed during driver initialization, so the initialization or lack of initialization can be an indicator of a problem.

If the computer doesn't boot due to incorrect drivers, corrupted files, or resource conflicts, it's time for **safe-mode startup**, which loads only the mouse, keyboard, standard VGA, and drivers required for the Device Manager.

If the computer boots from safe mode but not in normal mode, the problem likely fits into one of the following four categories:

- Network configuration—Disable the protected-mode networking drivers with Device Manager, and restart the computer.

- Protected-mode disk driver—Disable the protected-mode disk driver with Device Manager, and restart the computer.

- Video driver—Switch to the standard VGA driver. It this works, the display driver or its settings are incompatible with the system.

- Third-party VxDs—Comment out the entry for a third-party VxD in **system.ini**, and restart the computer. Continue this procedure with all other third-party VxDs until you find the problem driver.

Troubleshooting the initialization files

The central repository for all Windows 95 database information is the Registry. Even though Windows 95 has eliminated the need for **autoexec.bat**, **config.sys**, and INI files, they still remain for backward compatibility to run Windows 16-bit applications. The Registry files that relate directly to boot initialization are the **INF files** and the **INI files**.

People familiar with INI files are comfortable using and editing the INI files now located in the Registry. In fact, the Registry has improved these files' usefulness in several ways:

- The files have an unlimited size, and they can include binary and text values

- The files are arranged in a hierarchical order

- The files use more standardized values

- The **HKEY_USERS** key stores user-specific information

- The files can be remotely administered

Due to its complexity and the chance for syntactical errors, Windows 95 strongly recommends that users reconfigure settings with the Control Panel utility, although it is possible to do this through the Registry. Just make sure that you know what you are doing when you go there.

Concept Questions   *Semester 2, Unit 13, Lesson 64*

Demonstrate your knowledge of the concepts in this lesson by answering the following questions in the space provided.

1. Explain how to troubleshoot the boot process.

2. Explain how to troubleshoot the initialization process.

_____

_____

_____

_____

_____

_____

_____

_____

_____

_____

_____

_____

_____

_____

_____

_____

_____

_____

_____

Vocabulary Exercise   *Semester 2, Unit 13, Lesson 64*

Name: _____

Date: _____   *Class:* _____

Define the following terms as completely as you can.

bootlog.txt

_____

_____

INF file

_____

_____

INI file

_____

_____

safe-mode startup

_____

_____

Focus Questions

Semester 2, Unit 13, Lesson 64

Name: _____

Date: _____   *Class:* _____

1. What does it mean when you hear the POST beep code that is a repeated short beep?

_____

_____

_____

2. What does it mean when you hear the POST beep code that is one short beep with nothing on screen?

_____

_____

_____

3. What does it mean when you hear the POST beep code that is one short beep with video present but no booting?

_____

_____

_____

4. What does it mean when you hear the POST beep code that is two short beeps?

_____

_____

_____

5. What does it mean when you hear the POST beep code that is one long beep followed by one short beep?

_____

_____

_____

6. What does it mean when you hear the POST beep code that is continuous beeps?

_____

_____

_____

7. Describe some error messages that can occur during POST.

_____

_____

_____

8. Describe the files affected by the boot process.

_____

_____

_____

9. What **win.com** switch helps isolate an error condition?

_____

_____

_____

10. Describe some possible problems you might be having if you can boot in safe mode but cannot boot in normal mode.

_____

_____

_____

SEMESTER 2, UNIT 13, LESSON 65
Unit 13 Exam

If you have access to the online Aries A+ curriculum, contact your instructor for the Assessment System URL. If you do not have access to the online curriculum, please continue to Unit 14.

SEMESTER 2, UNIT 14

- Lesson 66: Procedures for Problem Avoidance and Recovery
- Lesson 67: Plug-and-Play Hardware
- Lesson 68: Troubleshooting Resources
- Lesson 69: Using the System Monitor and Troubleshooting Remote Windows 95 Computers
- Lesson 70: Unit 14 Exam

SEMESTER 2, UNIT 14, LESSON 66
Procedures for Problem Avoidance and Recovery

You have learned about troubleshooting during the boot process. Anticipating problems is an even better strategy. You've probably heard the old saying "an ounce of prevention is worth a pound of cure." This lesson will help you prevent problems from happening.

Registry backups

Responsible users continually back up files. Windows 95 has a built-in sense of responsibility: It is designed to back up the Registry each time it starts successfully. With each successful start, Windows 95 copies the current version of **system.dat** and **user.dat**. This means that if Windows 95 doesn't start, you don't have to panic. You can copy the backed-up Registry from the last successful startup and thus recover the most recent settings prior to the system failure.

If, on rare occasion, you have a badly corrupted Registry, you can use the Windows 95 startup disk to start the computer. Then you can use the **regedit.exe** utility on the startup disk to import a **.reg** file, using the following syntax:

- **/L:system**—Specifies the location of **system.dat**.

- **/R:user**—Specifies the location of **user.dat**.

- **File1.reg**—Specifies one or more **.reg** files to import into the Registry.

- **/e file3.reg**—Specifies the filename to which the Registry should be exported.

- **regkey**—Specifies the starting key from which to export a portion of the Registry.

- **/c file2.reg**—Specifies the **.reg** file to use to replace the entire contents of the Registry.

Another way to back up Registry files is to use the **Microsoft Configuration Backup** tool provided on the Windows 95 CD, located in the **\other\misc\cfgback** folder. This backup utility is designed to make periodic backups of the system Registry. Configuration Backup stores up to nine backup copies of a configuration. Although you can copy backups to other storage locations, you must copy them back to the *win_root* directory before they can be restored.

Windows 95 contains other files and utilities to help correct setup and startup problems. Besides using the startup disk, you can also try the following:

- Safe Recovery with Windows 95 Setup—If the setup fails, run the setup again and click Safe Recovery.

- Installed components verification—Automatic checking system that detects existing Windows 95 installations during the setup.

- Startup menu options—At the Starting Windows 95 screen, press F8 and choose from the eight options you can use to isolate error conditions from the command prompt.

Creating an emergency startup disk

Occasionally you run across machines with malfunctioning systems. This is when you need the emergency startup disk. This floppy disk contains troubleshooting utilities that load the operating system and present an MS-DOS prompt.

You can create a Windows 95 startup disk when prompted during the file copy phase of the Widows 95 setup, or you can use the Add/Remove Programs icon in the Control Panel after Windows 95 installation. Simply click the Startup Disk tab, insert a floppy disk, and click the Create Disk button. The following are the files that Windows copies onto a startup disk:

- **attrib.exe**—A file attribute utility

- **chkdsk.exe**—A disk status and repair utility

- **command.com**—A core operating system file

- **debug.exe**—A debugging utility

- **drvspace.bin**—A disk compression utility

- **ebd.sys**—A utility for the startup disk

- **edit.com**—A text editor

- **fdisk.exe**—A disk partition utility

- **format.com**—A disk format utility

- **io.sys**—A core operating system file

- **msdos.sys**—A core operating system file

- **regedit.exe**—A real-mode Registry Editor

- **scandisk.exe**—A disk status and repair utility

- **scandisk.ini**—A disk status utility configuration file

- **sys.com**—A system transfer utility

- **uninstal.exe**—A utility for uninstalling Windows 95

In addition to these files, you should copy the following files into a subdirectory on the startup disk:

- **system.dat**

- **autoexec.bat**

- **config.sys**

- **win.ini**

- **system.ini**

Troubleshooting procedures

Before jumping the gun and correcting the wrong problems, you should follow some common-sense problem-solving procedures:

- Analyze the symptoms and factors.

- Check to see if the problem is a common issue.

- Isolate the error conditions.

- Consult technical support resources.

How long would you continue to use the services of a physician who operated on your gall bladder when you really had a broken clavicle? If you expect to build a solid reputation as a computer technician, you must become very skilled at analyzing problems and asking the right questions. Under what conditions does the problem occur? What parts of the operating system control these conditions? Is the problem specific to a network, video, or sound? Is the condition chronic or sporadic? The answers to a myriad of questions can help pinpoint the problem.

Computer technicians can often get to a problem by checking for common, frequently occurring issues. A few problem areas follow:

- Specific driver problems

- Correct file versions

- Missing system files

- Missing required drivers

- Incorrect startup file entries

- System startup conflicts

- Device configuration problems

- Disk space problems

You can find details about these and other troubleshooting problems in the Windows 95 Resource Kit. Other common problems that you might encounter include the following:

- Inability to install Windows 95

- Problems starting or running Windows 95

- Network connectivity problems

- Local or network printing problems

- Application errors

- General protection faults

Windows 95 also includes online help for many common problems. Users can solve most problems from the Help button on the Start menu.

Resolving problems and conflicts in Windows 95

Even after analysis and checking for common problems, you might not find an immediate solution. The next logical step is to use the scientific method to test your hypotheses. Doing so requires isolating and testing the error condition.

Eliminated variables help you determine the actual cause of a problem. One way to isolate specific causes is to remove unnecessary lines from the **config.sys** and **autoexec.bat** files. Another way to test the cause is by changing a specific value and testing immediately to see if the problem is resolved or altered. Suppose you suspect that the Registry files have been damaged. You could simply restore the Registry files in **system.dat** and **user.dat** from backup files and retest.

If a component fails after upgrading to a new driver, replace it with the original driver and retest. If Windows 95 fails to load during startup, test the effects of not loading a device driver. You can do this by selecting the Step-By-Step Confirmation option during startup.

By testing individual modifications and making notes on the modifications and their effects, you can collect valuable data for solving the problem.

If you run into a problem or conflict you cannot solve, there are numerous support resources available, including resource people, online support, and Internet resources. If you meticulously follow the standard strategy for resolving conflicts by analyzing the symptoms and factors, checking for common issues, isolating the error, and consulting technical support, you have a good chance of resolving computer problems and conflicts.

Concept Questions   *Semester 2, Unit 14, Lesson 66*

Demonstrate your knowledge of the concepts in this lesson by answering the following questions in the space provided.

1. Explain some common problem-avoidance procedures.

2. Explain the two methods you can use to create an emergency startup disk.

_____

_____

_____

_____

_____

_____

_____

_____

_____

_____

_____

_____

_____

_____

_____

_____

_____

_____

_____

Vocabulary Exercise *Semester 2, Unit 14, Lesson 66*

Name: _____

Date: _____ *Class:* _____

Define the following terms as completely as you can.

autoexec.bat

_____

_____

config.sys

_____

_____

Microsoft Configuration Backup

_____

_____

regedit.exe

_____

_____

system.dat

_____

_____

system.ini

_____

_____

user.dat

_____

_____

win.ini

_____

_____

Focus Questions   *Semester 2, Unit 14, Lesson 66*

Name: _____

Date: _____   *Class:* _____

1. Describe how Windows 95 backs up the Registry.

_____

_____

_____

2. Describe some utilities to help correct setup and startup problems.

_____

_____

_____

2. Describe how you create a Windows 95 startup disk.

_____

_____

_____

3. What files are copied to the Windows 95 startup disk?

_____

_____

_____

4. Describe some troubleshooting procedures.

_____

_____

_____

5. Describe some common computer problems.

_____

_____

_____

6. Describe some methods of resolving problems and conflicts in Windows 95.

_____

_____

_____

SEMESTER 2, UNIT 14, LESSON 67
Plug-and-Play Hardware

You have learned about recovery procedures and some steps you can take to prevent problems. This lesson discusses one of the greatest preventive measures ever taken in the computer hardware domain: plug-and-play.

Microsoft prides itself on developing user-friendly products, and worked closely with hardware manufacturers to promote acceptance of the plug-and-play standard. Before plug-and-play, users had one hardware compatibility headache after another. Can you imagine buying a VCR that required all its components to be adjusted before it would function, only to find that it still wouldn't work with certain TV channels? Such was the situation in the computer world before plug-and-play.

The plug-and-play architecture

Microsoft played a key role in developing the **plug-and-play architecture**, but it needed the cooperation of the hardware industry. This occurred in 1993 when three other companies reached an agreement to support each other—Intel delivered plug-and-play chips, Phoenix Technologies delivered plug-and-play BIOS chips, and Compaq delivered plug-and-play PCs. Of course, since then many others have joined the bandwagon.

The philosophy underlying plug-and-play is very simple: Simply plug in the device, turn on the computer, and it works. The goal of plug-and-play is to enable PC configuration changes with no user intervention, making device installation an easy, trouble-free operation.

Under plug-and-play architecture, the user can change the system components without restarting the whole system. The system automatically adjusts to new devices and determines their optimal configuration. Gone are the days of tweaking **config.sys** files and refereeing between conflicting devices.

Understanding what plug-and-play does requires understanding some basics of the computer hardware architecture. The peripheral devices that use plug-and-play communicate with the CPU by one or more of the following means:

- Interrupt request (IRQ)—A hardware signal built in to the computer that deals with a Programmable Interrupt Controller (PIC), which can handle 16 interrupt signals. Table 14-1 shows the most common assignments.

- Direct memory access (DMA)—allows peripherals to work directly with the system memory instead of filtering through the system processor.

- **Input/output (I/O) ports**—Used when you want a device to perform input or output functions; they are mapped into a separate memory area.

- **Memory**—The original memory space allocated to the upper 384 KB of the address space.

Table 14-1   *IRQ signals*

IRQ Signal	Description
0	System timer
1	Keyboard
2	Cascade to second PIC
3	COM2 IRQ
4	COM1 IRQ
5	Parallel port 2
6	Floppy disk drive
7	Parallel port 1
8	Real-time clock
9	Cascade with IRQ2 and VGA/EGA
10	Open
11	Open
12	PS/2 mouse
13	Math coprocessor
14	HD controller
15	Open

Understanding the plug-and-play architecture requires understanding the multiple bus and device architectures that coexist in the system. One of the easiest ways to view these relationships is through a tree diagram, where each branch represents an object, or *device node*, that must be addressed by the plug-and-play architecture. To configure a device node, you need a unique identification code and resources allocated to the device node.

The plug-and-play process

If you have a machine made before summer 1995, you need to check whether the BIOS supports plug-and-play. Legacy ISA cards can coexist with plug-and-play cards, and user intervention may be necessary occasionally. Because legacy devices are less flexible in their resource requirements, legacy devices are assigned resources before plug-and-play devices.

PCs made after summer 1995 most likely operate with Windows 95 along with plug-and-play. Underlying the automatic functioning of plug-and-play lies an interesting process. We'll focus on ISA adapters as we outline the steps of the automatic configuration process:

1. Put plug-and-play ISA cards in configuration mode. Software identifies and configures devices, using commands. The data sequence writes to one of the ports (the initialization key), which enables the plug-and-play logic on the card.

2. Isolate one card at a time and assign a handle to the card. The isolation protocol uses a unique number on each card (a device ID and a serial number) to isolate one plug-and-play card at a time. After isolation the software assigns each card a handle. The handle eliminates the need for more complex isolation protocols.

3. Read the card's resource data structure to determine its resource requirements and capacity. Each card supports a read-only resource data structure that describes the supported and requested resources. The structure supports the idea of multiple functions per card. Plug-and-play resource information is provided to each logical device.

4. Allocate conflict-free resources to each card. When resource capacity and demands are known, resource arbitration begins to allocate resources to each ISA card. Command registers configure the ISA cards. If an ISA function cannot be reconfigured, equivalent resources are assigned, and the resource data structure informs the configuration software that it can't assign these resources to other plug-and-play cards. An I/O conflict-detection mechanism may be invoked. This ensures that there won't be conflicts with the devices and that card functions are either activated or deactivated.

5. Activate all plug-and-play ISA cards and remove them from configuration mode. When configuration is completed, plug-and-play cards are removed from the configuration mode. To reenable configuration mode, reissue the initiation key.

Plug-and-play components

In order for a computer to be fully plug-and-play functional, all the computer's components must be plug-and-play compatible. Among the essential components are the following:

- Operating system—For plug-and-play functionality, the operating system requires a configuration manager, hardware tree, bus enumerators, and resource arbitrators.

- BIOS—Enhanced to provide boot device configuration and dynamic event notification.

- **Bus enumerators**—May use existing drivers or BIOS services to access hardware.

- Hardware tree and Registry—Defines the standard scheme for identifying each device and its resource requirements and constraints.

- Devices and device drivers—Provide additional **APIs** required for plug-and-play device configuration. They must register with the configuration manager when first loaded, dynamically load and unload, and communicate with other components.

- Resource arbitrator—Interacts extensively with the configuration manager to allocate resource and resolve conflicts.

- Configuration manager—Coordinates the flow of all operations performed by the components involved in the configuration.

Plug-and-play devices

Many devices, including the following, are compatible with plug-and-play specifications:

- MicroChannel—A bus introduced with IBM's PS/2 series.

- EISA—A response to IBM's MicroChannel.

- SCSI—Used in many devices such as hard drives and CD-ROM drives.

- PCMCIA card—Small interface cards found in portables and other small computer systems.

- VL and PCI—The VESA Local (VL) bus allows high-speed peripheral connection. PCI succeeds VL and is used in most Pentium computers and Power Macs.

- IDE controllers—Provide a way to support multiple disk drives.

- Extended Capabilities Port specification—Supports plug-and-play devices as parallel ports.

- New technologies—Plug-and-play encourages evolving technologies.

Changing and configuring plug-and-play devices

Although it's usually not necessary (and is usually a bad idea) to change the configurations of a plug-and-play device, it is possible to do so. Go through the System icon in the Control Panel and click the Device Manager tab. From here you can change the configuration of any device onscreen. You can view the devices by their types or by their connections.

If you must change a configuration, it is probably best to view its connection because this more closely matches the Registry information. You can examine the Device Manager by clicking through the various screens, but be careful about changing the actual configurations. You don't want to hamper plug-and-play devices because they make the computer much more fun to work with.

Concept Questions   *Semester 2, Unit 14, Lesson 67*

Demonstrate your knowledge of the concepts in this lesson by answering the
following questions in the space provided.

1. Describe the history of plug-and-play from its early development

2. Explain the philosophy behind plug-and-play.

_____
_____
_____
_____
_____
_____
_____
_____
_____
_____
_____
_____
_____
_____
_____
_____
_____
_____

Vocabulary Exercise   *Semester 2, Unit 14, Lesson 67*

Name: _____

Date: _____   Class: _____

Define the following terms as completely as you can.

API

_____

_____

bus enumerator

_____

_____

EISA

_____

_____

I/O port

_____

_____

plug-and-play architecture

_____

_____

Focus Questions   *Semester 2, Unit 14, Lesson 67*

Name: _____

Date: _____   *Class:* _____

1. Describe some IRQs and their usage.

_____

_____

_____

2. Describe what is needed to configure a device node.

_____

_____

_____

3. Describe what happens with plug-and-play when the system includes legacy devices.

_____

_____

_____

4. Describe the plug-and-play process.

_____

_____

_____

5. Describe some essential plug-and-play components.

_____

_____

_____

6. Describe some plug-and-play devices.

_____

_____

_____

7. Describe how you configure plug-and-play devices.

_____

_____

_____

SEMESTER 2, UNIT 14, LESSON 68
Troubleshooting Resources

Beginning technicians may not feel confident enough to tear apart a Pentium processor and rewire an entire motherboard. Until that day arrives, many other more simple computer problems will come and go. You will encounter frustrated users who want instant service and instant satisfaction. Often you will be able to deliver. Sometimes you will venture into unknown territory. During such times, remember that you aren't alone. A wealth of information and support is just a few mouse clicks away. We will examine some of these troubleshooting resources in this lesson.

Microsoft recognized how intimidating the technological world can be, so it has equipped Windows users with a variety of supporting resources. Much of the information is shared among the resources, so you can access any of the following to get troubleshooting information as well as the latest product drivers and other services:

- **Windows 95 Resource Kit**—The definitive Microsoft book about Windows 95, which is often a one-stop reference guide for any software problem.

- **TechNet**—A monthly CD available by subscription.

- The Internet—Microsoft maintains WWW, FTP, and NNTP sites. You can find other helpful Web sites as well.

- The **Microsoft Network (MSN)**—An online service that contains information on numerous subjects, including forums on Microsoft and its products.

Microsoft TechNet

You should consider subscribing to Microsoft's TechNet if you are a computer professional who does any of the following tasks:

- Train and support users

- Administer networks or databases

- Integrate products and platforms

- Evaluate new products and solutions

Annual TechNet subscribers receive two CDs each month, containing many valuable resources, such as the following:

- A complete set of online Microsoft Resource Kits, loaded with technical references, utilities, and accessories to install and support Microsoft products.

- Microsoft Knowledge Base, which is the same library of technical support information developed and used by Microsoft's own engineers.

- A supplemental CD that contains the latest version of the Microsoft Software Library and includes the latest drivers, patches, and updates.

To subscribe to TechNet, contact Microsoft Corporation, PO Box 10296, Des Moines, IA 50336-0296; phone 800-344-2121.

Internet troubleshooting resources

As for almost anything you can think of, there is troubleshooting information and support on the Internet. Abundant Windows troubleshooting resources await your keyboard commands and mouse clicks. Microsoft maintains the Web sites listed in Table 14-2. Other Web sites concerning Windows 95 you may find useful include those listed in Table 14-3.

Table 14-2 *Microsoft Resource Web sites*

URL	Web Site Description
www.microsoft.com	Microsoft Corporation
www.microsoft.com/technet	TechNet online edition
support.microsoft.com/Support	Windows support home page
www.microsoft.com/windows	Windows product information, software library, support information.
www.microsoft.com/ie	Internet Explorer home page
home.microsoft.com	MSN home page

Table 14-3 *Windows 95 Web sites*

URL	Web site description
pcwin.com	Software downloads, tips, bulletin board, and so on
www.halcyon.com/cerelli	Software, tips, tricks, information, and other resources
www.worldowindows.com	News, information, tips, and resources

Besides these Web sites, you can use the various search engines to find other Web sites, check for bulletin boards on technical issues, join a newsgroup or e-mail list for computer technicians, and network via cyberspace to find other technical gurus and mentors.

MSN troubleshooting resources

Since Windows 98 came out, the appearance of MSN has changed to integrate itself into the Windows and Internet interfaces. Besides its news and entertainment functions, it contains technical support information on Windows programs through the Computing Central help desk. Users can get the latest information in the following forums:

- FAQ—Quick answers to common frequently asked questions

- Microsoft Knowledge Base—Contains thousands of articles with technical information about Microsoft products, as well as tutorials.

- Microsoft Software Library—Numerous free software add-ons, **bug** fixes, peripherals, updates, programming aids, and so on.

- Microsoft facilitated member-to-member interactions—Bulletin boards and chats to provide fast answers from other users.

Microsoft makes it extremely easy to join the MSN. One of the easiest ways is to select it in the Get Connected dialog box during Windows 95 setup. You can also install it after setup through the Add/Remove Programs in the Control Panel. As long as you have a modem and a phone line, you can connect to MSN by clicking on its icon. Benefits and features of MSN include the following:

- Familiar user interface—Users familiar with Windows 95 and Internet Explorer find MSN navigation a breeze.

- Multitasking—MSN takes full advantage of the Windows 95 multitasking function, so you can browse while another file is loading.

- Worldwide access—MSN is available everywhere that dial-up access is available.

- E-mail—Users can exchange email with other MSN members or with others who have Internet email.

- **Bulletin boards**—Users can join discussions on a variety of topics.

- **Chat** rooms—Users can converse in real-time.

- File libraries—Users can download graphics, software, product information, and so on.

- Internet use—Users can send mail to Internet users, post and reply to newsgroups, and obtain an Internet account.

Concept Questions   *Semester 2, Unit 14, Lesson 68*

Demonstrate your knowledge of the concepts in this lesson by answering the following questions in the space provided.

1. Explain the various troubleshooting resources.

2. Explain how to obtain maintenance updates and patches for Windows 95.

_____

_____

_____

_____

_____

_____

_____

_____

_____

_____

_____

_____

_____

_____

_____

_____

_____

_____

_____

Vocabulary Exercise   *Semester 2, Unit 14, Lesson 68*

Name: _____

Date: _____   Class: _____

Define the following terms as completely as you can.

bug

_____

_____

bulletin board

_____

_____

chat

_____

_____

MSN

_____

_____

TechNet

_____

_____

Windows 95 Resource Kit

_____

_____

Focus Questions   *Semester 2, Unit 14, Lesson 68*

Name: _____

Date: _____   *Class:* _____

1. Describe some Internet troubleshooting resources.

_____

_____

_____

_____

2. Describe some MSN troubleshooting resources.

_____

_____

_____

_____

3. Describe some benefits and features of MSN.

_____

_____

_____

_____

4. Describe the resource support provided by Windows 95 Resource Kit, TechNet, the Internet, and MSN.

_____

_____

_____

_____

5. Describe the ways you can use the Internet to troubleshoot Windows 95 problems.

_____

_____

_____

_____

SEMESTER 2, UNIT 14, LESSON 69

Using the System Monitor and Troubleshooting Remote Windows 95 Computers

So far we've focussed on troubleshooting individual Windows 95 PCs and software problems. In this lesson you'll learn about remote Windows 95 machines and how to monitor and troubleshoot a network of computers.

Using the System Monitor for performance profiles

Good physicians spend a great deal of time gathering data before offering possible diagnoses and a treatment plan. They have you fill out information, conduct an interview, perform a series of tests, and maybe even take an x-ray or CAT scan before discussing treatment with you. A similar process is necessary for troubleshooting individual PCs and networks.

By now you realize that troubleshooting computer problems requires gathering significant and accurate data. The **System Monitor** is a one-stop tracking tool that monitors the real-time performance of various computer components and functions and displays it visually with graphs and charts. System Monitor uses include the following:

- Monitoring system performance and comparing it with historical performance to identify patterns

- Determining system capacity

- Identifying bottlenecks

- Monitoring the effects of system configuration changes

The System Monitor can track performance data on the following categories, depending on what device drivers are loaded:

- The file system

- The kernel

- The IPX/SPX-compatible protocol

- The Memory Manager

- The Microsoft Network Client

- The Microsoft Client for NetWare Networks

- The Microsoft Network Server

- The Microsoft Network Monitor

Generating and interpreting performance data

Utilizing the System Monitor most effectively requires frequent viewing. Only through frequent viewing can you recognize the computer's typical performance and recognize and predict performance problems later.

To get in the regular habit of viewing the System Monitor, make it easily accessible on your desktop and run it while working under Windows 95. Add the System Monitor icon to your desktop, run the System Monitor, and use the commands on the View menu to either remove the title bar or make the window always appear on top.

The more you use the System Monitor, the more effective you will be at interpreting the data. Table 14-4 gives general guidelines and settings for troubleshooting.

Table 14-4   *Troubleshooting guidelines and settings*

Value	When to Check	Details/Solution
Kernel: Processor Usage	Computer seems slow	If the value is high when the user is not at the machine, a background application is dominating the computer.
Kernel: Threads	An application might not be freeing memory when finished	If thread count rises during application use, perhaps an application is not reclaiming its threads before starting new ones. Try closing the application.
Memory Manager: Page Faults	Computer is slow	High numbers and activity indicate that paging is slowing performance. Add RAM.
Memory Manager: Discards and Memory Manager: Page-outs	Hard disk accessed too frequently	High activity indicates that more RAM is needed.

Monitoring network performance

Although you can use the System Monitor to track the performance of remote computers with the proper administrative privileges, you would be much better off using the **Network Monitor**, which is an analyzer included in the Microsoft System Management Server. The Windows 95 CD also includes a Network Monitor agent and a protocol driver in the **\admin\nettols\netmon** folder. You can install the Network Monitor through the Network option on the Control Panel. Using the Network Monitor agent along with System Monitor generates some basic network performance data.

The Windows 95 Network Monitor agent functions as a data collector for two purposes:

- Recording general network broadcast statistics in the System Monitor.

- Sending network analysis information to a Network Monitor across a router. Network Monitor can only monitor the network on which it is running, unless the agent is installed on a remote subnet.

Troubleshooting remote computers

You can diagnose and troubleshoot remote computers with the **Registry Editor** and System Monitor as long as the following conditions are met:

- Both your computer and the remote computer support user-level security.

- The Remote Registry service is installed on both computers.

- The Remote Administration is enabled through the Remote Administration tab in the Passwords option under the Control Panel.

- Your username is on the administrators list on the Remote Administration tab.

Concept Questions   *Semester 2, Unit 14, Lesson 69*

Demonstrate your knowledge of the concepts in this lesson by answering the following questions in the space provided.

1. Explain how to use the System Monitor utility to identify bottlenecks.

2. Explain the similarities and differences of the System Monitor and the Network Monitor.

_____

_____

_____

_____

_____

_____

_____

_____

_____

_____

_____

_____

_____

_____

_____

_____

_____

Vocabulary Exercise   *Semester 2, Unit 14, Lesson 69*

Name: _____

Date: _____   *Class:* _____

Define the following terms as completely as you can.

Network Monitor

_____

_____

Registry Editor

_____

_____

System Monitor

_____

_____

Focus Questions   *Semester 2, Unit 14, Lesson 69*

Name: _____

Date: _____   *Class:* _____

1. Describe some uses of the System Monitor.

_____

_____

_____

_____

2. Describe what System Monitor can track.

_____

_____

_____

_____

3. Describe some functions of the Network Monitor.

_____

_____

_____

_____

4. Describe how you troubleshoot remote computers.

_____

_____

_____

_____

SEMESTER 2, UNIT 14, LESSON 70
Unit 14 Exam

If you have access to the online Aries A+ curriculum, contact your instructor for the Assessment System URL.

SEMESTER 2 GLOSSARY

GLOSSARY

Numbers and symbols

101-key enhanced keyboard   The standard layout for computer system keyboards, originally introduced by the IBM Corporation in 1986, that has since been copied by all PC-clone manufacturers.

104-key enhanced keyboard   A modified version of the 101-key enhanced keyboard with extra command keys added to support Microsoft Windows 95 and NT.

15-pin mini D-sub   The standard 15-pin connector used for connecting a video monitor to a video card.

25-pin serial port   A type of serial port that has 25 pins or contacts.

3D sound   Sound that seems to come from above, behind, and in front of you.

9-pin serial port   A type of serial port employing nine pins or contacts.

A

abacus   One of the earliest counting instruments, constructed of sliding beads on small wooden rods slated across a wooden frame.

AC (alternating current)   A form of electricity in which voltage alternates direction. The frequency of AC voltage is 60 Hz in the United States, and AC is generally the standard for electrical power in both residential and commercial buildings.

accelerator   The primary chip in the video chipset; which handles most of the video processing.

access list   A database that lists the authorized users and their permissions for a Windows NT network.

account   A file that holds records of users and resources.

acronym   A word that is made up of the first letters or syllables of the words for which it stands. For example, *RAM* stands for *random access memory*.

active partition   A DOS partition that is read at startup. The active partition should have the files required to boot the system.

adapter bracket   A brace or prop used to support and attach expansion cards to the chassis. It is a subassembly of the chassis.

adapter plate   A metal cover used to seal holes over unused expansion brackets. The plate prevents dust from entering the case and maintains proper airflow inside the computer's case.

Add New Hardware   A Windows 95 option that allows the user to install new hardware devices or configure hardware settings.

Add/Remove Programs   A Windows 95 option that allows the user to create a start-up disk, and add or remove programs and components.

address bus   A data bus used by the CPU to carry data that identifies the memory locations where the data bits are being sent to or retrieved from.

ADSL (Asymmetric Digital Subscriber Line)   A relatively new technology that allows more data to be sent over existing copper telephone lines than previously possible.

AGP (accelerated graphics port)   An interface specification developed by Intel Corporation, designed especially for the throughput demands of 3D graphics. It uses a dedicated point-to-point channel, and allows the graphics controller to directly access main memory.

AGP slot   A high-speed graphics port created by Intel that features a direct connection between the display monitor and memory.

alphanumeric key   A keyboard key that represents a letter or a number.

Alt   A key used simultaneously with a second key to produce a desired function.

Altair 8080   A microcomputer introduced by MITS in 1975. It is considered by many computer experts to be the first successful PC.

AMD (Advanced Micro Devices)   An Intel-clone - producing computer manufacturer.

analog   Signals that continually changing strengths or qualities, like sound waves or voltage.

analog-to-digital converter   A device that converts analog (sound-based) tones and pulses into digital (binary-based) data for computer use.

Analytical Engine   A programmable calculator designed by Charles Babbage in the 1830s.

antistatic bag   A bag used to prevent static electricity from passing to electronic components inside. They are used to help prevent ESD.

antistatic mat   A mat made of an antistatic material designed to provide a grounding source, used to absorbs static electricity and prevent damage to electronic components.

API (Application Program Interface)   The specific method an application program can use to make requests of the operating system or of another application.

Apple Computer   The manufacturer of the Apple II and the Macintosh. Steve Wozniak and Steve Jobs founded Apple Computers in a garage.

Apple II   The Apple Computer Corporation's second PC, introduced in 1977, believed by many to be responsible for popularizing the PC.

application　　A software program designed to carry out a task or produce a result such as word processing, creating accounts, database management, and/or inventory control.

application server　　A machine that holds the applications users frequently access.

apps.inf　　A Windows file that maintains information about popular MS-DOS programs.

arbitration　　The process the SCSI host adapter uses to set priorities in handling multiple read/write requests, simultaneously, from contending drives on the bus. Priorities are based on the SCSI ID of the devices, from 0 to 7, in order of increasing priority.

architecture　　A system's hardware, software, data-access protocols, and overall computer communications system designs.

archive　　A DOS system attribute that checks if a file has changed since the last backup and requires backing up. Also refers to files stored as backup.

ARCnet　　LAN technology from the Datapoint Corporation that uses a token-bus system.

ARP (Address Resolution Protocol)　　The protocol TCP/IP uses to get a domain name address when only an IP address is available.

ASCII (American Standard Code for Information Interchange)　　A standardized code, using binary values, for representing characters.

asynchronous　　Not occurring at predetermined or regular intervals. Also, communications in which an interchange of data can start at anytime instead of occurring at fixed intervals.

asynchronous communication　　Bidirectional data transmission between two devices, in which the length of time between transmitted characters is variable.

AT command set　　A standard body of commands that communication programs send to a modem to manipulate its internal logic. Also known as the Hayes command set.

AT tower　　A type of form factor associated with older technologies.

AT/desk　　A type of form factor associated with older technologies.

ATA-2 (AT Attachment Standard No. 2)　　An update of the IDE/ATA standard, or a disk drive implementation that integrates the controller on the disk drive itself. ATA-2 is also known as EIDE and fast ATA, depending on the manufacturer.

Atanasoff, John　　The inventor who, along with Clifford Berry, invented the modern computer.

ATAPI (ATA packet interface)　　The extension specification of the ATA-2 standard that defines the device-side characteristics for non-hard drive devices such as CD-ROMs or tape drives.

attribute　　A hidden code in a file that determines the file type and what operations are permitted for that file.

ATX   A computer form factor considered the forerunner of the Baby AT. The ATX's motherboard is rotated 90 degrees in the chassis, and the CPU and SIMM sockets have been relocated away from the expansion card slots. Therefore, all the slots support full-length cards. Most Pentium Pro boards use this form factor.

ATX motherboard   A standard, desktop computer, motherboard specification currently in widespread use.

autoexec.bat   A startup file that runs when DOS is loaded and tells the computer what commands or programs to execute automatically after bootup. **autoexec.bat** commands help a user configure the system to individual preferences.

B

Baby AT   A type of form factor associated with older technologies.

Baby AT motherboard   A motherboard specification that replaced the original IBM AT motherboard.

backbone   A computer network that links several networks. FDDI is a common backbone network. Also, a large transmission path in a network, into which smaller lines feed.

backup   A copy of a disk, program, or other data. Backups should be created on a regular basis in order to protect data.

backward compatible   An upgraded computer or software that can handle the commands of previous versions.

bad sector   A damaged disk area within a cluster, in a disk partition. Bad sectors cannot be used, but data can be routed away from them after they are identified.

bandwidth   The difference between the highest and lowest frequency available for transmission in a communications system.

basic mechanical switch   A switch that uses metal contacts in a transient contact arrangement. This is regarded as the simplest and most expensive type of keyboard switch, and provides excellent tactile feedback. It is also called a pure mechanical switch.

basis name   The first six characters of a filename, regardless of the name's length, that are retained when an MS-DOS program reads a Windows 95 program.

baud rate   The number of electrical oscillations that occur each second in digital communications. Each oscillation encodes 1 bit of information.

binary file   A file made up of codes, either 8-bit or executable.

binary number   A base-2 number that only uses the digits 1 and 0. Computers and digital devices work with binary numbers extensively.

binary system   A number system based on only two digits: 0 and 1. All values are expressed as combinations of these two numbers. For example, the letter A is expressed as 1000001.

BinderyNetWare   A server database that contains network information about users, groups, passwords, and access rights.

binding   A method for communicating between adapters, protocols, and networking services.

BIOS (basic input/output system)   Built-in computer software that determines what functions a computer can perform without accessing programs from a disk. The BIOS contains the code required to control the display screen, disk drives, keyboard, serial communications, and a number of miscellaneous functions.

bit   A basic unit of information in the binary system—either a 1 or a 0. A bit is the smallest piece of information that a computer can understand. It takes 8 bits to equal 1 byte, which is the amount of disk space to store one character of information.

bitmap   Individual data pieces collected together to produce an image.

bitmap font   A typeface designed pixel by pixel, intended for computer-monitor display. Also called raster or screen font.

blackout   Complete failure of electric power for a region.

block mode PIO (programmed I/O)   Two essential interface signals used to indicate the status of two connected drives on an IDE controller channel. This allows the master and slave IDE drives to coordinate their data transmissions on the bus.

boot   To load and start the operating system on a computer.

boot partition   A primary partition on a hard drive that has been set to active, or bootable, by the partitioning utility. The BIOS searches for the operating system's bootstrap loader on this partition.

boot sector   Another term for the master boot record. Cylinder 0, head 0, sector 1 is considered the beginning of the hard drive containing the initial boot program that the system BIOS loads to begin the boot process.

bootstrap   An early computer industry term that means to start up and load a computer's operating system.

bps (bits per second)   The same as the baud rate when 1 bit is transmitted per modulation change.

bridge   A piece of equipment used to connect segments of a single network or to connect similar entire networks to each other.

brownout   A type of power event in which the voltage falls below the nominal voltage carried by a power line.

browse master   A utility that acts in an administrative capacity in peer-to-peer networks to list all the servers in the network.

buffer   A temporary storage area usually located in RAM, which acts as a holding area that allows the CPU to manipulate data before transferring it to a device.

bug   An error or defect in software or hardware that causes a program to malfunction.

bulletin board   A computer that can be accessed by a modem to share and exchange messages or other files.

bus   A pathway between many devices when used in relation with a network. An assortment of wires through which data is transmitted from one part of a computer to another.

bus enumerator   A device driver that identifies devices located on a specific bus and assigns a unique code for each device.

bus network   A network in which computers are arranged "down a line," without a centralized hub.

byte   A grouping of 8 bits that usually contains a single letter, number, or other symbol. The amount of space that it takes to store one character of information.

C

cable modem   A modem designed to function in unison with the coaxial cable lines owned by cable TV companies. It is not a true modem, but uses a network adapter interface to link to the Internet through the high-bandwidth coaxial cable medium.

cache   A storage area for frequently accessed information for faster response. Motherboard cache memory is extra-fast RAM that maintains a copy of recently requested bits from regular RAM.

case   The plastic housing that encloses and protects the CRT and associated electrical circuitry.

case sensitive   When an operation distinguishes between upper- and lowercase letters.

CAU (controlled-access unit)   A Token Ring network's central hub

CCITT (Consultative Committee on International Telephone and Telegraph)   Older name for the ITU.

CD-ROM (compact disc—read only memory)   A round, flat, disc medium designed to store up to 650 MB. CD-ROMs are also called CDs.

CD-ROM (compact disc—read only memory) drive   A peripheral device that uses a read-only optical storage medium to access data, including text, audio, video, and graphics. This type of device can have either an IDE or a SCSI interface.

CGA (color graphics array) The first graphics standard, introduced in 1981; it became obsolete when VGA was introduced in 1987.

character In serial communications, a byte of data or 8 data bits preceded by 1 start bit and ended by 1 stop bit.

chat To "talk" on the Internet with another person who is online at the same time.

circuit board A thin, rectangular plate usually made of silicon, on which chips and other electronic components are placed.

click and drag To move a selected image or block of text with a mouse. By clicking on an item and holding down a mouse button, a user can use a mouse to slide text or images to a designated screen position.

client A user's microcomputer on a network.

Client for NetWare Networks A mechanism that allows a machine to be connected to a NetWare Network.

client software A program that exists on a remote computer in a network.

client/server network A number of individual workstations or client computers that are connected to each other and exchange information via a central server.

clock signal Voltage supplied by the motherboard to a quartz crystal in order to make it vibrate at a predetermined speed. The vibrations of the quartz crystal help control the speed of the CPU.

close program A command in the dialog box that allows you to end a program.

cluster A unit of storage on a disk that contains sectors of data. Clusters are the smallest group of sectors within a partition.

cmd.exe The Windows NT command processor.

CMOS (complementary metal oxide semiconductor) chip A battery-powered memory and clock chip that is used to store system clock settings and configuration data. Another term for this is RTC/NVRAM chip. A commonly used term for the stored system configuration settings that are set up in BIOS.

CMOS setup Another term for the BIOS or system setup utility. The term is technically incorrect, but it is used because the system setup configuration is stored in the CMOS chip.

cold boot Starting up a computer by turning on the power button.

collisions When information is sent by two Ethernet-network computers at the some time, the data "collides." The network waits a random amount of time, and then tries to re-send the data.

color gradation   The perceptual factor involved in a monitor's color display design, but more specifically regarding the limited range of a digital display, and the near-infinite number of color shades for analog displays.

COM   The name used by MS-DOS to designate serial ports.

COM1, COM2   Serial communications ports on the motherboard that can be configured in a number of ways. Multi I/O connectors.

command interpreter   Another term for command processor.

command line   A DOS function that waits for user commands to be typed according to DOS-specific codes.

command processor   The central command file for the operating system kernel, which accepts and executes the operating system commands. This file is accessed directly from a command prompt.

command prompt   Also called the command line, the command prompt is the text-based screen interface for an operating system.

command queue   The memory buffer used to line up read/write requests from SCSI hard drives until the host adapter processor has time to attend to them.

command.com   The MS-DOS command processor. It is also one of the three MS-DOS operating system files that the MS-DOS bootstrap loader searches for in the root directory of the boot disk and loads into memory.

command-line execution parameters   Parameters that change the function of a batch file. They are passed to the batch file from the command line of the batch file.

complete trust domain model   An arrangement of clients and servers that allows reciprocal trust relationships between multiple domains and resources.

compound document   An organized collection of user interfaces that form a single, integrated environment containing text files, audio files, video files, and so on.

computer   An electronic device that enables users to input, manipulate, store, and output information.

computing pen   An input device similar to a mouse that is usually used to enter data on a small portable computer.

concatenate   To join in sequence. For example, Disk Defragmenter concatenates data so that all the data for each file is physically located together on the disk.

conductive   Having the capability to transmit electricity, heat, sound, and so on.

conductor   Material that transmits electricity, heat, sound, and so on.

config.sys   A DOS file that configures some computer resources and loads drivers to control computer-specific hardware.

configuration   The way in which a computer and peripherals are connected and programmed to operate. The way a computer's operating system is set up, and the variety of components contained within the system and how they are set up.

connect network registry   A command in the Registry Editor that permits the user to edit the Registry of a remote computer.

connectivity   The capability of files, data, and resources to be shared and exchanged across a network.

connector   Another term for electrical leads and plugs.

container   A file that contains linked, common-purpose files or other objects.

container object   A file that contains linked common-purpose files or other objects. Also called a *container*.

contiguous   Sharing a boundary, next to each other.

control circuitry   The dedicated electrical component that reads the output from the video card RAMDAC chip and controls the electron beam scanning the CRT. External controls can manipulate the brightness, contrast, screen shape, and color of this output.

Control Panel   A utility represented by an icon in the Windows 95 My Computer default window. It allows users to configure a computer's color, fonts, mouse, desktop, sound, date and time, and other system features.

conventional memory   A computer's first 640 KB of memory; contains essential programs, data, and operating system areas.

cooperative multitasking   A type of multitasking that requires the currently running task to give up control of the processor and allow other tasks to run.

copy protected   Software containing a developer-implanted lock to keep users from unauthorized copying.

CP/M (Control Program for Microcomputer)   The first PC operating system, written by Gary Kildall in 1973.

cps (characters per second)   The measure of speed of dot-matrix printers. How many characters of a certain quality the printer can output each second.

CPU (central processing unit)   A microchip is a tiny computer chip that acts as a computer's brain. A CPU carries out commands, performs calculations, and communication with all the hardware components needed to operate a computer. A CPU is sometimes referred to as a microprocessor.

CPU cache   A memory bank that bridges the CPU and main memory. It is considerably faster than main memory and allows data and instructions to be read at a higher speed.

crash   For a hard drive or a program to suddenly fail to work while it is running.

CRC (cyclic redundancy check)   An error-detection technique used by modems on every block of data sent between them. Detected errors force the re-sending of the bad data.

CRT (cathode ray tube)   A glass cylinder that hosts an electron gun at the rear, which emits an electron beam to activate the phosphor-coated screen at the front to create an image. Also, any type of monitor that utilizes the component.

CSA (Canadian Standards Association)   A Canadian standards development and certification organization.

CSEL (cable select)   One of two key interface signals used to indicate the status of two connected drives on an IDE controller channel. This allows the master and slave IDE drives to coordinate their data transmissions on the bus.

CSMA/CD (carrier sense multiple access collision detect)   An Ethernet feature that, after listening for silence, sends packets, re-sending them if a collision is found.

Ctrl + Alt + Del   A combination of keys to use simultaneously to close down programs that are hung and/or to reboot the machine, depending on the operating system.

cut-sheet paper   Individual-page paper fed into the printer engine one sheet at a time from a manual or tray feeder.

Cyrix   A computer manufacturer that produces a Pentium-clone computer, the Cyrix 6x86.

D

DASP (drive active/slave present)   One of two key interface signals used by hard drives on the IDE bus. The DASP device signals the presence of a slave drive at startup, and is used by both drives after startup to indicate whether they themselves are active.

data   In the world of computers, any information that goes into or is taken from the computer.

Data Compression Standard   The ITU standard for data compression that provides a mathematical algorithm to compress the data to one quarter its normal size over a modem connection.

data integrity   The accuracy of data after being transmitted or processed.

DB (data bus)   The number of pins on the connector.

dB (decibel)   The logarithm of a ratio of power, voltages, current, and so on. A 3-db increase in power represents a doubling in power.

DC (direct current)   Electrical current that travels in only one direction, as opposed to AC. It is generally used in electronic circuits.

debounce   A programming routine used by a keyboard controller to neutralize the side effects of rapid keyboard switch pressing—a condition that causes the switches to bounce rapidly on and off the circuit contacts.

decimal system   A common base-10 numbering system using the digits 0–9.

Decompression   The process of restoring the contents of a compressed file to its original form.

defacto   A standard generally used in the computing industry, although not officially sanctioned by a standard-setting organization.

default   Settings or parameters that are used automatically by a system until it receives different instructions.

default system icon   An onscreen graphic depicting a group of linked, common-purpose container objects, such as My Computer, Recycle Bin, and Network Neighborhood.

default.pif   A Windows file that stores information about MS-DOS programs that are not contained in the apps.inf file.

deflection coil   The portion of the CRT that deflects the electron beam. The deflection causes the beam to strike a specific screen area. Also called the *yoke*.

defragment   To rewrite files to a disk so they are in contiguous order.

Delete key   A computer keyboard key used to remove alphanumeric characters and other onscreen objects.

demodulation   The means by which a modem converts analog data signals into digital signals.

desktop   The onscreen space that underlies all work done on the computer. Like an actual desktop, the computer's desktop gives a computer user a location to put and organize work. The Windows 95 desktop is the first Windows 95 logon screen.

despool   To remove documents from the print spool before sending them to the printer.

developer unit   A small roller near the drum that feeds toner onto the drum from a storage bin above it. The storage bin is called the *toner hopper*.

device contention   An enhanced panel option that configures how the system should handle resource conflicts.

device driver   A program that controls various devices, including the BIOS, BIOS extension, and operating system.

device font   A fast type of printer font stored inside the printer. Also called a *hardware font*.

Device Manager   A Windows 95 System Properties utility that notifies the user of device conflicts. It also allows the user to change a computer's properties and the devices attached to it.

DHCP (Dynamic Host Configuration Protocol)   A protocol that allows network administrators to centrally manage and automatically assign IP addresses in an organization's network.

diagnostic software disk   A disk containing software designed to run system diagnostics and display the results on a monitor or by means of printouts. It provides diagnostics for a computer's memory, processor, disk storage, operating system, and peripherals.

diagnostic test   Software used to diagnose problems within the system; for example, antivirus software.

dialog box   An onscreen window, displayed in response to a user request, designed to provide options currently available to the user, and/or the progress of the system's execution of a command.

Dial-Up Networking   An object in the Windows 95 My Computer default container that permits user access to modem and Internet resources.

Difference Engine   An early steam-powered calculation machine designed by Charles Babbage.

differential backup   One type of Microsoft Backup command. Differential backup backs up only files changed or created since the last full backup.

digital   Data that is kept as a collection of numbers. For example, a digital image is kept as a collection of numbers that determine the color of each point. Digital signals and information consist of electronic pulses of energy designed to represent the bits and bytes of binary code.

digital computer   A computer that accepts and processes data that has been converted into binary numbers. All modern-day computers are digital.

DIMM (dual inline memory module)   A small circuit board that holds memory chips. A DIMM chip generally has a 64-bit data path. A DIMM has a 64-bit path to the memory chips, in contrast to a SIMM, which has a 32-bit path to the memory chips.

directory   An inventory of file names that indexes organized and grouped files for information retrieval.

Disk Defragmenter   A Windows 95 program that defragments disks.

disk platter   Media disks that store data in the hard drive. The disks are typically constructed of a rigid composite material covered with magnetically sensitive, thin-film medium.

display monitor   Another term for video display monitor, monitor, or video monitor.

displayable resolution   A manufacturer's resolution specification that states the maximum physical resolution a monitor model can display.

DLL (dynamic link library) files   Small files containing codes common to several Windows programs.

DMA (direct memory access)   A means by which data moves between a system device such as a disk drive and system memory, without direct control of the CPU. This frees up the CPU for other tasks.

DMM (digital multimeter)   A device used to measure and test voltage, resistance, and amperage of electrical components.

DNS (Domain Name System)   Internet computer–locating software that allows users to find specific computer users on the Internet by either a domain name or an IP address.

dock   To connect a laptop or notebook computer to a docking station, which contains a power connection, expansion slots, and peripheral connections.

docking station   A desktop unit into which a laptop computer connects, which allows the user to use a full-size monitor, keyboard, mouse, and expansion slots.

Documents   A Start menu option that lists the computer's most recently used or created documents.

domain   An arrangement of client and server computers, with a specific reference name, that share a security permissions database.

domain controller   A server that authenticates workstation network logon requests by checking the user accounts database for username and password verification.

DOS (Disk Operating System)   Another term for *MS-DOS*.

DOS parameter   A parameter that changes how a batch file functions, sometimes referred to as an *environment variable*. Set in autoexec.bat, DOS parameters specify both DOS and batch file functions.

DOS prompt   An onscreen prompt in the command prompt window which indicates that the system is ready to receive a user's DOS-driven commands.

dot   The smallest elements of a CRT. Dots are the small red, green, and blue phosphorus spots on the inside of the monitor.

dot pitch   The distance between adjacent sets of red, green, and blue dots in a given pixel. Dot pitch defines how fine the dots are that make the image on a video display. The smaller the distance between the dots, the sharper the image.

dot-matrix printer   A type of printer that creates characters and graphics by striking pins against an ink ribbon. The striking pins print closely spaced dots in the appropriate shapes of characters.

double-click   To rapidly choose and open a program by pressing and releasing a mouse button twice in close succession.

downloadable font   A font downloaded to a printer's memory as needed from a disk. Also called a *soft font*.

DPMS (display power management system)   A power management signaling specification developed for monitors by VESA. This system allows a computer to monitor a video display for inactivity, and power it down until used.

drag   To position a mouse pointer over an object, hold the mouse button down, and move the pointer to another screen location. Also known as *drag and drop* and *click and drag*.

drive   A device used to write to and/or read information from magnetic platters or disks. It is usually located inside the system unit. Types of drives include hard drives, floppy disk drives, CD-ROM, and optical drives.

drive bracket   A brace or prop used to attach a drive to the chassis.

drive command   A device command in the system BIOS used to manage hard disk drives through the controller interface.

drive status light   An indicator light on the front bezel of the system case that denotes whether a drive is active or at rest. Generally, when the light is on, the drive is in use. A light that is off indicates that the drive is not in use.

driver   A device or program that controls another device. Individual drivers allow a computer to utilize specific devices, such as printers or disk drives.

DriveSpace3   A Windows 95 utility used to compress data.

drum   A magnetic media storage device

DSP (digital signal processor)   A very fast digital-processing chip used in devices such as sound cards, cellular phones, and high-capacity hard disks.

dual boot   A configuration facility that allows a computer to boot up in either Windows or previously installed MS-DOS.

dual ported   A memory architecture design for video memory, especially VRAM and WRAM, that has two access paths and can be written to and read from simultaneously.

dust plate   A plate that covers each hole on the back of the computer that is not being used by an expansion card. Another term for an *adapter plate*.

duster   Compressed air or carbon dioxide in a can that is used to blow dust off electronic components.

DVD (digital video disc)   A two-sided optical disc the size of a standard CD, but featuring considerably more storage space. DVDs are considered the next generation of optical disc storage technology.

Dvorak keyboard   A keyboard layout designed in the 1930s by August Dvorak and his brother-in-law, William Dealey. It is not widely used.

dynamic electricity   Electricity that results from moving charges within conductors.

dynamic IP address   A current-session-only IP address.

E

econo-mode   A low-resolution print mode for inkjet printers that prints at a lower density and uses less ink.

EDO RAM (extended data output RAM)   A type of RAM that is faster than conventional RAM. Unlike conventional DRAM, which only allows 1 byte to be read at a time, EDO RAM can copy an entire block of memory to its internal cache. While the CPU is accessing this cache, the memory can collect a new block to send. EDO RAM is faster than the usual DRAM, but generally slower than SDRAM.

efficiency   In a power supply, the ratio of input power to output power.

EGA (enhanced graphics array)   The second graphics standard, introduced in 1984; it became obsolete when VGA was introduced in 1987.

EIA (Electronics Industry Association)   An association that has members from various electronics manufacturers and is based in Washington, DC. It sets standards for electronic components.

EIDE (enhanced integrated drive electronics)   The same as the ATA-2 standard.

EIDE interface   The 40-pin interface connector that is keyed by the removal of pin 20 on the male drive connector site for the IDE drive and the motherboard controller.

EISA (extended industry standard architecture)   A standard bus architecture that extends the ISA standard to a 32-bit interface.

electrode   A device that emits or controls the flow of electricity.

electron   A subatomic particle that has a negative electrical charge.

electron gun   A device in a computer monitor that produces an electron beam.

e-mail (electronic mail)   General e-mail features and files transmitted electronically by means of a network or phone line.

EMF (enhanced metafile format) spool   A method of print spooling used by Windows 95 that returns application control to the user more quickly than the spooling method used in Windows 3.1.

EMI (electromagnetic interference)   An electrical disturbance created by electromagnetic signals, resulting in reduced data integrity and increased error rates on transmission channels.

Energy Star   An energy conservation standard created by the U.S. Environmental Protection Agency for computer efficiency. Devices that draw no more than 30 watts when inactive can be certified for this standard and display the logo.

Entire Network   A file in the Windows 95 Network Neighborhood default container. It holds other workgroups, servers, and shared network resources.

environmental variable A variable that changes how a batch file functions. Set in autoexec.bat, DOS parameters specify both DOS and batch file functions. Usually called *DOS parameters*.

EPROM (erasable programmable ROM) A type of ROM that retains its contents until it is exposed to ultraviolet light. Once exposed to ultraviolet light, its contents are cleared, making it possible to reprogram the memory.

ergonomic Devices designed and arranged with special attention to their safe and efficient human use.

error correction standard The ITU V.42 standard for error correction in modem communications.

ESD (electrostatic discharge) The flow or spark of electricity that originates from a static source such as a carpet and arcs across a gap to another object.

Ethernet Currently the most popular technology for computer networking. An Ethernet can take either a bus or star configuration.

expansion adapter A device that serves as an interface between the system unit and the devices attached to it. Also called a *circuit board* or *circuit card*.

expansion card A printed circuit board designed to be inserted into a computer's expansion sockets to provide a computer with added capabilities. Examples include video adapters, graphics accelerators, sound cards, and internal modems. Expansion cards are sometimes referred to as *adapters*, *cards*, *add-ins*, and *add-ons*.

extended memory A computer's memory above 1 MB. 386-enhanced mode requires at least 1024 KB extended memory; standard mode requires 256 KB extended memory.

extended partition A partition on a hard disk that is used to hold files. It cannot contain operating system software, and can be subdivided into multiple partitions.

extension A three-character designation added to the end of a filename and preceded by a period that identifies the file as belonging to a particular type or category.

external drive unit A peripheral device such as a floppy disk drive that attaches to the system unit and is used for input and output, such as storage of data.

external lever switch One of two kinds of power on/off switches. It is connected to the older AT form factor power supply.

F

fan-fold paper Another term for *tractor-feed paper*.

FAQ (frequently asked questions) Information posted in an attempt to answer questions that are common to many users of a newsgroup or Web site.

fast SCSI-2   A variant of the SCSI-2 standard that supports data rates of 10 MBps over an 8-bit bus, and uses the 50-pin interface connector.

fast wide SCSI-2   An extension of the SCSI-2 standard, sometimes called SCSI-3, that features a 16-bit bus and supports data rates of 20 MBps over the wide SCSI-2 68-pin interface connector.

FAT (File Allocation Table)   A catalog of the locations and sizes of all the hard drive files. An operating system, looking for a file, checks the FAT. The FAT file system is the only formatting DOS can use.

FAT32   A 32-bit FAT system that allows partitions larger than 2 GB and supports long filenames.

fax (facsimile)   A transmission of text or graphics over telephone lines in a digitized form. Also, the equipment used for these transmissions.

FCC (Federal Communications Commission)   An independent government agency responsible for the licensing and regulatory authority of television, radio, wire, satellite, and cable in the United States.

FDC (floppy drive connector)   A multi I/O parallel connector on a motherboard.

FDDI (Fiber Distributed Data Interface)   A technology for computer networking, typically used to link several networks. Based on a ring configuration without a central hub, it is a token-passing network architecture that uses fiber-optic lines to transmit data at 100 Mbps. It can support many users and is a very fast networking architecture.

fdisk   A Windows 95 utility that allows the user to create partitions.

fdisk.exe   A DOS program file used to partition and activate hard drives for installing an operating system.

FIFO (first in, first out)   A method in which items are removed in the same order in which they were added; for example, the first in would be the first out.

file   A compilation of saved data with a designated name.

file handle   An open file; sometimes, a device.

file management system   A portion of an operating system that translates an application's requests into specific tasks. Also refers to the complete structure that names, stores, and organizes files. It includes directories, files, and the information for locating and accessing them.

File Manager   A Windows 3.1 utility for simplifying file organization.

file set   A set of files that have been backed up and stored in sets by the Microsoft Backup utility for later retrieval.

file system   Also known as a *file management system*, it is the portion of the operating system that translates an application's requests into specific tasks, and acts as the file tree structure that names, stores, and organizes files.

Find   A Start menu option that offers users options for locating various computer features, files, and folders.

fixed disk drive   An alternate term for a hard drive, used by IBM.

fixed drive   A disk, like a hard drive, that is a fixed, permanent part of the computer.

fixed refresh rate   A design specification for a display monitor that has only one scanning frequency. This limits the monitor's ability to display higher resolutions without image flicker due to the fixed vertical and horizontal scan rates.

flash BIOS   A type of memory chip called an EPROM that allows the BIOS to be updated by files from the manufacturer.

floppy disk   A removable, reusable magnetic storage media used by floppy disk drives to read and write data. Also called *disks* or *diskettes*.

floppy disk drive   A type of disk drive that uses floppy disks. Commonly called a *floppy drive*.

floppy drive controller   Electronics that control the floppy disk drive and negotiate the passage of data between the floppy disk drive and the computer.

flow control   A method of managing the rate at which the host system sends data to the modem.

flux   The magnetic polarity of the particles in the thin-film media of hard drive platters.

flux pattern   The pattern of flux reversals or transitions encoded into the thin-film media of the hard drive platters. The timing of these transitions represents the stored data bits.

flux reversal   A switch in the magnetic polarity of the particles in the thin-film media of hard drive platters.

FM (frequency modulation) synthesis   Synthesizing sound by creating a wave close to the original sound's wave.

foam buffer key switch   A mechanical switch similar to the tactile feedback mechanism. It uses foam with a foil laminate in place of a metal plate to strike the contacts. It is also called a *foam element key switch*.

folder   A computer's storage place for programs and files. Indicated onscreen by a graphic file folder.

font   A character set with a common typeface, style, and weight.

form factor   The physical dimensions of a system unit. Two computers with the same form factor are physically interchangeable.

format.com   A DOS program file used to create a FAT file system on a hard drive or floppy disk.

Formatting   An external DOS command that uses the **format.com** file to prepare a disk to store information and create a FAT.

frame buffer   The storage area inside video memory where information is stored about the video image itself.

front bezel   A faceplate that covers the front of the chassis and provides attachment points for standardized components.

front case bezel   The portion of the computer's case through which the CD-ROM drive and floppy drives are accessed. It may also contain various LED indicators, the reset button, and the on/off switch.

FTP (File Transfer Protocol)   A protocol used to transfer files over a TCP/IP network, to download files from or upload files to remote computer systems. It includes functions to log on to the network, list directories, and copy files. It can also convert ASCII and EBCDIC character codes.

full backup   An option of the Microsoft Backup command that backs up all hard drive files.

full duplex   An updated sound card characteristic, wherein, as in a telephone line, sound can travel in both directions, and do so simultaneously via two channels.

full tower   The largest of the tower form factors.

full-duplex mode   A mode in which high-performance modems send and receive data at the same time. This is accomplished by sending data bits out of one wire and receiving data in the other wire in a two-wire phone line.

fuse   A device used as part of the power supply's internal overload protection circuitry. When the maximum allowable current is exceeded, the fuse intercepts the overload of current and intentionally fails. This interrupts the circuit and protects a power supply's circuitry.

fuser   In a laser printer, a pair of hot rollers that affixes the toner into the paper via heat and pressure.

G

ganged   A term for the stacked way that read/write heads are attached to the end of the head actuator assembly of a hard drive. They move in unison as a gang.

Gates, Bill   The multibillionaire and Harvard-dropout CEO of Microsoft Corporation.

gateway   A device used to connect networks whose protocols differ. Also, a network point (often a proxy server) that acts as an entrance to another network.

GB (gigabyte)   A measurement equal to 1,024 MB or 1,073,741,824 bytes.

GDI (graphics device interface)   A system that provides graphics support in Windows 95. As it relates to printing, the GDI assists in EMF spooling, to return application control to the user more rapidly.

GDI Manager   A core file whose job is to draw images and TrueType fonts, mainly for icons and other windows features, such as dialog boxes and buttons.

GPF (general protection fault)   An error a user receives when an application attempts to access an area not designated for its use. Also called a *general protection error*.

grabber   File picture-taking software that transfers a single video onscreen image to a disk file.

graphics tablet   An input device that has a touch-sensitive surface. When the user draws on the tablet's surface using a special pen, it relays the image that is drawn to the computer, where it can be manipulated in a graphics application.

gray code   A binary number system in which the code for a specific number and a number that is one greater differs by exactly 1 bit. It is used to avoid errors that may result from ambiguous readings from a disk platter.

ground   Any contact point that is electrically neutral.

grounding strap   A device, usually worn on the wrist, that prevents the buildup of ESD.

group   Files organized by their file extensions that help organize program icons and menus that run and start programs.

GUI (graphical user interface)   A user interface that utilizes a mouse and graphics such as icons and pull-down menus. It is currently the industry standard for interacting with computers.

H

HAA (head actuator assembly)   The hard drive mechanism composed of the read/write heads, the arms that hold them, and the voice coil actuator, which moves these accurately across the hard drive platters.

half duplex   An early sound card characteristic, in which, as in a two-way radio, sound travels in both directions, but only in one direction at a time.

handshake   An electronic exchange of signals that takes place initially when one modem contacts another over telephone lines.

handshake mode   A request/acknowledgement method that a SCSI host adapter uses to negotiate an asynchronous data transfer with a SCSI device on the bus.

hard disk   A device comprised of several rotating, nonremovable magnetic disks used for storing computer data.

hard disk drive   A high volume, non-removable, internal disk drive with fixed media. Often called a *hard drive*.

hard disk drive LED   An electronic device that lights up when electricity is passed through it to indicate that the hard drive is in use.

hard drive   A high volume, non-removable, internal disk drive with fixed media.

hard drive controller   Electronics that control the hard disk drive and negotiate the passage of data between the hard disk drive and the computer.

hardware   The physical components of a computer, including monitors, keyboards, motherboards, and peripherals, such as printers and modems.

hardware font   A fast type of printer font stored inside the printer. Also called a *device font*.

hardware profile   Data that is used to configure computers for use with peripheral devices.

harmonic distortion   A change in an electrical signal that occurs periodically.

Hayes command set   Another term for the AT command set.

HDA (head disk assembly)   The sealed chamber of a hard drive, containing the disk platters, spindle motor, heads, and head actuator mechanism. It is a single logical component only serviceable by the manufacturer.

heat sink   Heat-absorbing material used for chip-generated heat absorption on computer motherboards.

Help   A Start menu option that provides a Windows information resource.

hex (hexadecimal) system   A base-16 numbering system using the digits 0–9 and A–F. It is often used to represent the binary numbers that computers use.

hidden   A DOS system attribute that prevents a file's appearance in the directory. This attribute is usually assigned to system files or other files that require protection against accidental deletion.

hierarchical network   A network where one host computer controls a number of smaller computers, and these smaller computers may be a host to a group of PC workstations.

HKEY_CLASSES_ROOT   A subdirectory in the Registry structure that contains configuration information about OLE, shortcuts and the GUI.

HKEY_CURRENT_CONFIG   A subdirectory in the Registry structure that contains hardware configuration information.

HKEY_CURRENT_USER   A subdirectory in the Registry structure that points to another subdirectory, **HKEY_USERS**, for the currently logged-on user.

HKEY_DYN_DATA   A subdirectory in the Registry structure that contains plug-and-play configuration information and points to **HKEY_LOCAL_MACHINE**.

HKEY_LOCAL_MACHINE   A subdirectory in the Registry structure that contains specific information about installed hardware, software settings, and other information.

HKEY_USERS   A handle key containing user configuration information.

hold time   The time during which a power supply's output voltage remains within specification following the loss of input power.

horizontal scan rate   The rated speed at which the scanning electron beam can write the image across the screen horizontally.

host computer   The main computer within a system of computers that are connected by communication links.

host drive   A file created by DriveSpace to hold compressed data on the hard drive.

hot wire   An ungrounded lead wire used to connect the transformer and electrical devices or appliances by means of an electrical outlet and power plug.

HTML (Hypertext Markup Language)   A document format used on the Web, primarily to construct Web pages. HTML defines the page layout, fonts, graphic elements, and hypertext links to many documents on the Web.

HTTP (Hypertext Transfer Protocol)   A protocol used for connecting servers on the Internet.

hub   Another name for the spindle to which the disk platters are mounted. The term *hub* is also used in networking to refer to a connection that joins network communication lines in a star configuration.

hung   Wedged or locked up, not responding.

I

I/O (input/output)   An assortment of wires connecting the CPU with external devices, including all I/O connectors such as drive controllers, serial ports, parallel ports, and keyboard connectors connected to the ISA and PCI buses or adapter cards installed in the ISA and PCI bus slots.

I/O bus   A bus for data that is composed of data paths and storage units. It can either be internal or external.

IANA (Internet Assigned Numbers Authority)   The IP address registry.

IBM (International Business Machines)   The world's largest computer company, which dates back to Herman Hollerith's adding machine.

IBM compatible   A computer with a microprocessor that is compatible with the original IBM PC 8088. Not manufactured by IBM, they are often referred to as *IBM clones*, and are usually compatible with IBM software.

ICMP (Internet Control Message Protocol)   TCP/IP's protocol that sends error and control messages.

icon   A small onscreen graphic image used to access the computer's applications or devices.

IDE (integrated drive electronics)   A type of drive interface ratified in 1989, called the ATA standard. The standard gave specifications for the integration of the old ST-506 disk controller circuitry onto the hard drive; it was superceded by the ATA-2 standard in 1995.

identify drive   An ATA-2 standard drive command issued by the system BIOS to the EIDE hard drive, requesting it send a 512-byte data block identifying its make, model, and drive geometry. A command sent by the BIOS to the IDE hard drive to query the drive for its operating parameters and drive geometry.

IEEE (Institute of Electrical and Electronic Engineers)   The world's largest technical professional society, it promotes the development and application of electrotechnology and allied sciences.

impact printer   A printer in which the print heads physically strike the paper.

Import/Export   A command in the Registry Editor that allows the user to save data in a text file and restore it, either to the same or another computer.

incremental backup   A backup that backs up only files changed or created since the last full or incremental backup.

INF file   A Windows 95 or 98 file that contains device installation and configuration information.

Information Superhighway   Another name for the Internet, the world's largest computer network, made up of smaller computer networks.

infrared connection   A port on a motherboard that enables an infrared signal to transmit data from one device to another, without the use of cables.

INI file   A text-based initialization file used by Windows to store system-specific or application-specific information.

initialization   The process of assigning values to variables and data structures in a program when it first starts up.

inkjet printer   A type of non-impact printer that uses liquid ink to spray characters onto the page.

input   Data that is sent to the CPU for processing from an outside source such as a keyboard, CD-ROM, or modem.

input connector   The 15-pin mini D-sub video cable connector on the back of the monitor.

input device   A device used for entering data into a computer, such as a keyboard, mouse, or joystick.

input signal   Manufacturer specification for the type of video input the monitor uses. The standard for modern analog monitors is RGB Analog. This is opposed to the old TTL digital standard.

insulator   A nonconductor of electricity.

integrated circuit   An electronic circuit in which more than one transistor is placed on a single piece of semiconductor material.

intelligent hub   A hub in a star-based network that monitors the network for problems and removes network access from a problem-causing computer.

interlaced   A scanning mode in which the scanning beam goes across the screen from top to bottom but alternates every other line, requiring two passes across the screen. The first scan is for even lines, and the second is for odd. This allows monitors to support higher resolutions at lower frequencies, but leaves the undesirable flicker.

internal register   High-speed memory bits inside a microprocessor.

Internet   The world's largest computer network, made up of smaller computer networks. The Internet began in the early 1970s as a network connecting government agencies, called the Advanced Research Projects Agency Network. Also called the *Information Superhighway* and the *World Wide Web*.

internetwork   To communicate between two separate computer networks via PCs.

InterNIC (Internet Network Information Center)   A joint endeavor to provide information services, directory and database services, and registration services for the Information Superhighway. InterNIC is made up of AT&T, General Atomics, and Networks Solutions.

interoperate   To function between two systems.

interrupt   A communication to the system from the processor that signals a problem or service request.

intuitive interface   An easy-to-use user interface in which an object's purpose it denounced by its appearance. For example, the files and folders in Windows look like physical files and folders.

Invar   Shadow mask metal manufactured by Hitachi that can bear high temperatures without distortion.

io.sys   One of the three MS-DOS operating system files that the bootstrap loader searches for in the root directory of the boot disk and loads into memory.

ion   An atom or a molecule that has gained or lost electrons and has a positive or negative charge. In general, negative ions have an excess of electrons, and positive ions lack electrons.

ionizer   An electrical device used to generate ions into the air. It helps prevent static buildup and ESD.

IOS (input/output system)   Built-in software that determines what a computer can do without accessing programs from a disk. The I/O system contains all the code required to control the display screen, disk drives, keyboards, serial communications, and a number of miscellaneous functions.

IPv6 (IP version 6)   An update of Internet Protocol version 4.

IPX/SPX (Internetwork Packet Exchange/Sequence Packet Exchange)   A networking protocol that interconnects Novell networking clients. SPX is a transport-layer protocol built on top of IPX.

IrDA (Infrared Data Association)   A group of device manufacturers that developed a standard for sending data by means of infrared light waves.

IRQ (interrupt request)   A signal generated by a hardware device to tell the CPU that a request needs to be executed.

ISA (industry standard architecture)   A bus standard for IBM compatibles that extends the XT bus architecture.

ISA bus   The bus used in the original IBM PC and still in widespread use.

ISA card   A card that attaches to a computer's motherboard to expand the computer's functions. A sound card, for example, allows a computer to produce sound effects, music, and voices.

ISA expansion slot   An industry-standard architecture expansion slot on the motherboard that connects to the I/O bus.

ISDN (Integrated Services Digital Network)   An international communications standard for sending voice, video, and data over digital telephone lines.

ISO (International Organization for Standardization)   A worldwide organization founded in 1946 that representing more than 100 countries and promotes standards for communications protocols.

isopropyl alcohol   A type of alcohol used as a solvent.

ISP (Internet service provider)   A company that provides access to the Internet for computer users for a monthly fee. It provides an access telephone number, a username, and a password for a modem-equipped user to log on to the Internet and use the Web, transfer files, and access news and email services.

ITU (International Telecommunications Union)   Formerly called the CCITT, an organization which sets the modulation standards that govern the basic rate of speed for modem communications.

J

Joule   A unit used for measuring energy. 1 watt of power lasting for 1 second supplies 1 Joule of energy.

joystick   An input device that is used to control onscreen movement. It is usually used in game applications to control the movement of some object such as an animated character.

K

kernel   The heart of the operating system, it launches applications, allocates system resources, and manages memory, files, peripheral devices, and a the date and time.

key matrix   A grid array of key switches that collectively form the keyboard.

keyboard   An input device that allows the user to type in text or enter commands into the computer. Although based on the typewriter keyboard, a typical PC keyboard also contains special keys that are used with computer programs.

keyboard interface   A serial port, unlike standard COM ports, that handles serial communications between the keyboard and motherboard.

keylock   A security device that when locked with a key, locks all access to system input devices.

KHz (kilohertz)   A measure of transmission speeds of electronic devices: 1 KHz = 1,000 cycles per second or 1,000 Hz.

L

LAN (local-area network)   A data network designed to connect workstations, peripheral devices, terminals, and other devices in a single building or other geographically limited area.

LAPM (Link Access Procedure for Modems)   An error-correction standard established by the ITU called V.42 that defines how parity-checking methods are to be used in modem transmissions.

large drive connector   A large 4-pin power supply connectors that connect to the hard disk or floppy disk drives, and uses a 12-volt motor.

laser printer   A type of non-impact printer that uses a laser to draw an image on an electrically charged drum, which is transferred to electrically charged paper using toner.

laser scanning assembly   The part of the print engine in a laser printer that transcribes the array of dots into a printable image on the photoreceptor drum.

LBA (logical block addressing)   A method used to support IDE hard disks larger than 504 MB on PCs, to provide the necessary address conversion in the BIOS.

LCD (liquid crystal display)   A monitor type that uses a polarized, molecular structure liquid, held between two see-through electrodes, as its display medium.

LED (light-emitting diode)   A device that illuminates when electrical current passes through it. Depending on the material used, the color can be visible or infrared. Used as indicator lights on many types of electronic devices.

legacy application   An older application that is still in use after the system has been upgraded.

line conditioner   Equipment that provides some type of filtering and/or regulation from an AC power source.

line interactive UPS   Another term for *online UPS*.

line noise   Undesirable communications channel signals that occur on an electrical circuit.

Linux   A UNIX-like operating system that was designed to provide PC users with a low-cost or free operating system.

load   To copy a program from some source into memory for execution.

load resistor   A device that maintains and regulates the electrical power flow at a predetermined, minimum operating limit.

load runtime   The amount of time a UPS can supply the system with electricity by using battery power only.

loader   Another name for the **win.com** file that starts Windows and contains the **win.cnf**, log, and run length encoded files.

local loop   The local analog telephone line segment of the telephone network from the nearest PSTN switch. These are the telephone lines between homes or businesses and the telephone company's central switches.

local printer   A printer that is connected to one computer, as opposed to a network.

lockup   A computer condition in which applications and hardware become temporarily inoperable or incapable of proceeding without intervention. A lockup is different from a crash. If the system crashes, it becomes unable to function; if the system locks up, it is incapable of making progress with a specific computing task.

logic board   A circuit board with soldered-on or socketed silicon chips.

logical drive   A drive that has been named as such by the system, whether or not that is its actual form.

logout   The action of closing an operating system that has been running on a network. Also called *logoff*.

loopback connector   A device that enables testing of the circuit or leads. It does this by sending signals out and recognizing whether the correct input is received back.

low profile   Another term used for a Slimline form factor.

low radiation   A manufacturer specification that indicates a monitor's compliance with international standards for very low frequency and extremely low frequency magnetic emissions. Because these are potentially harmful types of long-term radiation, this standard is designed to minimize exposure.

LPT (line print terminal)   Used by MS-DOS for designating printer ports.

LPT1, LPT2, LPT3   The names reserved by MS-DOS for the parallel printer ports.

LUN (logical unit number)   The physical number of each device connected in a daisy chain of drives.

M

make directory   A command that creates a directory on a drive or disk. Also called the **md** or **mkdir** command.

MAN (metropolitan-area network)   A high-speed network that can include one or more LANs. A MAN is smaller than a WAN, but usually operates at a higher speed.

mandatory user profile   An administrator-created profile with a **.man** filename extension that prevents the user from modifying the profile.

master boot code   The initial boot program, located in the master boot record, that the BIOS loads and executes to start the boot process. This program seeks the boot partition with the bootstrap loader and transfers control to the loader for starting the operating system.

master boot record   Another term for *boot sector*.

master domain model   An arrangement of client and server computers that allows resources to have separate domains.

master partition table   A table located in the master boot record that contains the descriptions of the partitions contained on the hard disk.

MB (megabyte)   A unit of measurement used to gauge amounts of storage and data transfers. When used to describe data storage, 1 MB is equal to 1,048,576 bytes. When used to describe data transfer rates, 1 MB is equal to 1,000,000 bytes.

Mbps (megabits per second)   A measurement of data transmission speed: 1 Mbps = 1,000,000 bits per second.

MBR (master boot record)   The information on the first sector of any disk or hard disk that provides information about the operating system so it can be loaded into the computer's main storage or RAM. Also called the *partition sector* or the *master partition table*.

MCA (microchannel architecture)   A computer-expansion slot interface developed by IBM for its PS/2 line.

MDA (monochrome display adapter)   The first display standard, introduced in 1981 by IBM Corporation as a character-only video display with no graphics capability.

media   Plural of *medium*. The physical material on which computer data is stored, such as floppy disk or CD-ROM.

membrane keyboard   A variant of the rubber-dome keyboard design in which the keys are integrated into a continuous sheet that sits directly atop the rubber dome sheet.

memory address   The numeric identity of a particular memory or peripheral storage location.

menu   An options list from which users select desired actions, commands, or formats.

MHz (megahertz)   A measure of transmission speeds of electronic devices: 1 MHz = 1,000,000 cycles per second.

microphone   A device that changes sound energy into electrical signals and that is used to input sounds into a computer.

microprocessor   The computer's CPU, which can be thought of as the computer's brain. Intel created the first microprocessor in 1974.

Microsoft Backup   A Windows 95 utility used to create backup copies of data.

Microsoft Plus   A Windows 95 utility that enhances the capabilities of DriveSpace, Compression Agent, and System Agent.

Microsoft Windows 95 Resource Kit   Microsoft's definitive guide to Windows 95.

.mid   The file extension for MIDI files.

MIDI (musical instrument digital interface)   A hardware specification that makes it possible to connect synthesizers and other electronic musical equipment to a computer. MIDI data is stored in files with **.mid** extensions.

MIDI-In   Delivers the data to an instrument.

MIDI-Out   Sends the data out from an instrument that it originally came from.

MIDI-Thru   Sends an exact copy of the data coming into the MIDI-In and passes it on to another instrument or device.

mid-tower   The medium size of the tower form factor.

mini-DIN (Deutsche Industries Norm) connector   A connector for a motherboard, mouse, or keyboard. On PS/2 systems, this type of connector is a 6-pin connector.

mini-tower   The smallest of the tower form factor.

MMX (Multimedia Extensions)   An enhancement to the architecture of Intel Pentium processors that improves the performance of multimedia and communications applications.

modem (modulator/demodulator)   An electronic modulator/demodulator device used for computer communications via telephone lines. It allows data transfer between one computer and another. Typically, it converts digital data to analog signals, and then back to digital data.

modulation   The process a modem uses to convert a digital computer signal to analog form, for transmission over phone lines.

monitor   Another term for a video display monitor, display monitor, or video monitor.

motherboard   A computer's main circuit board that holds the microprocessor, main memory chips, and other essential computer elements.

motherboard connector   A power supply lead that connects to a motherboard inside a system unit. The number of them varies, depending on the type of motherboard and power supply used.

motherboard ground screw   A special hexagonal screw used to ground the motherboard to the mounting plate at specific points.

motherboard manual   A booklet or CD containing specifications, instructions, and diagrams for the motherboards, the devices attached to them, and their configuration. Each motherboard model and form factor has a corresponding manual.

motherboard mounting pan   Another term for a *motherboard mounting plate*.

motherboard mounting plate   Part of the case that provides the attachment surface for the motherboard.

mounting bay   A recess or an indentation in the front bezel or face plate of the case for inserting a drive into an drive bracket.

mounting chassis   The outer bracket of the hard drive that contains the head disk assembly and includes the mounting screw holes to secure the drive into the drive brackets.

mounting points   Holes in the motherboard that are used to secure it to the motherboard mounting plate by means of ground screws and stand-offs.

mouse   An input device that allows the user to point to and select items onscreen. It is used primarily with GUI programs to select icons and menu commands. It is also used with most drawing and paint programs.

mouse pointer   The mouse's onscreen representation. The pointer usually takes the form of an arrow.

MOV (metal oxide varistor)   The active component in a surge suppressor that limits pass-through voltages due to a line surge in voltage. It is capable of absorbing large currents without damage.

MPC (Multimedia PC)   Shorthand for the Multimedia PC Working Group, of the Software Publishers Association. It sets industry standards for multimedia PCs.

MPC1   The original multimedia PC standard set by the MPC.

MPC2   The MPC's second standard level of performance specifications.

MPC3   The MPC's third standard level of performance specifications.

MPEG (Moving Picture Experts Group) codec   Standards for digital video and digital audio compression.

MPRII   An international standard for low-radiation emissions developed for monitors by the Swedish regulatory agency, SWEDAC. It is now the compliance standard for many worldwide manufacturers for their monitors.

MSAU (multistation access unit)   The central hub for IBM-computer-station Token Ring networks.

mscdex.exe   A file loaded in MS-DOS mode. **mscdex.exe** loads installed CD-ROM drives and Windows 95–installed mouse drivers.

MS-DOS (Microsoft Disk Operating System)   The first operating system developed and licensed for the IBM compatible computer system.

MS-DOS prompt   A Start menu option that lets the user access MS-DOS commands.

ms-dos.sys   One of the three MS-DOS operating system files that the MS-DOS bootstrap loader searches for in the root directory of the boot disk and loads into memory.

MSN (Microsoft Network)   An online information service created and maintained by Microsoft.

MTBF (mean time between failure)   The average failure rate of a power supply established by the actual operation or calculation from known standards. It is expressed in hours.

multifrequency rate   The ability of a monitor to support many different horizontal and vertical scan frequencies, and therefore many resolutions.

multiple master domain model   An arrangement of client and server computers in which more than one domain has access to various resource domains.

multiprogram   To run two or more programs on a single computer at one time. Another term for *multitask.*

multitask   A technique used in operating systems for sharing a single processor to accomplish several independent tasks.

multithreaded   More than one thread working simultaneously to accomplish a task.

multi-word DMA mode 2   A direct memory access mode drive transfer operation used by some advanced ATA-2 hard drives and incorporated into UDMA hard drives.

My Computer   A default Windows 95 desktop icon, a container object, that holds all the computer's resources.

N

navigate   To move around in the Windows environment in order to access and use programs, utilities, and hardware.

NDIS (Network Device Interface Specification)   A programming interface for different protocols sharing the same network hardware.

near letter quality   A print-quality mode for dot-matrix printers that is between draft and letter quality.

negotiation   A process modems use to arrive at a common modulation standard.

NetBEUI (NetBIOS Extended User Interface)   A new version of NetBIOS that allows computers to communicate within a LAN, using a frame format.

NetWare   Novell's network operating system, developed in the early 1980s, that is a cooperative, multitasking, dedicated server, network operating system with wide client support.

Netwatcher   A peer-to-peer networking tool that shows the system's sharing status, and allows users to create or disable shared resources.

network   To link computers and their peripherals by means of wires, cables, or telephone lines.

network adapter   A network card.

Network Backups   Software used to safeguard the data and configurations stored on a peer-to-peer network.

Network Monitor   A BackOffice product included with Microsoft System Management Server that servers as a protocol analyzer.

Network Neighborhood   A default Windows 95 desktop icon, a container object, that holds all the computer's network-accessible devices.

neutral wire   In a circuit, the wire that is connected to an earth ground at the power plant and at the transformer.

NFS (Network File System)   A client/server application that lets a user view, store, and update files on a remote computer, as if it were local. It also allows local file systems to be exported across the network.

NIC (network interface card)   A card that fits into a computer's motherboard to provide a port for the computer's network access.

node   A device connected to the network that can communicate with other network devices.

noise   The signal degradation that occurs when stray electrical signals, such as signals caused by fluorescent lights, interfere with data movement.

nonconductor   Material that does not transmit electricity, heat, sound, and so on.

non-impact printer   The class of printers in which nothing in the printer actually impacts the paper to form characters. This class includes laser printers and inkjet printers.

noninterlaced   A scanning mode in which the scanning beam moves across the screen from top to bottom, continuously, over each line. This is currently the standard scanning mode in quality monitors.

nonpreemptive multitasking   A type of multitasking in which a task does its job until finished before relinquishing control to the processor.

non-user definable   Box screens that provide information about a system's BIOS configuration. Box screens are activated when a system's BIOS does not offer configurable choices for the user. Examples include the autodetect video fields and keyboard fields of the main BIOS setup screen.

NOS (network operating system)   An operating system on the server in a LAN that coordinates the activities of computers and other devices attached to the network.

notification area   A portion of the Taskbar just left of the system clock. It displays icons relating to status information about system functions.

NT Server   The Windows NT server version.

NT Workstation   The Windows NT client version.

NTFS (New Technology File System)   A file system introduced by Microsoft with the Windows NT operating system in 1993.

numeric tail   An abbreviation, denoted by its file extension, at the end of a filename that has been converted by a DOS-based program.

O

object   A folder, file, program, printer, modem, or process represented by an icon in Windows 95.

Object menu   The list of options offered when the mouse is right-clicked on a desktop object's icon.

octal system   A base-8 numbering system that uses the digits 0–7.

octet   An piece of data that is exactly 8 bits.

offline UPS   A type of UPS that operates offline. Also called a *standby UPS*.

OLE (Object Linking and Embedding)   A protocol for transferring information among applications that either links or embeds the information into the file it has been transferred to. Embedding differs from linking in that, for example, when a graphic is linked to a word processing file, changes made to the original graphics file automatically appear in the linked version. On the other hand, when one file is embedded in another, the embedded file is a copy of the original, and changes made in the original do not automatically appear in the embedded copy.

online UPS   A type of UPS that always runs off the battery. This is the more desirable type of UPS.

Open Program Title Box   The Taskbar button for every open program in Windows 95.

operating system boot disk   A disk used to initialize or start the operating system software.

optimize   To improve the performance of a hard drive by rearranging data. Also called *defragment*.

OS (operating system)   The software that runs a computer, receives command requests through the user interface, analyzes commands, and then sends out instructions to the various computer components.

OS Executive   Another name for the kernel, which is regarded as the heart of the operating system. It launches applications, allocates system functions, and manages a computer's memory, files, and peripheral devices, and maintains the date and time.

OS/2 (Operating System 2)   An operating system jointly developed and introduced by Microsoft and IBM in 1987 that was intended as a replacement for DOS.

oscillation   A change in the electrical signal that occurs periodically.

OSI (Open System Interconnect) model   An international seven-layer model of functions in a telecommunications system.

outlet tester   A device that tests for proper conductor connections of electrical outlets. Lights on the tester indicate proper or improper wiring of the outlet.

output   The processed data from the CPU that is displayed on the monitor. Other forms of output include information sent to a printer or fax/modem.

output device   An internal or peripheral device attached to the system unit that allows the user to view results.

overload protection   Protection provided on all outputs against short-circuits.

overvoltage protection   A feature of the power supply that shuts down the supply or clamps down on the output when its voltage exceeds a preset limit.

P

page description language   A language designed to transcribe the layout and contents of a printed page and send commands to the printer for the desired results.

page format   The layout of a page, including the fonts, spacing, paper size, margins, text layout, and graphics.

page printer   Another term for *laser printer*.

paging file   Another term for *swap file*.

paper path   The channel through which the paper feeds and is transported through a printer.

paper transport mechanism   The electromechanical means by which the paper is moved through the paper path in a printer.

paradigm   An established way of thinking or a widely accepted belief system. For example, the Windows paradigm is based on its intuitive interface's array of objects that suggest their functions to a user.

parallel port   A parallel interface for connecting an external device, capable of transmitting more than 1 bit of data at a time. Printers are usually connected to computers using parallel ports.

parallel processor   An architecture in a PC that can perform multiple operations simultaneously.

parity checking   A method of ensuring that data that was transmitted via a modem from one computer to another is error free. Parity is achieved by adding a 1 or a 0 bit to each byte as the byte is transmitted. At the other end of the transmission, the receiving modem verifies the parity and the accuracy of the transmission.

partition   An area of space on a hard drive that is allocated for system use. Also, to configure a free area of disk space for system use.

Pascal, Blaise   A French mathematician who invented the first recorded calculation machine, called the pascaline.

pascaline   A calculating machine developed in 1642 by French mathematician Blaise Pascal.

passive hub network   A network that joins wires from several stations in a star configuration. There is no dedicated device on a passive network to support networking.

pass-through   To go on to the next phase without stopping.

patch   A temporary solution to a technical problem. Also, a sample of an instrumental sound sometimes found on a music synthesizer.

PC (personal computer)   A computer that meets the IBM standard.

PCI (peripheral component interconnect)   A bus created by Intel to provide superior performance to an ISA, and to allow peripheral devices to automatically configure themselves through the plug-and-play process.

PCI IDE (peripheral component interconnect and integrated drive electronics) A bus used for communication between peripherals and PCs. IDE is the hardware that connects peripherals to a PC.

PCL (Printer Control Language) A proprietary page description language developed by Hewlett Packard for its inkjet and laser printers.

PCMCIA (Personal Computer Memory Card International Association) An organization that creates devices that conform to its standards and plug into specially configured slots in PCs. A PCMCIA modem is about the size of a credit card.

PDC (primary domain controller) A domain server that can authenticate workstations and usually contains master copies of security, computer, and user account databases.

peer-to-peer network A network of two or more computers that use the same program to share data and resources, and in which computers share equal responsibility in acting as a server to other computers in the same network.

Pentium Intel's fifth-generation 80x86 CPU. It followed the 486 processor and began Intel's "fast" CPU line.

Pentium II Intel's follow-up to its initial Pentium chips series. Built-in multimedia extensions and easier upgrading capabilities characterize the Pentium II processor.

Performance A tab in the Control Panel's System utility that offers options to set virtual memory values.

peripheral A computer's hardware device that is separate from the CPU or working memory. Some examples of peripherals are disks, keyboards, monitors, mice, printers, scanners, tape drives, microphones, speakers, and cameras.

PIF (program information file) A Windows file that provides information on how a DOS application should be run.

PIF Editor A configuration utility that produces PIFs, which give Windows instructions on how to handle DOS applications.

pixel Short for picture element, it is the smallest element of a video image and is composed of three primary phosphor color dots.

pixel rate The speed at which the RAMDAC chip can draw the pixels, commonly expressed in MHz.

plug-and-play A feature designed to simplify installing hardware allowing the operating system and the BIOS to automatically configure new hardware devices, thus eliminating system resources conflicts.

PM (Presentation Manager) An ineffective graphical interface to the initial OS/2 system.

popup A type of menu called for and displayed on top of the existing text or image. When the item is selected, the menu disappears and the screen is restored.

port   A parallel or serial interface where data is transferred. Generally, a port is located on the back of a computer system.

portable computer   A compact version of a desktop computer. Also referred to as *laptops*, portable computers retain most standard, desktop computer features and can operate on either battery or household current.

POST (power-on self-test)   A self-check the BIOS performs in the preboot stage to ensure that the machine is working properly

Postscript   Adobe's page description language used in all computer platforms. It is the commercial typesetting and printing standard.

power button   A button located on the front of the computer that controls electrical current to the power supply.

power cord socket   A receptacle or cavity used to connect the power supply to an external power source such as a wall outlet, generally via an electrical cord or lead.

power cycle   A reboot.

power on/off switch   A lever that allows electrical current to the power supply to be turned on and off.

power supply   A device inside a computer's system unit that converts AC electricity from a power outlet to DC electricity used by the computer.

power supply lead   A wire capable of conducting an electrical current that connects the power supply to the computer's internal components and drives.

power supply mount point   The shelf or ledge on which the power supply rests when it is attached to the chassis.

Power_Good delay   The period during which the **Power_Good** signal is delayed until all voltages have stabilized after the system has been turned on.

Power_Good signal   A +5v signal sent by the power supply after it has passed a series of internal self-tests. It is sent to the motherboard, where it is received by the processor timer chip controlling the reset line to the processor.

ppm (pages per minute)   A measure of laser printer printing speed that tells how many pages per minutes the printer can output at a given resolution.

PPP (Point-to-Point Protocol)   A protocol for communication between computers using a serial interface, most often a PC connected by a phone line to a server.

PPTP (Point-to-Point Tunneling Protocol)   A VPN protocol built in to Windows NT that ensures secure data transmission.

preemptive multitasking   A type of multitasking in which a controller interrupts and suspends a running task in order to run a new task, thus facilitating smoother computer operations.

primary partition   The portion of a hard disk that contains the operating system. The system boots from the primary partition. A disk can have up to three primary partitions, but only one of them can be designated active, or in use, at any given time.

print engine   The mechanism that transcribes the array of dots created by the printer controller into a printed image.

print head   The part of the printer that either physically impacts the paper surface through a ribbon, directs ink to the paper, or burns toner onto the paper.

Print Manager   A Windows 3.1 system for managing printer operations and configuring settings.

print spooler   Software that manages files sent to a printer.

printable screen font   A font used onscreen that has a printer font equivalent.

printer   An output device that produces paper printouts from computer software applications such as word processors and spreadsheets.

printer controller   The command center in a laser printer that reads the data output from the host computer and then interprets the commands for the page format and then sends them to the print engine.

printer font   A font stored in the printer.

Printers folder   An object in the Windows 95 My Computer default container that provides a means to configure printers to be used with the operating system and icons for currently installed printers.

program   A software application designed to perform some work or achieve some function on a computer.

program icon   A small onscreen image that provides the user access to a specific computer program.

Program Manager   The main control shell used to perform operations, such as starting programs and organizing files, in Windows 3.1 and Windows NT. It is the onscreen interface for **progman.exe** and is called Windows Explorer in Windows 95/98.

programming language   One of many computer languages designed to write computer instructions and programs in which programmers express data with symbols. Some examples of programming languages include BASIC, C++, and COBOL.

projector   A peripheral device that enables computer data to be displayed on a large remote screen for presentation purposes.

prompt   A text symbol in the DOS command prompt window which indicates that the system is ready to receive commands.

properties   The characteristics of a file, an application, or a device, such as size, creation date, and type.

proprietary   A product or design that is owned by and unique to a specific company.

proprietary standard   A specification set for a specific company's product.

protected mode   An Intel-based operational state that allows the computer to address all its memory, while preventing an errant program from entering the memory boundary of another.

protected-mode driver   A driver that supports protected mode, which has more advanced features than real mode.

protocol   A special set of rules for communicating that components use when sending signals. Often described in an industry or a national standard.

protocol stack   Layers of specialized sets of rules for computer communication that occur during a session.

PS/2 connector   Another term for *mini-DIN connector*.

PSTN (public switched telephone network)   The international telephone system made up of digital and analog telephone lines.

pulse code modulation method   A way to sample and digitize sound digitally by recording successive digital sample differences.

PUN (physical unit number)   A device connected directly to the SCSI bus. It is the same as the SCSI ID.

punch card   An early storage medium made of thin cardboard cards that read data as a series of punched holes.

Q

QIC (quarter-inch cartridge)   A type of tape used for data backup.

quantization noise   Signal degradation that occurs during analog-to-digital conversion across the PSTN backbones. It limits traditional modem communications to 33.6 Kbps.

queue   A storage area designed to hold temporary data.

Qwerty keyboard   The standard English-language typewriter keyboard. The letters Q, W, E, R, T, and Y are the letters on the top-left, alphabetic row of the keyboard. It was designed in 1868 by typewriter inventor Christopher Shoals.

R

RAM (random access memory)   Computer memory that is both readable and writable. When the computer shuts down, RAM data is no longer retrievable.

RAMDAC (RAM digital-to-analog converter)   A device that converts the digital images in video memory to analog signals and sends them to the video monitor.

RARP (Reverse Address Resolution Protocol)   The protocol TCP/IP uses to get an IP address when only a domain name address is available.

RAS (Remote Access Server)   Windows software that permits remote access to a server using a modem.

raster font   A typeface designed pixel by pixel, intended for computer monitor display screens. Scaling raster fonts lessens image quality. Also called *bitmap* or *screen fonts*.

rasterization   The last preprinting stage in a laser printer, where the printer controller converts the page format to a dot array before burning it to the drum.

raw   The print spooling used in Windows 3.1; it is a slower method of printing than the EMF method used in Windows 95.

raw spool files   Files created in Windows 3.1 when the **print** command is given.

read multiple   An ATA-2 enhanced BIOS drive command that enables the controller and drive circuitry to support multiple-sector disk writes concurrently.

Read/Write Head Req/Ack (Request/Acknowledgement)   The method a SCSI host adapter uses to negotiate an asynchronous data transfer with a SCSI device on the bus. For each data transfer request, the host adapter sends a request to the device, and the device controller responds with an acknowledgement.

read-only   An attribute that, when enabled, prevents a user from deleting or altering a file. As the name implies, the user is only allowed to open and read the file, but not alter it in any way.

real mode   An Intel-based mode of program operation in which the processor can execute only one program at a time and access no more than 1 MB of memory. Such programs are usually part of the operating system or the special application subsystem and can be trusted to know how to update system data.

real-mode driver   A driver that supports real mode, an older operating mode that enables the processor to execute only one program at a time. They were often the source of system crashes as they did not include memory boundary protection.

reboot   To shut down the computer and immediately restart it.

recommended resolutions   Part of the manufacturer's resolution specification, the list of display resolutions that the manufacturer recommends for a monitor model.

Recycle Bin   A default Windows 95 desktop icon that holds all deleted hard drive files. It retains deleted files until they are either retrieved or deleted permanently.

refresh   To redraw a screen at intervals to keep its phosphors irradiated.

refresh rate   The number of times per second that the video screen display is redrawn.

Registry A Windows 95 internal database that contains data on the hardware and characteristics of the computer. Windows programs continually reference the Registry during normal operation.

Registry Editor Software that lets a user edit the Registry's entries.

rema The DOS **remove** command.

remote button switch The remote, power on/off switch found on Slimline and ATX computer models.

repeater A communications device used to extend the distance of data transmission. It amplifies or regenerates a data signal.

reset button A button that you press to activate the reset line that sends the message to the CPU to reboot the system.

reset switch connector A switch located on the front case bezel that is used when the computer locks up so that the system can be rebooted.

resolution An onscreen image's degree of sharpness, expressed as a matrix of horizontal and vertical dots. A reference to the size of the pixels in a display at a given screen size. The higher the resolution, the smaller the pixels.

resource A utility, file, or peripheral that is useful to a client.

restart A command that causes the computer to reload its operating software.

RFI (radio-frequency interference) A form of EMI that creates noise on an electronic circuit. It can be created by an appliance in the computer's vicinity.

ring in A point in a Token Ring network where the data flows into the MSAU.

ring network A LAN where all the nodes are connected in a closed loop, or ring.

ring out A point in a Token Ring network where the data flows out from the MSAU.

ripple Another term for *noise*.

roaming user profile A profile that is stored and configured to be downloaded from a server. It allows a user to access his or her profile from any network location.

ROM (read only memory) A type of nonvolatile storage that can only be read from. It is a nonvolatile storage system, and contains important data that must be saved even when the power is shut off. It is used to hold critical data such as the CMOS setup and other boot-up data for the computer.

root directory The base of any file system directory structure.

router A piece of equipment used to connect networks to each other. It makes more sophisticated data routing decisions than do bridges.

RPC (remote-procedure call)   A protocol that allows a program running on one host to cause code to be executed on another host, without the programmer needing understand network details.

rpm (revolutions per minute)   The number of times the drive platter spins completely in 1 minute.

RTS/CTS (request-to-send/clear-to-send)   Signals sent between the modem and host system to manage the rate of data flow. *See* flow control.

rubber dome switches   A variant of the foam buffer design, in which the spring is eliminated from the plunger and a rubber dome is used in place of the foam and foil laminate pad. The rubber dome sits atop the contacts on the circuit board.

Run   A Start menu option that provides one method of opening programs.

run length   An encoded bitmap file data compression technique used to minimize file sizes by encoding multiple consecutive occurrences of a given symbol.

S

safety ground wire   A safety ground wire that connects the earth ground to the chassis of an electrical appliance or device via an electrical outlet and plug. It is used to ensure that no electrical hazards exist between the chassis of the electrical device and the earth ground.

sag   A type of power event in which a decrease occurs that equals 80% below the normal voltage carried by a power line. It is sometimes referred to as a *brownout*.

SAM (Security Accounts Manager)   The module of the Windows NT executive that authenticates a username and password in the account database.

sample   In computers, to change analog signals to digital format by measuring samples at regular intervals.

sample size   The amount of storage designated to a single sound sample when converting analog signals to digital signals.

sampling rate   In computerized sound, the frequency at which sound samples are taken. The more sound samples taken per time unit, the closer the digitized sound will match the original analog sound.

SBIC (SCSI bus interface controller) chip   A logic chip that governs the SCSI controller circuitry on a SCSI drive.

scan code   A unique binary code sent to the motherboard by the onboard keyboard processor, based on the key switch position in the key matrix. When the key is pressed, the processor reads the position and sends the appropriate scan code to the motherboard.

ScanDisk   A Windows 95 utility that can repair certain kinds of disk errors.

scanner   An input device that reads printed information such as pictures or text and translates them into digital data the computer can understand.

scanning   The movement the electron beam makes across the video screen as it writes the image. The scanning movement can be interlaced or noninterlaced.

scanning frequency   A manufacturer specification listing the horizontal and vertical scan range of a monitor model.

scheduling   Pertaining to Windows 3.1, this refers to an enhanced panel option that specifies how much of the system's resources are reserved for the foreground application.

screen font   A typeface designed pixel by pixel, intended for computer monitor display. Also called *raster* or *bitmap font*.

screen size   The actual physical size of the monitor screen as measured in inches, from one corner diagonally to the other.

screen treatment   A manufacturer specification for CRT monitor screens that details the monitor's type of screen coating. Quality monitors generally have tinted screens featuring antistatic and antiglare surface treatments.

script   A program that contains a set of instructions for an application or a utility.

SCSI (small computer systems interface)   A bus interface standard initially ratified in 1986 that uses a 50-pin connector and allows up to eight devices to be connected in a daisy chain. Also called SCSI-1 to differentiate it from the SCSI-2 and SCSI-3 revisions.

SCSI bus interface controller   A logic chip that governs the SCSI controller circuitry on a SCSI drive.

SCSI host adapter   The electronic gateway between the SCSI bus and the host system's I/O bus.

SCSI ID   A number set with jumper pins on the SCSI device; it can range from 0 to 7. The order of service priority by the SCSI host adapter is determined in increasing order of number. Also called a *PUN*.

SCSI-1   The first SCSI bus standard, ratified in 1986.

SCSI-2   The second SCSI bus made standard, ratified in 1994. The enhancements included increased device support and a common set of BIOS commands.

SDRAM (synchronous DRAM)   A type of RAM that incorporates features that allow it to keep pace with bus speeds as high as 100 MHz. By allowing two sets of memory addresses to be opened simultaneously, data can be retrieved alternately from each set, eliminating the delays that normally occur.

sector   The smallest unit of space on the hard disk that any software can access; it is 512 bytes in size.

sector translation   A method used by the enhanced BIOS of computer systems since the mid-1990s to overcome the drive geometry limitations in the BIOS. This allows the BIOS to acknowledge drive sizes beyond 504 MB.

security provider   A Windows NT domain or workgroup computer that delegates user group resources and permissions.

segment   To split a large Ethernet network into more manageably sized segments connected by bridges and routers.

serial interface   An interface used for the serial transmission of data. In this type of transmission, only 1 bit is transmitted at a time.

serial port   A general-purpose 9- or 25-pin interface that can be used for serial communications with peripheral devices including modems, mouse devices, and some printers.

server   A network computer or program that is accessible to many network users and fulfills users' requests for information access and transfer.

server-on-a-LAN   A computer that runs administrative software that controls the workstations of the network. On the Internet, it's a server that responds to commands from the clients.

servo mechanism   A control system where the final output is mechanical movement. It uses gray code to control the position and the acceleration of the hard drive.

session   An active connection between a client and a peer (often a server) during which data and files are exchanged.

settings   A Start menu option that allows users access to Control Panel, Taskbar, and printer features.

setup   The process of preparing an application or a program so that it will run on a computer.

shadow   Similar to a shortcut, it creates a connection to an actual object on another computer.

shadow mask   A masking design composed of fine metal mesh on the inside of the monitor screen that helps to focus the electron beam on the correct pixels.

share-level security   A form of network security used on Windows 95 systems in which a network administrator holds passwords for folders and disk drives on the network.

shell   A program that provides access to the operating system.

shortcut   A user-created desktop icon that gives quick access to a Windows 95 object, such as a program or file.

shut down   A Start menu command for closing the operating system.

SideKick   A popup program that first appeared as a multitasking shell accompanying DOS programs in the mid-1980s.

signal   An electrical impulse used to transmit data over a physical medium for the purpose of communication.

signal-to-noise ratio   The number of bits of correct data divided by the number of bits of noise.

silicon   Material used as the base for most microprocessor chips.

SIMM (single, inline memory module)   A small circuit board that holds a group of memory chips. On Macintosh computers, SIMMs can hold up to eight chips. On PCs, they can hold up to nine chips; the ninth chip is used for parity error checking.

sine wave   A waveform whose amplitude varies, proportionally to the sine of the time elapsed. Visually, it appears like the letter *S*, rotated 90 degrees.

single tasking   The limitation of an operating system to perform only one operating task at a time.

single-domain model   The simplest arrangement of client and server computers, which operates in one unit.

single-ended SCSI   The normal SCSI signal standard, in which one cable wire is used to carry the signal from end to end.

sinusoidal   Of, relating to, or shaped like a sine curve or sine wave.

Slimline   A type of form factor in current use.

small drive connector   A small 4-pin power supply connector found on current 3 1/2-inch floppy drives.

SMTP (Simple Mail Transfer Protocol)   A protocol that governs e-mail transmission and reception.

Socket 3   A motherboard socket where older-technology CPUs connect to the motherboard.

Socket 7   A motherboard socket where older-technology CPUs such as the Intel Pentium P54C and P55C series CPUs connect to the motherboard.

Socket 8   A motherboard socket where more recent technology Pentium Pro CPUs connect to the motherboard.

software   Computer instructions that fall into two categories: systems software and applications software. Systems software includes the operating system and all the utilities that make the computer function. Applications software includes individual programs designed to perform specific functions for a user.

sound card   A multimedia card added to the motherboard that allows a computer to record and play WAV or MIDI files.

speaker   A device that enables users to hear sound.

spike   A sudden burst of power lasting between .5 and 100 microseconds.

spindle   The central post or hub on which a disk drive's platters are mounted.

spindle motor   The motor in the head disk assembly that powers the spindle to rotate the drive platters.

spool file   A file created by the spooler when the **print** command is given.

spray contact cleaner   A liquid solvent used to clean electronic connections that has a rapid drying time and does not leave a residue.

SRAM (static RAM)   A type of memory that is faster and more reliable than RAM. It needs to be refreshed less often than RAM.

standby UPS   A type of UPS that runs off its battery only when the AC mains exhibit problems.

stand-off   A small piece of hardware that is used to attach the motherboard to the motherboard mounting plate on the chassis.

star network   A network configured like a star, with a centralized hub to which each computer on the network has access.

start bit   In a serial communications session, the binary number 0 that precedes every byte to tell the receiving system that the next 8 bits constitute a byte of data.

Start menu   Located at the left end of the Taskbar, a menu offers access to almost every program on the computer.

startup disk   A floppy disk that contains copies of the computer's operating system files and can be used to start up the computer in case of a crash. Also called a *system disk*.

static electricity   Stationary electricity that happens when electrons build up on conductive material.

stop bit   In a serial communications session, a data bit that follows the byte (or character) to signal to the remote system that it was sent.

support resolutions   The range of resolutions supported by the monitor model, as specified by the manufacturer.

surge   A type of power event in which a voltage increase above 110 % of the normal voltage occurs.

surge suppressor   A device used to protect equipment from transient power surges that travel from AC power lines and telephone circuits.

SVGA (super video graphics array)   Enhancements to the VGA standard that increased resolution to 1024 x 728. (The VGA's resolution is only 640 x 480.)

swap file   A hard drive file that holds parts of program and data files that do not fit in memory.

synchronous   A form of data communication in which exchanges of data bits are strictly timed by a clocking signal.

sysedit.exe   A configuration utility for simultaneous configuration of some DOS and Windows configuration files.

system   A group of related components that interact to perform a specific task. Also, the controlling program or operating software on a computer.

system board   Another name for the *motherboard.*

System Monitor   A peer-to-peer networking device that allows observation of a number of system behaviors that can point to potential and actual problems.

system policy   A policy that controls what a user can do and controls the user's environment. It can be applied to a specific user, a group, a computer, or all users.

System Policy Editor   A utility located in the Administrative Tools group that is used to create system policies.

System Resources   A Program Manager feature that lists the system's available resources.

system unit   A computer's case and internal components that allow the computer to process information, store data, and communicate with other parts of the computer. It can include the power supply, motherboard, CPU, RAM, ROM, and one or more disk drives.

system.dat   A Registry file that contains information about hardware and software.

system.ini   A Windows 3.1 file that stores system-specific information on the hardware and device driver system configurations.

SYSX (system exclusive) data   Data that a manufacturer uses to transmit private information about its products.

T

Tab   A key used simultaneously with the Alt key to cycle through each active program.

tactile feedback mechanism   The metal clip-and-spring mechanism located beneath the plunger of a key switch, designed to provide a slight spring-fed feel of resistance when the key is pressed.

Tandy   A manufacturer of PCs and electronics.

TAPI (Telephony Application Programming Interface)   An interface that facilitates communication between computers and telephone equipment.

Taskbar   A Windows 95 graphic bar that displays all active programs and allows users to switch between programs.

TCP/IP (Transmission Control Protocol/Internet Protocol)   A routable protocol in which messages transmitted contain the address of a destination network and a destination station. This allows TCP/IP messages to be sent to multiple networks within an organization or around the world, hence its use in the Internet.

TechNet   A worldwide information service designed for information specialists who support or educate users, administer networks or databases, create automated solutions, and evaluate information technology solutions.

Telnet   A program used to access another computer, with the correct permissions.

terminate   To seal the ends of an electrical bus to maintain the correct impedance for signal propagation, and to prevent signal echoes that degrade the quality of data exchange.

text file   A text character file, such as a word processing or ASCII file.

thin-film media   The extremely fine layer of magnetically sensitive cobalt alloy deposited on hard drive platters for data encoding and decoding.

thread   A data structure used to prioritize multiple demands for a computer resource. Task requests are placed in order—either a first in, first out or a last in, first out.

token   A small token ring frame that makes one-way trips around the ring to be seized by a network computer waiting to send a message.

token passing   A type of networking system where bits of information are inserted into an empty frame that is examined by successive workstations and passed on.

token ring   A type of computer network based on a star configuration in which a token ring's computers are connected to either a central controlled-access unit, a multistation access unit, or a smart multistation access unit.

toner   In laser printers, a very fine powder of plastic particles that is attached to the paper via a charged drum and then fused into the paper by a fuser.

toner hopper   In laser printers, a toner storage bin that sits atop a developer unit and feeds toner to the drum for transference onto the paper.

topology   A configuration formed by the connection between devices on a LAN.

touch screen   An input device that allows users to interact with a computer by touching the display screen.

trackball   A type of mouse that the user manipulates by rotating the ball with the thumb, fingertips, or palm of the hand. Its buttons are used to perform basic clicking actions such as selecting commands from a menu.

tractor-feed device   The sprocket mechanism in dot-matrix printers that pulls or pushes the paper through the paper path and past the print head.

tractor-feed paper   Also called fan-fold paper, tractor-feed paper has perforated edges that can be torn away after the paper has been printed. It is commonly used with dot-matrix printers.

transfer time   Pertaining to an offline UPS, the elapsed time between AC main failure time and resumption of power from the battery source.

transient   A momentary variation in power, which ultimately disappears. Surges, spikes, sags, blackouts, and noise are examples of transients.

transistor   A small, solid-state component with three leads, in which the voltage or current controls the flow of another current.

TrueType font   A font that possesses a printed copy appearance identical to its onscreen appearance.

trust   Short *for trust relationship*, which is an administrative link that joins two or more domains.

TSR (terminate and stay resident)   A type of DOS utility that stays in memory and can be reactivated by pressing a certain combination of keys.

tunnel   To transmit data structured in one protocol format within the format of another protocol.

tunneling protocol   A data transmission protocol that is designed to serve as a carrier for other data stream protocols.

TUV   A German-based service organization that tests and certifies product safety to meet standards and specifications of the European Union.

typeface   The name given to a specific print characters design. Aria, for example, is the typeface for an Arial, italicized, 10-point font.

U

UART (universal asynchronous receiver/transmitter)   A buffered computer chip that handles asynchronous communications through a computer's serial ports and contains both the receiving and transmitting circuits required for asynchronous serial communication.

UDMA (ultra direct memory access, or ultra DMA)   A protocol developed jointly by Intel and Quantum that promotes bypassing the I/O bus bottleneck during peak sequential operations on EIDE hard drives. It also enables read-and-write data transfers through DMA channels with and without bus mastering.

UDMA mode 2   The highest transfer rate mode supported by the new Ultra DMA protocol through DMA channels on ATA-3 hard drives, using bus mastering.

UL (Underwriters Laboratories)   An independent not-for-profit agency in the United States that tests and certifies products for safety.

Underwriters Laboratories of Canada   The Canadian division of Underwriters Laboratories.

uninstall   To remove a software program. Windows 95 provides the efficient Add/Remove Programs feature for eliminating unwanted software programs.

UNIX   A powerful, multitasking operating system that is widely used as the master control program in workstations and servers. It is less popular in PCs.

Update Information tool   A tool in Windows 95 that allows you to find exactly which files you have installed and which version of Windows 95 you have.

UPS (uninterruptible power supply)   A backup device designed to provide an uninterrupted power source in the event of a power failure.

USART (universal synchronous/asynchronous receiver/transmitter)   A module that contains both the receiving and transmitting circuits required for synchronous and asynchronous serial communication.

USB (universal serial bus)   An external bus standard that supports data transfer rates of 12 million bits per second. It allows peripheral devices, such as mouse devices, modems, and keyboards, to be plugged in and unplugged without resetting the system. It is expected to eventually replace serial and parallel ports.

user control   A manufacturer specification that refers to the range of controls in adjusting the operating parameters of the monitor. User controls typically include the power switch, horizontal/vertical size, horizontal/vertical position, pincushion, contrast, and brightness controls.

user friendly   A system that is easy to learn and easy to use.

user interface   The command-line or graphical representation of software that controls the allocation and use of the computer's hardware. The user interface, the file management system, and the kernel form the operating system.

user profile   A device that is used to save each user's desktop configuration.

user.dat   A Registry file that contains information that is reflected in user profiles.

user's manual   A booklet that accompanies a new computer and generally contains information such as how to set up and use a computer.

user-level security   A form of security used on network systems in which a user or an administrator can use passwords to secure a network. Only authorized users have access to system-shared files and resources.

utility   A software program that takes care of the internal maintenance of the computer system such as editing files, compressing files, and undeleting files.

V

V.42bis   The ITU data compression standard supported in all modern modems.

vacuum tube   An electronic device used as a switch.

variable frequency synthesizer circuit   A motherboard circuit that multiplies the clock signal so that the motherboard can support several speeds of CPUs.

vector font   Another name for TrueType font; it has a printed appearance identical to its onscreen appearance.

vertical scan rate   The number of times an image is refreshed or redrawn in 1 second. It is measured in Hz and is also called the *vertical scan frequency.*

VESA (video electronics standards association)   An organization founded in 1989 by the nine leading video board manufacturers to standardize the technical issues surrounding the SVGA video display. This organization has also been involved in other issues since then.

VESA BIOS extension   A BIOS extension to the VGA standard introduced by member companies of VESA in 1989 to resolve incompatibilities in the implementations of the SVGA display technology. This provided a standard interface for programmers to write the drivers for their SVGA video adapters.

VESA DPMS   A power-management signaling specification that VESA developed for monitors.

VFAT (Virtual File Allocation Table)   A virtualized 32-bit FAT, which makes it possible for Windows 95 to support long filenames.

VGA (video graphics array)   The first analog video graphics standard, introduced by IBM Corporation in 1987. The hardware that determines a monitor's screen resolution and color range capability. A VGA-supported monitor displays at least 256 separate colors, and 640 x 480-dpi resolution.

video adapter   An expansion board that plugs into a computer system to give it display capabilities. In conjunction with the display monitor, it forms the video system for the computer.

video bandwidth   The maximum display resolution of a video screen, generally measured in MHz and calculated by multiplying horizontal resolution times the vertical resolution times the refresh rate per second.

video BIOS   The BIOS on the video card that provides a set of video-related functions that are used by programs to access the video hardware. This is much the same way the system BIOS provides the functions that software programs use to access the system hardware.

video card   A printed circuit board that converts images created in the computer to the electronic signals required by the monitor. Sometimes called *video adapter* or *video board.*

video chipset   The logic circuit that controls the video card. It almost always includes an internal processor that performs various video calculation functions before the RAMDAC chip outputs to the monitor.

video display monitor   Another term for *monitor*, *display monitor*, or *video monitor*.

video driver   Software that functions between the video card and other computer programs. It works with the video card to help draw Windows objects on the monitor.

video memory   The amount of RAM on the video card used by the video chipset to draw the requested screen display.

viewable area   A monitor's display area that is usable for a screen image. This differs from a monitor's screen size, due to the black border around the perimeter of each monitor that is unusable.

virtual memory   Memory made available by borrowing space from a computer's hard disk. It allows the computer to run programs larger than the system would ordinarily have the RAM to support.

virus scanning and repair disk   A disk used to start a virus detection program. It is usually bootable, and it may also have an **fdisk** utility to run tests and repair the hard disks.

VM (virtual machine)   An abstract program that runs a computer that doesn't exist physically, yet operates independently as a fully functional unit.

VM manager   The interpreter that executes commands for the VM.

voice coil actuator   The device that moves the head actuator assembly with read/write heads across the hard disk platters by electromagnetic attraction or repulsion of its wire coils against a magnet. This positions it precisely over the required track.

voltage inverter   A device that converts DC voltage from the battery to AC voltage that can be used by the power supply.

voltage switch   A lever located on the back of the power supply unit that allows the user to switch between 120v and 220v electrical power.

volume   A fixed amount of storage on a disk, created by formatting a partition. It contains the actual file-management system used by an operating system.

volume boot code   The bootstrap loader that launches the operating system.

VPN (virtual private network)   A means by which to set up private networks on the World Wide Web, using encrypted transmissions.

VRAM (video RAM)   A specialized DRAM memory chip on video boards designed for dual port access; it helps provide two access paths so information can be written to and read from simultaneously.

W–Z

wait state   A clock tick during which nothing happens. It occurs between cycles and is used to ensure that the processor does not get ahead of the rest of the computer.

WAN (wide-area network)   A communications network that connects clients both countrywide and worldwide.

warm boot   To start up a computer by using the restart button or by pressing Ctrl + Alt + Del.

.wav   The file extension for sound files stored as waveforms.

waveform   A representation, usually graphic, of a wave's shape. It indicates the wave's frequency and amplitude.

wavetable synthesis   State-of-the-art sound synthesis using actual instrument sound rather than recorded instrument sound.

Web (World Wide Web)   A huge internetwork that consists of all the documents on the Internet. Written in HTML, the Web locates documents by their uniform resource locator (URL) addresses. Routers are able to decide on data's best pathway across networks.

Web site   A server that contains Web pages and other files that is online to the Internet 24 hours per day.

wide SCSI-2   A variant of SCSI-2 that utilizes the 16-bit bus standard over a 68-pin connector.

wildcard   A character such as an asterisk or question mark that takes the place of a letter or word. It allows the user to conduct a broad search for files that share common characteristics and/or extensions.

win.com   Also called the *loader*, the **win.com** file starts Windows and contains the **win.cnf**, **lgo**, and **rle** files.

win.ini   A Windows 3.1 file that stores information about the appearance of the Windows environment.

win_root   A folder in which the Registry Editor is stored.

Win32   An application interface that is common to all of Microsoft's 32-bit operating systems.

window   A display area where a program or utility can function.

windowed display   One of the separate viewing areas on a display screen in a system that allows multiple viewing areas as part of its GUI.

Windows   The Microsoft family of software programs, including Windows 3.1, 95, 98, NT, and 2000.

Windows 2000   The latest generation of Windows NT.

Windows 95   Microsoft's successor to the Windows 3.1 operating system for PCs. Released in 1995, Windows 95 ushered in a new level of GUI sophistication and ease of use for PC users.

Windows 95 Resource Kit   Microsoft's definitive guide to Windows 95.

Windows 98   The newest generation of Windows 95.

Windows Explorer   The file manager in Windows that helps users find and manipulate system files and folders.

Windows NT (New Technology)   Microsoft's 32-bit operating system designed for high-end workstations, servers, and corporate networks.

Windows NT security   Measures taken to protect the NT network against accidental or intentional loss, usually in the form of accountability procedures and use restrictions.

WINS (Windows Internet Name Service)   A part of the Windows NT Server that manages and assigns IP addresses to workstation locations without any user or administrator being involved in the configuration.

word   A computer's natural storage unit, typically consisting of 8 bits, 16 bits, 32 bits, or 64 bits.

workgroup   A group of network users who share network resources.

workstation   A computer intended for individual use, but faster and having more functionality than a PC.

WRAM (window RAM)   A modification of VRAM that improves performance, reduces cost, and is designed specifically for use in graphics cards to allow for higher-performance memory transfers.

wrap plug   Another term for *loopback connector*.

write multiple   An ATA-2 enhanced BIOS drive command that enables the controller and drive circuitry to support multiple-sector disk reads concurrently.